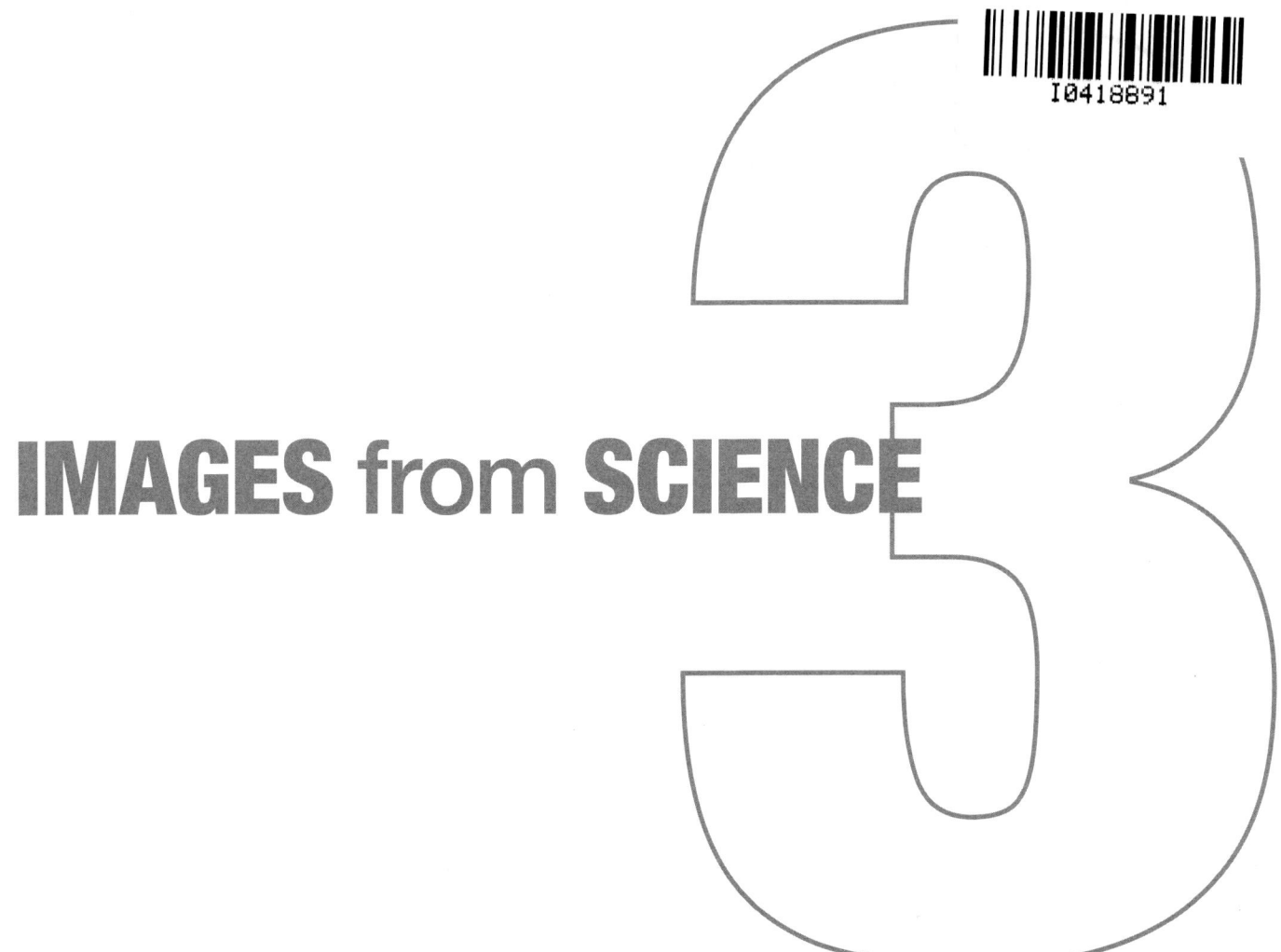

IMAGES from SCIENCE

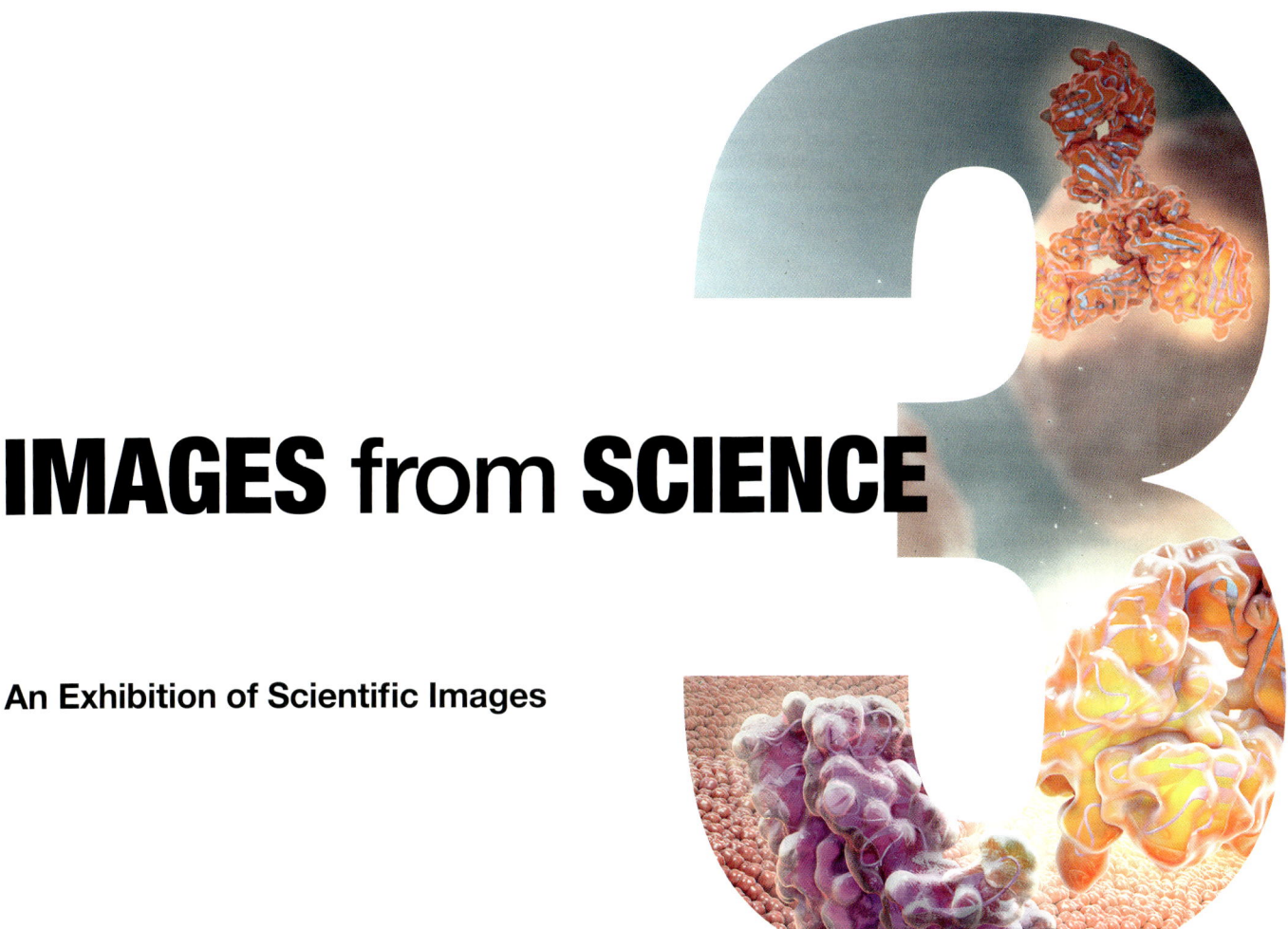

IMAGES from SCIENCE

An Exhibition of Scientific Images

Organized by the School of Photographic Arts and Sciences
at Rochester Institute of Technology
and Johns Hopkins University and School of Medicine

RIT Press
Rochester, New York

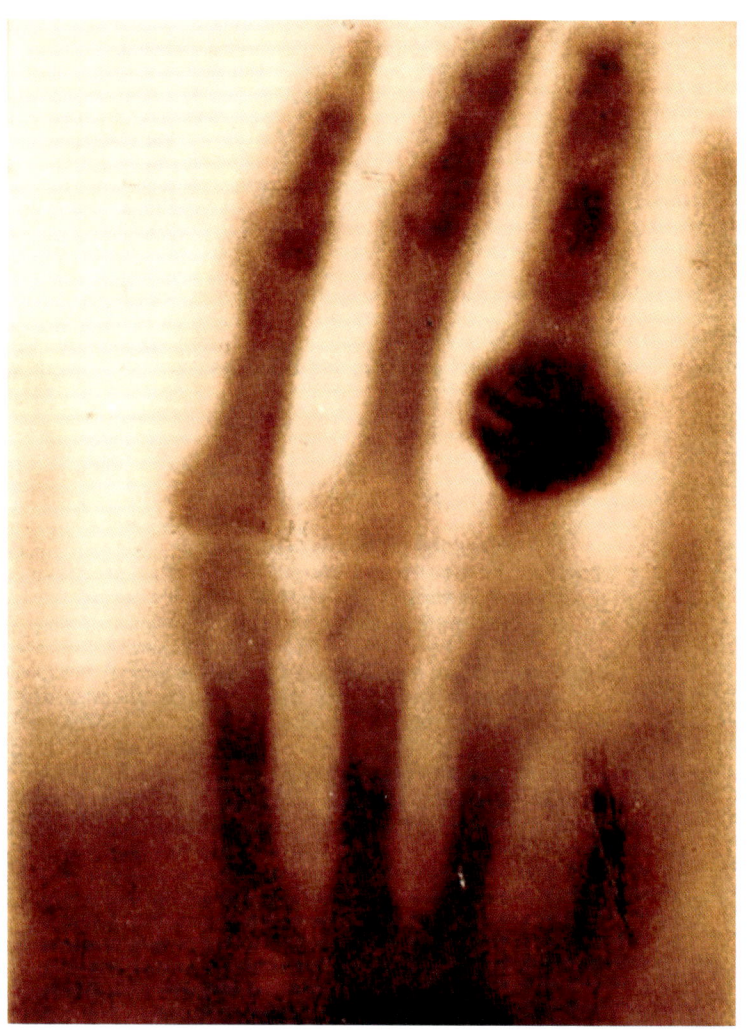

The radiograph features the hand of Mrs. Wilhelm Röntgen, captured in the first X-ray image, made in 1895. This image was originally reproduced in Otto Glasser's *Wilhelm Conrad Röntgen and the Early History of the Roentgen Rays*, London, 1933. Image courtesy of the History of Medicine Collection, US National Library of Medicine, National Institutes of Health.

Foreword

The role of photography in science has been a largely overlooked story in the literature of photographic history. Part of the story told well is the consequential role of nineteenth-century scientists in developing the early building blocks of the medium—optics, chemistry, camera technologies, and the theories of light and color. They, along with artists and enterprising promoters, instinctually understood the possibilities of photography for seeing the unseen, whether in the far-flung reaches of the celestial skies or in the molecular functions and structures of human and natural life. As a result, early science photographs, including the first photograph of the moon, taken by American scientist John W. Draper from his observatory in 1840, and the first X-ray image by German physicist Wilhelm Röntgen in 1895—among many other "photo science firsts"—held persuasive and pervasive power in advancing new avenues of scientific discovery and profoundly influencing the course of human knowledge.

The story of photography's role in science has continued unabated from then to now, and at an ever-quickening pace and with increasing cultural importance. From picturing the invisible realm of human DNA to exploring the rings of Saturn or viewing Earth's global warming, photography and science are indispensable partners whose evolving story continues to shape the ways we know ourselves and our seen and unseen world.

The exhibition and allied publication *Images from Science*, now in its third installment, seeks to reveal the contemporary storylines of photography in science and in new frontiers of scientific imaging. Leading experts from the fields of astronomy, medical photography and illustration, material sciences photography, and related industries serve as judges of an international online competition to gather the best and most thought-provoking images, animations, and short form moving media currently at large in science photography and imaging. As in past iterations, a primary goal of *Images from Science 3* is to produce a touring exhibition with international breadth. This was certainly true of *Images from Science 1* and *2*, which traveled to more than 35 venues worldwide. New to *Images from Science 3* is an enduring website that better relates the importance of online technologies, social media, and evolving moving media forms to furthering the reaches and import of science photography to an attentive public.

A collaborative initiative in organization and support, *Images from Science 3* counts among its sponsors a consortium of imaging powerhouses:

Rochester Institute of Technology (RIT)
Johns Hopkins University and School of Medicine
Carl Zeiss Microscopy, LLC
RIT Chester F. Carlson Center for Imaging Science
BioCommunications Association
Association of Medical Illustrators
Service Photo, Inc.
Science Source Images, Inc.
RIT School of Photographic Arts and Sciences
RIT School of Art
RIT Press
Histolite

With faculty and practitioners engaged in teaching and exploring scientific photography and imaging, these institutions confirm the interdisciplinary nature of the medium that posits new visual data across human and natural science by expanding evolving technologies in novel ways.

Images from Science 3, with its multiple allied pursuits, joins a growing scholarly and public interest in the present and future of science photography and imaging. Certainly, digital technologies of the late twentieth and early twenty-first centuries laid out a path for new visual discoveries, but so too did the professionalization of the discipline fields and the original means of display and image distribution. For almost 200 years, the partnership of science and photography has been nothing less than transformational. Beyond the ways it has informed visual culture, it shapes human knowledge and understanding, with new sight to observe the world and ourselves.

Therese Mulligan, PhD
Director, School of Photographic Arts and Sciences
Rochester Institute of Technology

About the *Images from Science 3* Project

On October 12, 2002, the first *Images from Science (IFS)* exhibition opened in the William Harris Gallery at Rochester Institute of Technology (RIT). Professor Michael Peres and Professor Emeritus Andrew Davidhazy created the project with the intent of promoting a wider appreciation of scientific photography by showcasing beautiful, data-rich—but rarely seen—images drawn from oceanography, geology, biology, engineering, medicine, and physics in the traveling exhibition.

At a professional conference in April 2018, the idea to create an *Images from Science 3* exhibition was discussed. *Images from Science 3* aspired to build on the successes of *Images from Science 1* and *2*. *Images from Science 1* was launched at the infancy of the internet and contained 59 photographs. It traveled to 22 venues in seven countries until 2007 when it was retired. Because of the success of *IFS 1*, Davidhazy and Peres produced *Images from Science 2,* which premiered in the fall of 2008. It was displayed in 13 venues before being lost in shipping from the United Kingdom to the Netherlands in 2014. Both exhibitions were produced as experiments to explore the power of the internet as the sole tool used to advertise, identify, and ultimately display some of the world's most interesting photographs of science.

Much has changed since those exhibitions were mounted. The explosion of new imaging methods and technologies has been nothing short of extraordinary. Coupled with new optical techniques and more advanced imaging software, almost anything is now possible in the creation of images for science. The dynamic release of new imaging equipment including the smartphone, along with the explosive adoption of social media, such as Twitter and Instagram, has made it possible for images of all types to be shared with worldwide audiences. One could make a compelling argument that imaging has become a science unto itself and is an integral part the work of every contemporary organization, science image maker, and research center. NIH, NSF, NASA, and many other important organizations share massive amounts of data on various platforms, keeping their followers engaged with their messaging, research, and images.

Similar to its predecessors, *Images from Science 3* was organized to celebrate the production of beautiful images featuring science. At its core mission, the project explored the interface of science, technology, art, design, and communication. Science images, unlike most other genres of images, rarely find their way into art galleries. With little more than the enthusiasm to re-explore the project, the organizers reached out to many organizations, seeking sponsors, collaborators, a gallery space, and a publisher. Many individuals and organizations embraced the opportunity, including Rochester Institute of Technology; RIT Press; the RIT City Art Space; Johns Hopkins University and School of Medicine; the RIT Chester F. Carlson Center for Imaging Science; Carl Zeiss Microscopy, LLC; the BioCommunications Association; the Association of Medical Illustrators; Service Photo, Inc.; Science Source Images, Inc.; the RIT School of Art; the RIT School of Photographic Arts and Sciences; and Histolite. Without their generosity and advice, this project would not have gotten off the ground.

Professors Michael Peres, Norman Barker, Ted Kinsman, and Bob Rose are the organizers of *IFS 3*. They have enjoyed long careers in this unique field as photographers but also as authors, educators, and industry leaders. Because of their interest in science images, and along with noted RIT professor of graphic design Chris Jackson, they collaborated to produce the third installation of the exhibition, sharing images created by those who work at the frontier of contemporary science.

The organizers of *IFS 3* hoped to identify 75 examples of images that revealed science in new and unique ways. Similar to past *IFS* projects, it used the internet as its primary voice for promotion. Different than *IFS 1* and *2*, this exhibition features moving images, animations, and illustrations, as well as photographs. An international panel of seven experts from around the world selected 81 images. Creating an international exhibition on a tight budget created some unique challenges. The success of the exhibition required constant innovation and problem solving.

Image solicitation began September 1, 2018, and concluded January 15, 2019. At the end of the collection phase, more than 380 files from 130 contributors who lived in 19 countries had been submitted for consideration.

Judging was accomplished online. The panel of *IFS 3* judges included photography editors, scientists, physicians, science photographers, and business owners, who live in Europe, Australia, and North America. You can find more in the section "The Judges" on page 190. Each judge received minimal instructions and was asked to select images for inclusion based on aesthetics, uniqueness, degree of difficulty in making, and myriad other hard-to-quantify subjective metrics. In addition, each judge selected their favorite image for special commendation; each of these images received a Juror Selection Award. Judging took place from February 1 to February 28,

2019. Seventy one contributors from 15 countries were invited to submit their images for the Exhibition.

IFS 3 is presented in an exhibition catalog, a traveling print exhibition, and an online gallery. The *Images from Science 3* print exhibition opened on November 1, 2019, at the RIT City Art Space in downtown Rochester, New York. Following the first installation, it traveled to Johns Hopkins University in Baltimore, Maryland. The exhibit is available for travel to other venues.

Michael Peres, Norm Barker, Ted Kinsman,
Bob Rose, and Chris Jackson
November 2019

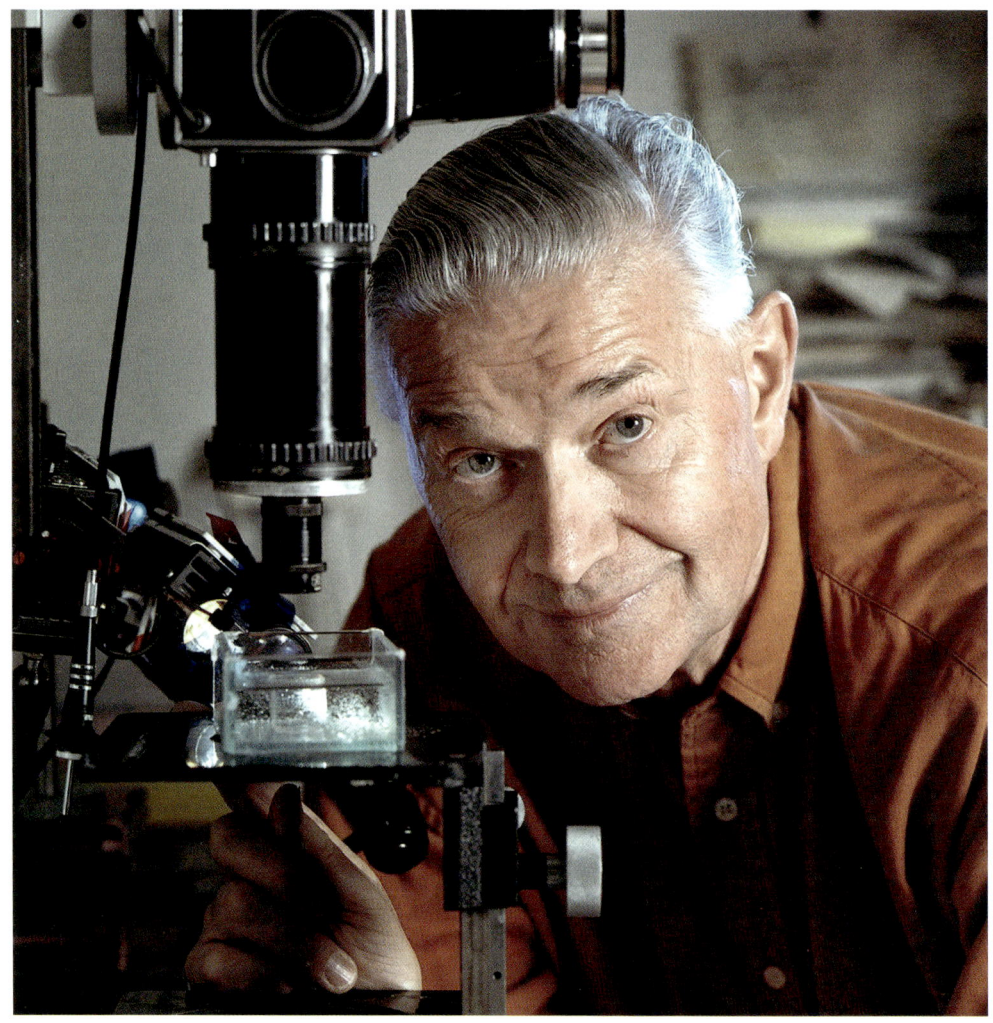

Lennart Nilsson in his laboratory, 1997. Image courtesy of Jacob Forsell.

Dedication

Many important image-makers created pictures of science, beginning possibly with Michelangelo in the late 1400s. A Who's Who of the most famous would include photographic image-makers spanning two centuries, such as Anna Atkins (1799–1871), Eadweard Muybridge (1830–1904), and Roman Vishniac (1897–1990), among others.

These and other giants pushed the envelope, making science visible to the societies of their time. Now, looking through the lens of history, we can see how important their contributions were. Their innovations and their extraordinary skills and passion pushed society's knowledge forward.

The organizers of this exhibition dedicate *Images from Science 3* to Lennart Nilsson (1922–2017), a groundbreaking scientist, explorer, and photographer. Compared to Carl Linnaeus and Leonardo da Vinci, the Swedish photographer is widely regarded as one of the most influential science photographers in history. Nilsson held a modest opinion of himself and would say "I'm just a photographer who happened to become fascinated with mankind."

Nilsson was given his first camera when he was 11. He initially worked as a feature photographer and became well-known as one of Sweden's best visual narrators. An early assignment gave him international exposure when he photographed a polar bear hunt on Spitsbergen, an island in the arctic Norwegian archipelago of Svalbard. The photos were equally exquisite and disturbing. Nilsson's reputation was that of the photographer who dared go closer, further, and deeper than any other. In ways, he was similar to the American photographer Ansel Adams (1902–1984) who, using powerful landscape photography, helped further establish national parks in the United States. Nilsson helped shape Scandinavian practices and attitudes about managing arctic animal populations by using his photographic voice.

In the 1950s, his interest in experimenting with new photographic techniques and science gained momentum. In 1953, *LIFE* magazine printed his first photograph of an embryo and in 1954 published another early photograph of battling soldier ants in terrifying detail. This work marked the starting point of Nilsson's life's work. An important result of this early work was his book *A Child is Born*, one of the world's best-selling photographic books. Beginning with the first edition (1965), it has been translated into more than 20 languages and printed in five editions, reaching millions of readers. In 1965, *LIFE* magazine also published the photo essay *Drama of Life Before Birth*, a milestone for both Nilsson and photographic history. The entire issue sold out, and the sensation caused by his photographs was on a par with pictures from the first moon landing.

In the following years, Lennart Nilsson maintained a contract with *LIFE* and furthered his pioneering work in scientific photography. His interest in technological innovations enabled him to photograph with a degree of detail that no one had seen before. He said, "I am driven by a desire to illustrate vital functions that are invisible processes using the highest degree of accuracy possible in making the invisible, visible. Such processes took place inside the human body or in the life that existed on earth." Nilsson continued to make new work until the end of his life in 2017.

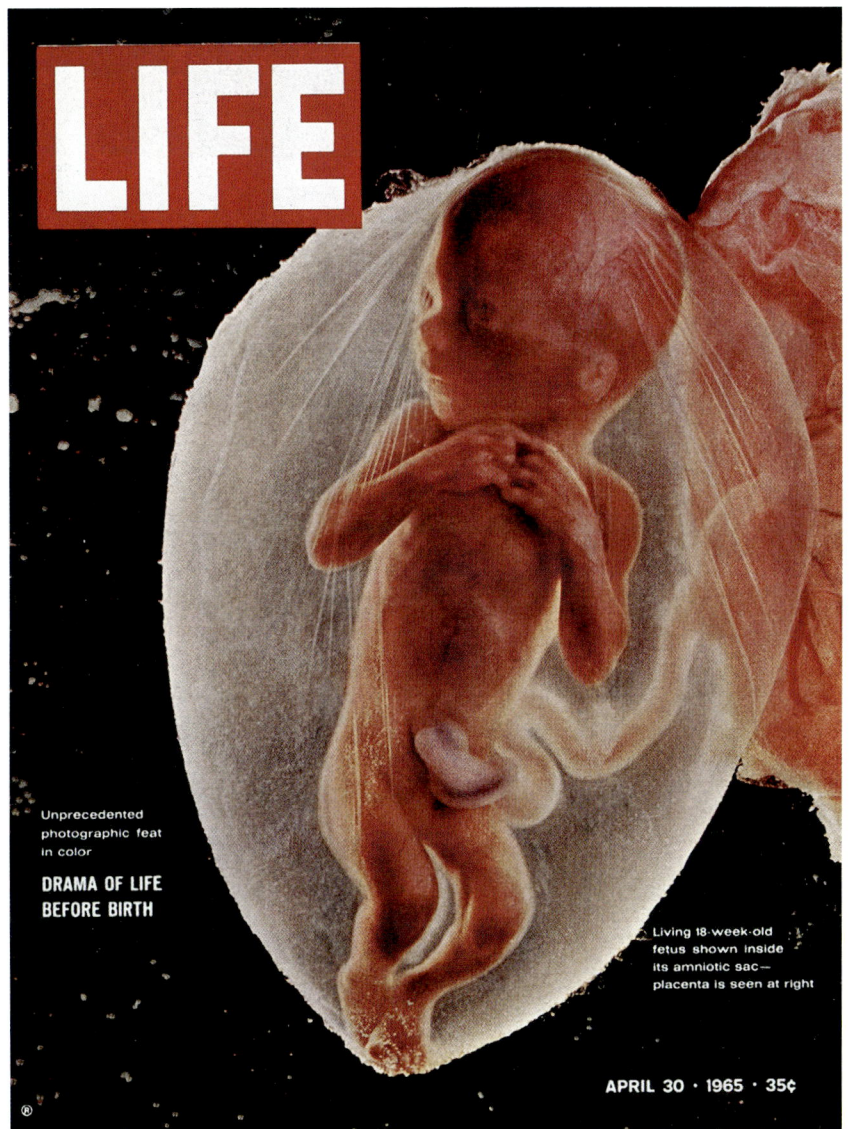

Lennart Nilsson's photograph featuring human development was on the cover of *LIFE* magazine, 1965. Within days of the initial publishing, eight million copies were sold. Image courtesy of *Time Life* / Lennart Nilsson Photography.

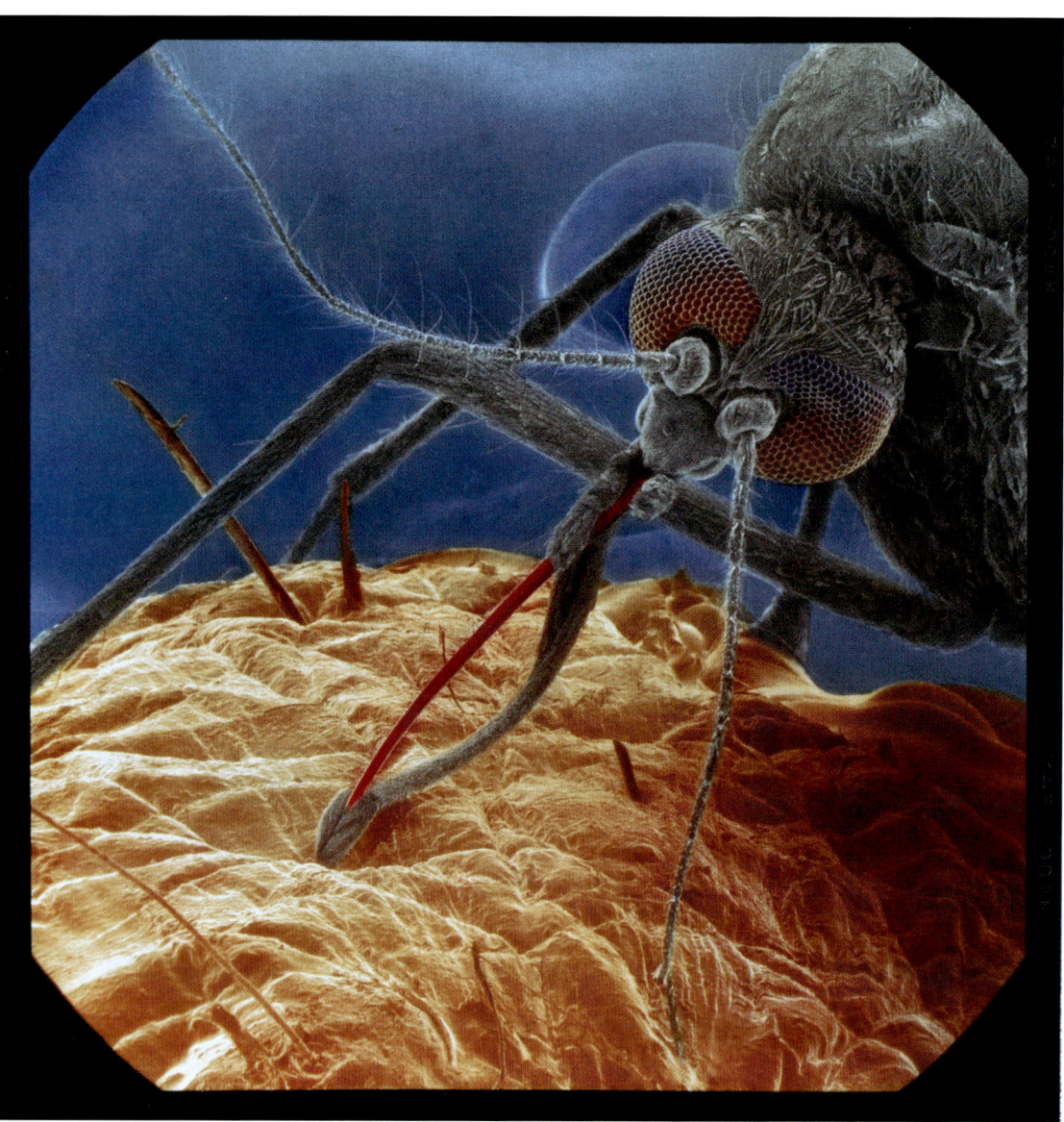

12

Nilsson's photographic goals remained constant during his lifetime: "to reveal that which was familiar in unique and new ways." Nilsson's efforts required all the obsessiveness learned in his previous projects. His goal was simply to take the first microscopic picture of a mosquito biting a human. Surprisingly, obtaining live mosquitoes proved far more difficult than finding human subjects willing to be bitten. He and his friend Berndt Ödarp, an entomologist at the Swedish Museum of Natural History, took their finely meshed nets to coastal islands and dense woods and, when it got too cold for mosquitoes in Stockholm, even flew to Denmark. Back at Nilsson's lab at the Karolinska Institute, Ödarp served as the first victim. As soon as a mosquito pierced the skin on Ödarp's arm, Nilsson slapped a vial over it and then glued its legs in position. A doctor injected Ödarp with a local anesthetic and then cut out a small flap of skin containing the intact mosquito. This sample was frozen in liquid nitrogen, and then dried using the method called critical point drying; finally it was put into the scanning electron microscope and photographed. Ödarp felt no pain and donated 12 pieces of skin before four other volunteers were enlisted. After 45 mosquitoes and 45 attempts, Nilsson had his perfect picture.

The image of a mosquito sucking human blood was photographed by Nilsson using a scanning electron microscope and published for the first time in 1979. It was originally photographed in black and white and colored by Swedish photographer and colorist Gillis Häägg, who used a special technique of adding colors onto the different layers of black and white film. The photograph was published in *National Geographic* in the mid-1980s. Image courtesy of Lennart Nilsson Photography.

Acknowledgments

It has been our experiences that large projects typically start slowly, and then they take on a life of their own. More importantly, we have also learned that to achieve all of a project's objectives, it takes the help of an entire community. From our experience with *Images from Science 1* and *2,* we were acutely aware that if we were going to achieve our mission, this project would again require sponsorships and collaborators.

The decision to produce another *Images from Science* exhibition occurred after a meeting between Michael Peres and Norman Barker, who was visiting RIT in April 2018. After Barker agreed to participate, they moved ahead with numerous organizational and promotional details related to mounting the exhibition. Shortly after their agreement, Ted Kinsman, Chris Jackson, and Bob Rose joined the team.

For the sake of brevity, we cannot thoroughly express our heartfelt gratitude to all the various contributors and supporters who made this exhibition and the production of the catalog possible. From the beginning, colleagues—at Rochester Institute of Technology, at Johns Hopkins University and School of Medicine, and in the industry—shared encouragement for our idea, and each offered generous financial help to move us ahead, with the expectation of another successful outcome.

We are proud of our exhibition and would like to recognize the following *Images from Science 3* partners for their generous financial support. James Sharp, president, and John Morreale, vice president of business development, of Carl Zeiss Microscopy, LLC, were on board right from the start. Zeiss frequently advertised the exhibition using various Zeiss channels. Dave Messinger, director of the RIT Chester F. Carlson Center for Imaging Science, also was an enthusiastic partner. The Center has been a partner in all three *Images from Science* projects. The BioCommunications Association and the Association of Medical Illustrators, too, were very generous with their contributions and promotional assistance. Service Photo, Inc., Science Source Images, Inc., RIT School of Photographic Arts and Sciences, and the RIT School of Art were also vital partners. All of these sponsorships together allowed us to produce a very high-quality traveling exhibition of prints and an impressive catalog. We also thank RIT Press for its immediate endorsement of the project and willingness to take on the publishing this third IFS catalog. In particular, we would like to recognize Molly Cort, RIT Press managing editor, and Marnie Soom, marketing and design specialist. Their oversight and suggestions enabled us to produce this beautiful catalog. We also want to recognize the excellent work of Susan Matheson, our copy editor, for her work in conforming the writing from literally around the world.

We would also like to thank Therese Mulligan, director of RIT's School of Photographic Arts and Sciences, for extending her personal support and for writing the exhibition's foreword.

One of our goals was to include video, animation, illustration, and photography. Electronic submissions of this size could *not* have been accomplished without the RIT Information and Technology Services group, who assisted us in creating a secure and customized system for transfer of very large files. This system of image transfer was used by more than 75 percent of the contributors. Similarly, the College of Art and Design's IT team was helpful beyond words from the beginning to end of the project.

The opportunity to be part of this project was all we had to offer award-winning photographer Felice Frankel of the Massachusetts Institute of Technology, who volunteered to write the guest essay for the exhibition. Frankel's career of over 25 years as a scholar, author, and scientific photographer made her uniquely qualified to write this essay.

Once the images were submitted, image selection became the work of our invited panel of international judges, who were charged with identifying the best images from the nearly 390 submissions. Our world-renowned panel included Chloe Coleman, Paul Crompton, Jonathan Epstein, Steve Gerard, Staffan Larsson, David Malin, and Nick Woolridge. We thank them all for their time and aesthetic expertise in identifying the 81 best pieces.

We would be remiss not to recognize the extraordinary work of the contributors. Without their interest in sharing their work, this exhibition would not have been possible. Entries were received from 19 countries, and the final curation of the exhibition reflects the noteworthy skills and motivations of the contributors.

The exhibition panels were professionally printed by students and staff in the RIT Photo Imaging Systems Lab. Their attention to detail and pride in producing prints that share a complete richness and fidelity to the original image in this collection is to be commended and greatly appreciated by all involved.

A big thank you especially to John Aäsp, director of the RIT City Art Space, who offered enthusiasm to display *Images from Science 3* even before the project was official. His endorsement of the Exhibition and commitment to display the Exhibition were important validators and one of the reasons we decided to proceed.

There are also many people who worked out of sight and whose contributions were vital. While Chris Jackson is part of the team, we want to offer a special thank you to him, our project's web and print designer, who made all of the content look so great in sharing this impressive collection of science images.

Michael Peres
Norman Barker
Ted Kinsman
Bob Rose
Chris Jackson

More Than Pretty Pictures

I was recently asked a thoughtful question during the question-and-answer session following a presentation about my new book, *Picturing Science and Engineering.* In the book, I describe in detail everything that I have learned about making science images and figures. My "mission," if I may use that word, is to nudge researchers to consider the value of making their "visual explanations"—images, graphs, figures, and illustrations—more communicative, not only to their colleagues but, just as importantly, to the public. The question was: "Do you first think about the aesthetics of the image you are about to make or do you first think about the science?" I had to think a bit before responding and then realized that I simply cannot separate the two. The science in the images that I capture is primary, and that science already has a stunning aesthetic component if I represent it carefully, honestly, and with the intention of communicating the information. The image should always be about the aesthetics *and* the science. You, the reader, should understand I am consciously not using the word "art." I use the word "aesthetics" with the intention of suggesting "beauty."

Over the years, I have observed many representations of science coming from various laboratories across the globe, where both the science and beauty are obscured. I have always believed my job as a scientific illustrator is to clarify the science and discover the existing beauty of an object or phenomena, to refine both of these qualities, and then nudge them to a place where viewers will want to look more deeply. With careful composition, editing, and lighting techniques, I can compose the information that is already present within the science. When I am effective, I can better communicate the information, while always maintaining scientific integrity.

Sometimes I wonder why the science and beauty are often difficult to see in images created by scientists. After all, most researchers are already seduced by the aesthetics of the phenomena they are studying. So why do we not always see that characteristic in their pictures? After conducting a series of master classes for many years on my campus and elsewhere, I've come up with some initial questions that I present to science and engineering students to help these scientist photographers gain a greater awareness of the value of creating more effective illustrations—without complicated set-ups.

The first question I ask is: "Have you read your equipment manual?"

I have been surprised by how little researchers know about the basic operation of their expensive imaging equipment. I am not referring to astronomers, microscopists, or others whose knowledge about their equipment *is* the science and an essential component of their research. But I have found that those working at their research benches—fabricating devices, observing changes over time, studying various structures, or using cameras or electrons to document what they see—are generally missing the basics of imaging practices. For example, when I pose questions regarding f/stops to those using cameras, I sometimes get blank stares. And when I ask what file size their scanning electron microscope (SEM) produces, it's clear that some scientists are unaware that they can change the resolution of their SEM in order to capture a higher-resolution image (and produce a larger file) for a journal cover image. For

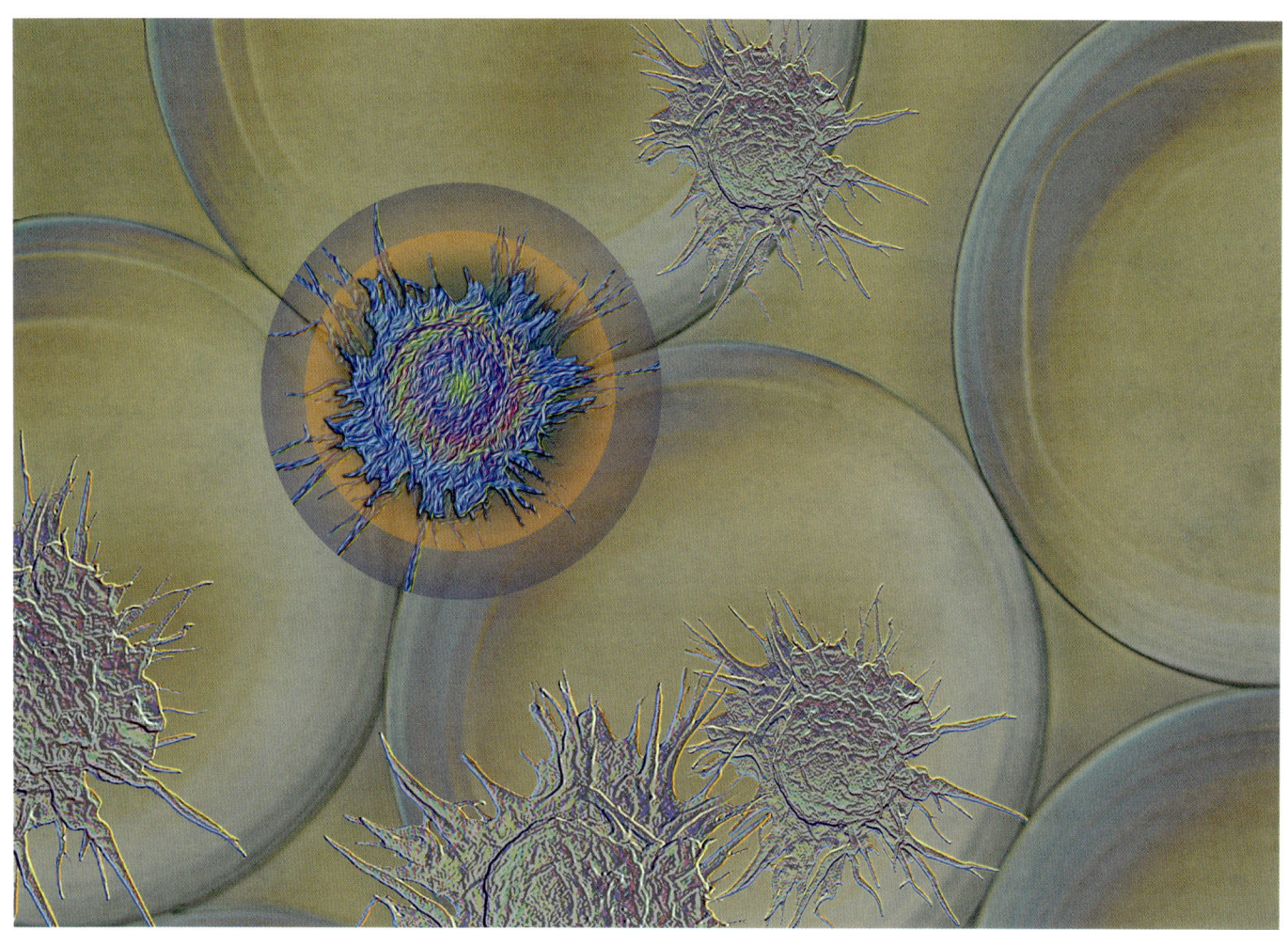

many of these dedicated scientists, committing time to better understand their tools always seems to be tangential. To achieve better images, that attitude needs to change.

I next ask: "What is the first thing you want the viewer to see?"

The answers vary but, because scientists know exactly what to look for in their own images, they assume the viewer will see all the same things. This is a problem. My biggest challenge is to persuade researchers they are creating images and figures with too much information. In essence, they are making it difficult for viewers to "read" their images. When viewers see an image or figure for the first time, their view is not directed; they look at everything. There is no way of directing a viewer where to look or what to initially observe. In my attempt to urge better editing, I get polite nods of agreement, but later I see that few changes were made. The problem is that a researcher wants a viewer to see all the work they have produced, no matter if the content of one image is redundant to that of another. However, multiple images of similar fields do not necessarily communicate more information.

Often, rather than relying on straight photographic documentation, I have to use other means to depict a scientific idea or concept because the concept itself cannot be photographed. This image, which appeared on the cover of *Nature Materials*, is a combination of photomicrographs, creating a metaphor to tell the "story" about the research. The scientists developed a technique to chemically protect an implanted device against the body's natural mechanism of fighting any foreign material, depicted by metaphorically "deactivating" the macrophage on the left. Research: Joshua Doloff, et al. MIT. Image reproduced courtesy of Felice Frankel.

Another question I am curious about is: "Why do you not push the envelope?"

Too often, scientists perpetuate the notion that "this is the way it's always been done." They don't consider the possibility that their images or graphics can better communicate their science if they re-evaluate "the way it's always been done" and adopt a more contemporary process. Just because the software spews out colors for a visualization that a software engineer, and not an imaging expert, developed does not mean that it should remain the best practice. Consider, for example, the images created with an atomic force microscope (AFM). The software in this type of microscope always displays a rust-tinted visualization. The image is actually a grayscale rendition, but for some reason the tint was added years ago when the equipment was first developed. I raise the question in many workshops, "Why not convert this type of image to grayscale to make it more readable?" The common response is that an AFM image is recognizable because of its color. Should that be the reason to perpetuate a questionable aesthetic? Changing conservative minds is a slow process, but once a scientist sees the value in adopting more effective imaging practices, powerful and new imaging outcomes are possible.

Another question I ask, which can start some interesting conversations, is: "How far can scientists go when enhancing science images?"

How far a scientist can enhance, adjust, or "touch up" an image is a critical question in science and needs more attention in research communities. Moreover, we need to engage non-experts in the conversation as well. In our visually bombarded daily lives, where everyone sees themselves as a photographer, we need to discuss the ethics of image enhancement of any kind. In my book, I include an entire chapter about image enhancement; I begin by referencing a stunningly beautiful Hubble Space Telescope image that has been color enhanced. You might not know that almost all Hubble images are enhanced. I write:

If you think about it, the very nature of making an image involves a subjective decision from the start of recording evidence. It takes the form of deciding what and when to photograph. Thus it is a mistake to get bogged down with the idea that no enhancement whatsoever should be permitted. You already have edited the evidence by not including this, or that, within the frame. If we can agree that the purpose of visuals is not only to show evidence but also to communicate that evidence, then we can permit some enhancement to help the viewer read the information, as long as we specify exactly how the image was enhanced. How many times, while photographing a sample, have I left out an imperfection? Is that decision unethical? Am I manipulating the evidence? Or is it for clarity? The one important thread throughout the journals' guidelines is that researchers must always indicate when any "enhancement" is applied to a photograph.

I push the envelope a bit more by asking: "Are researchers making their pictures a priority?"

Planning to make the best visuals for a journal submission or presentation should not be left as a last-minute exercise. It should be part of every researcher's thinking from the beginning of an investigation. The power of pictures as a communication tool should not be underestimated. For that reason alone, learning to make science images that are compelling, informative, and accessible should be part of every researcher's education. It is a skill that is as important as the writing component of a journal article.

When I first began this amazing and joyful journey as a science photographer 25 years ago, I was confronted with a strange idea that was presented by many young researchers. They thought that some of my pictures were "too beautiful" and that the science within the image would not be taken seriously because the work seemed to focus on aesthetics. I am delighted to report that that peculiar thinking has almost completely dissipated from conversations about my work. I believe science illustrators should scream to the world how astonishingly beautiful science is! And what better way to say it than with pictures.

This exhibition is testament to those who subscribe to pushing the boundaries of what is possible in communicating both science and the beauty already within the science.

Felice Frankel
Massachusetts Institute of Technology

Science photographer Felice Frankel is a research scientist at the Massachusetts Institute of Technology where she works in the Departments of Chemical Engineering and Mechanical Engineering. She is a fellow of the American Association for the Advancement of Science, a Guggenheim Fellow, a Senior Research Fellow in Harvard University's Faculty of Arts and Sciences, and a Visiting Scholar at Harvard Medical School's Department of Systems Biology.

In her collaboration with scientists and engineers, Frankel's images have appeared on journal covers, in journal articles, in web spotlights, and in various other international publications, including *National Geographic*, *Nature*, *Science*, *Angewandte Chemie*, *Advanced Materials*, *Materials Today*, *PNAS*, *Newsweek*, *Scientific American*, *Discover Magazine*, *Popular Science*, and *New Scientist*, among others.

The Exhibition

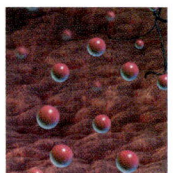

Edmond Alexander and Cynthia Turner

T Cell Activation and Tumor Attack, 2017

Digital illustration
Adobe Photoshop CS6

Alexander & Turner Medical Illustration Studio
Santa Rosa Beach, Florida, United States

This poster reveals how tumor cells produce antigens that are captured by antigen-presenting cells (APCs). The specific APCs that activate T cells are typically dendritic cells. T cells cannot recognize or respond to free soluble antigens, but they can recognize and respond to antigens that have been processed and presented by APC dendritic cells. Once T cells undergo activation, they proliferate and migrate to the tumor cells, releasing apoptosis-inducing proteins.

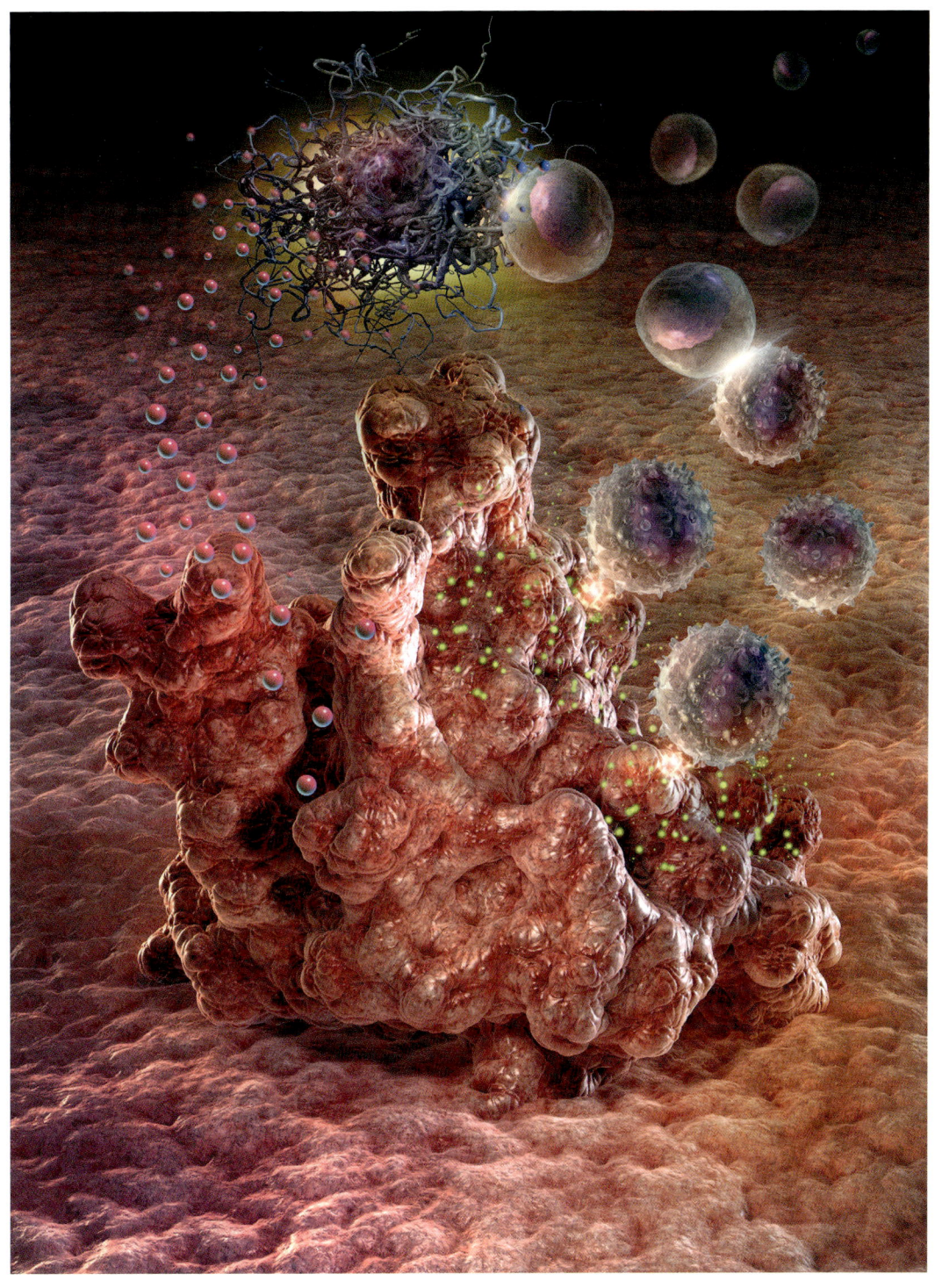

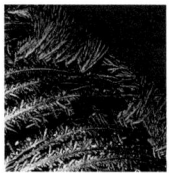

Márkus Bálint

Melarsomine Crystal, 2016

Photomicrograph
Image is a composite of 113 images that were focus stacked and stitched together

Tata, Hungary

This photomicrograph shows a microscopic melarsomine crystal that was examined using polarized light. Melarsomine is a relatively expensive drug and is used in veterinary medicine for the treatment of heartworm infections in dogs. Melarsomine contains arsenic and is highly toxic. This crystal was approximately 3 millimeters in size.

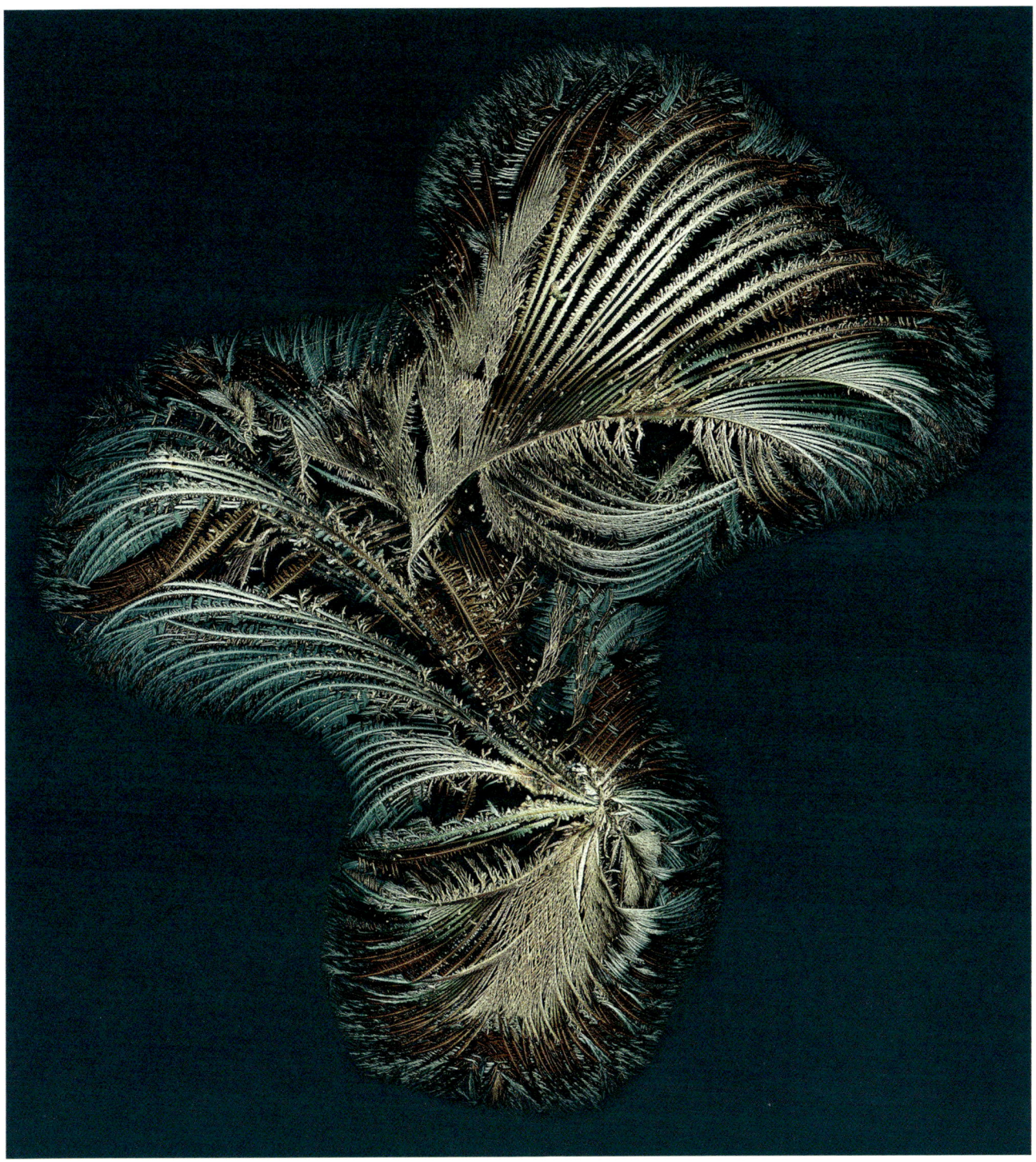

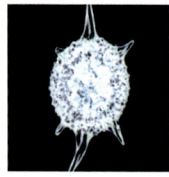

Stefano Barone

25 Radiolarians Micromanipulated and Mounted by the Author on a Permanent Microscope Slide, 2018

Photomicrograph
Capture magnification x250; darkfield illumination produced from a Zeiss Axio Imager.A2 research microscope; Canon EOS 5D Mark III DSLR camera

Diatom Lab, www.diatomlab.com
Palazzo Pignano, Cremona, Italy

This photomicrograph shows 25 Radiolarians collected from marl, a sedimentary rock collected in Barbados, an eastern Caribbean island. They are fossil Radiolarians and have mineral skeletons.

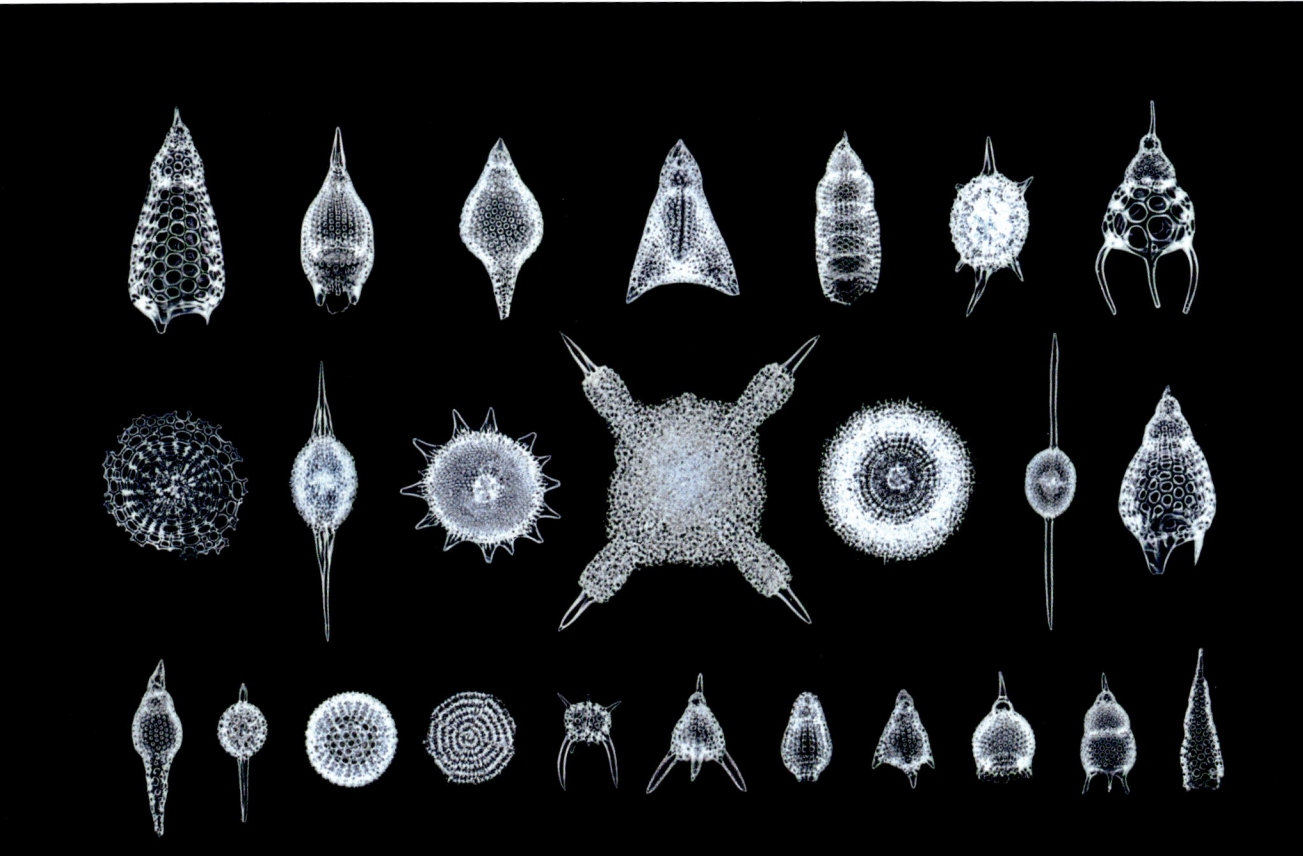

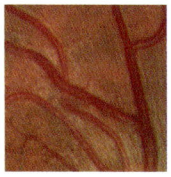

Chris Barry

Bear Tracks Hypertrophy, 2018

Retinal fundus photograph
Digital retinal fundus camera

Lions Eye Institute
Perth, Western Australia, Australia

This image features the fundus, or back, of a human eye, revealing congenital retinal pigment epithelial hypertrophy, also called bear tracks. This anomaly is a condition in which areas of excessively pigmented retinal pigment epithelium resemble paw prints. It does not affect vision.

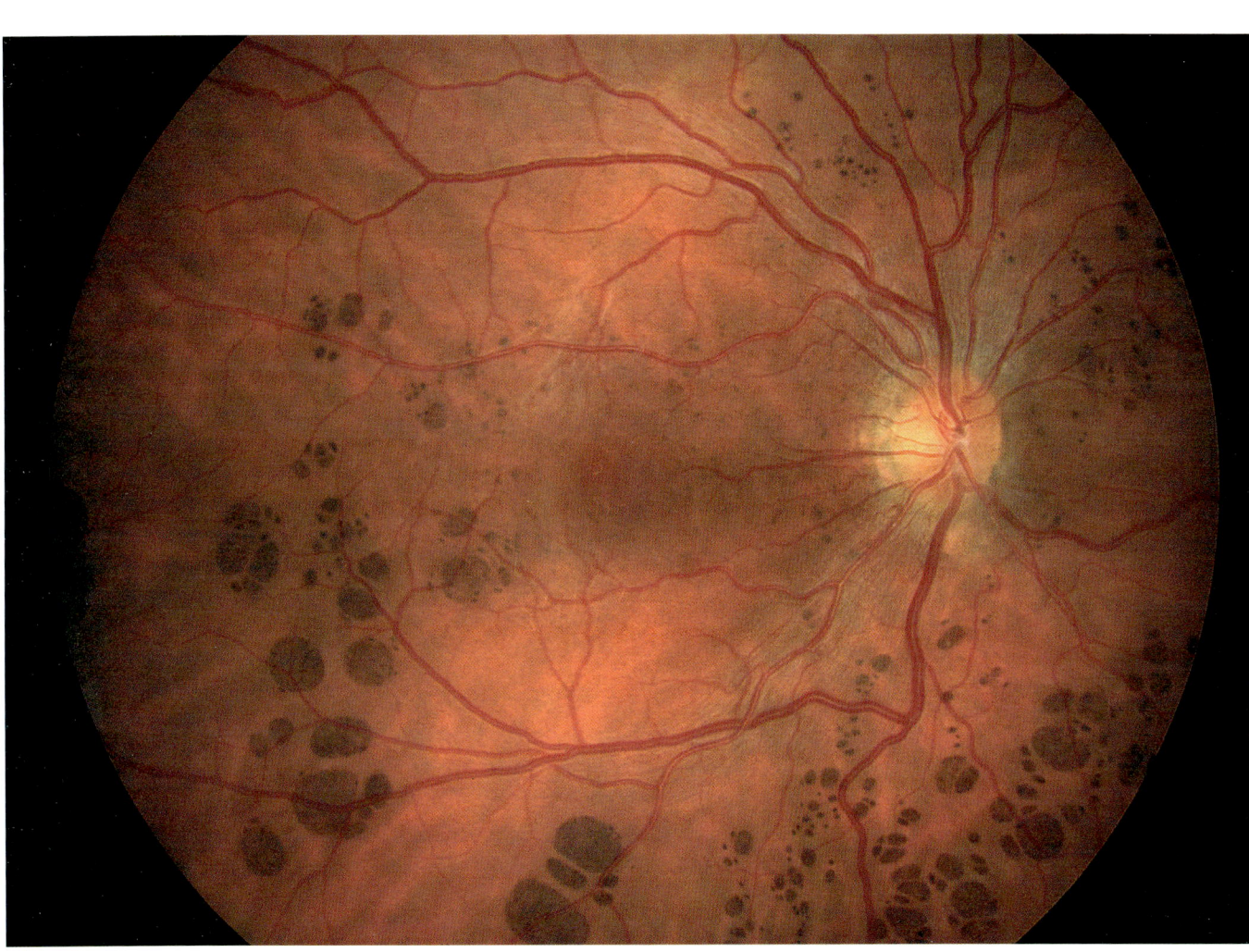

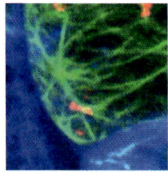

Elison Blancaflor

Chemical Disruption of Actin in Plant Cells, 2018

Confocal photomicrograph
40x water immersion objective; capture magnification ~x400

Noble Research Institute, LLC
Ardmore, Oklahoma, United States

This photomicrograph features a five-day-old Arabidopsis thaliana seedling after exposure to latrunculin B, a metabolite isolated from red sea sponge. Latrunculin B blocks the assembly of actin monomers into filamentous structures. The green, red, and blue colors mark distinct regions of the plant cell. The green color marks the filamentous actin (F-actin) cytoskeleton, and the red and blue colors show autofluorescence from chloroplasts and cell walls, respectively. Note that thick actin bundles accumulate in distinct regions within the cytoplasm. The width of the elongated cells is approximately 40 micrometers.

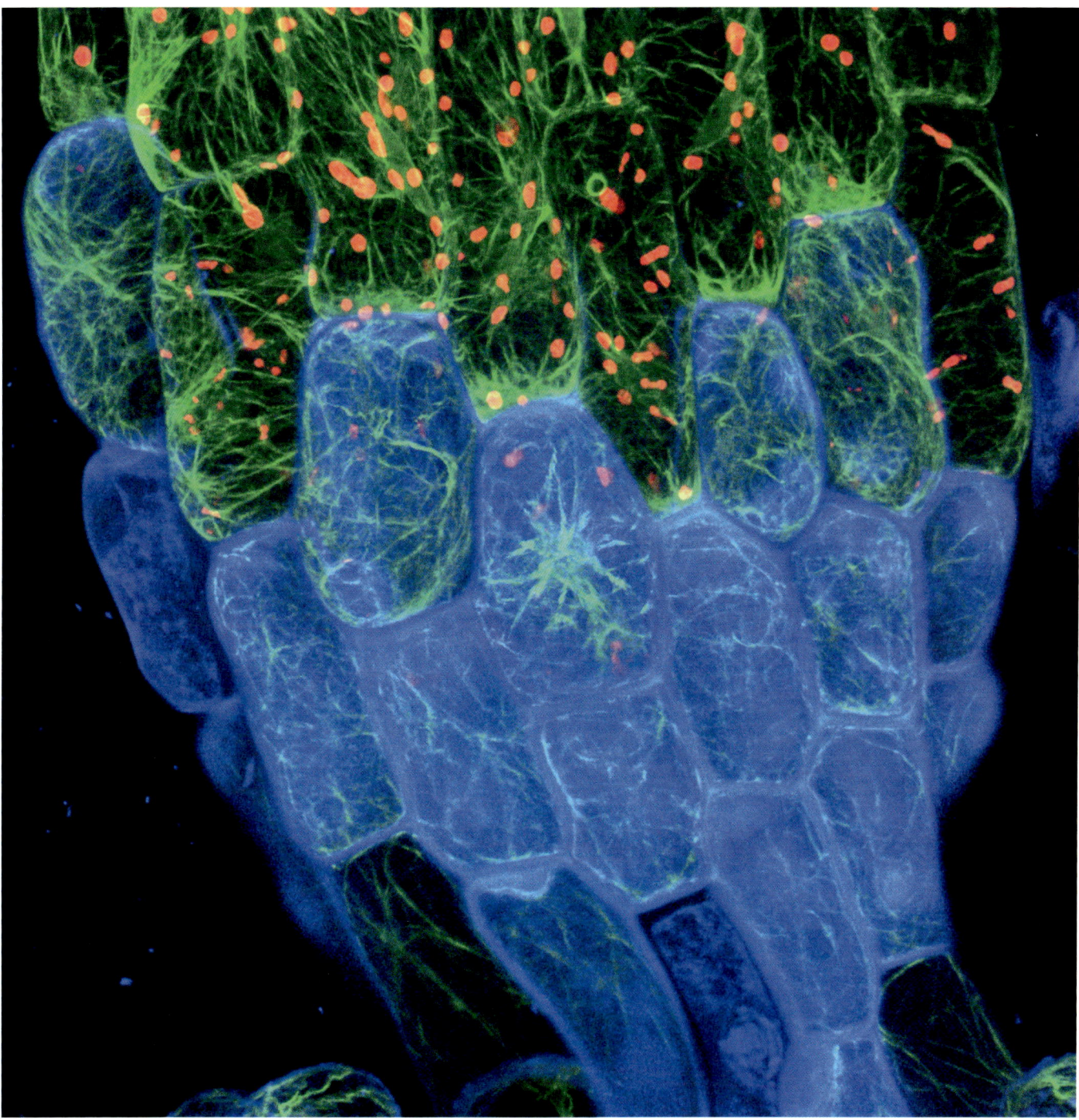

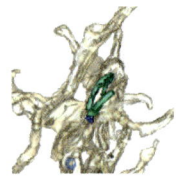

Giulia Bolasco

3D Nanostructure of a Microglia Cell Body, Processes, and Internal Organelles, 2018

Confocal photomicrograph
Serial block-face scanning electron microscope workflow; correlative light and electron microscopy; field of view 32x24x23 microns; anisotropic resolution 5 nanometers in *xy* orientations and 25 nanometers thick

Microscopy Facility, Epigenetics and Neurobiology, European Molecular Biology Lab
Rome, Italy

This photograph shares a 3D model of a segmented microglia cell body, its processes, and internal organelles.

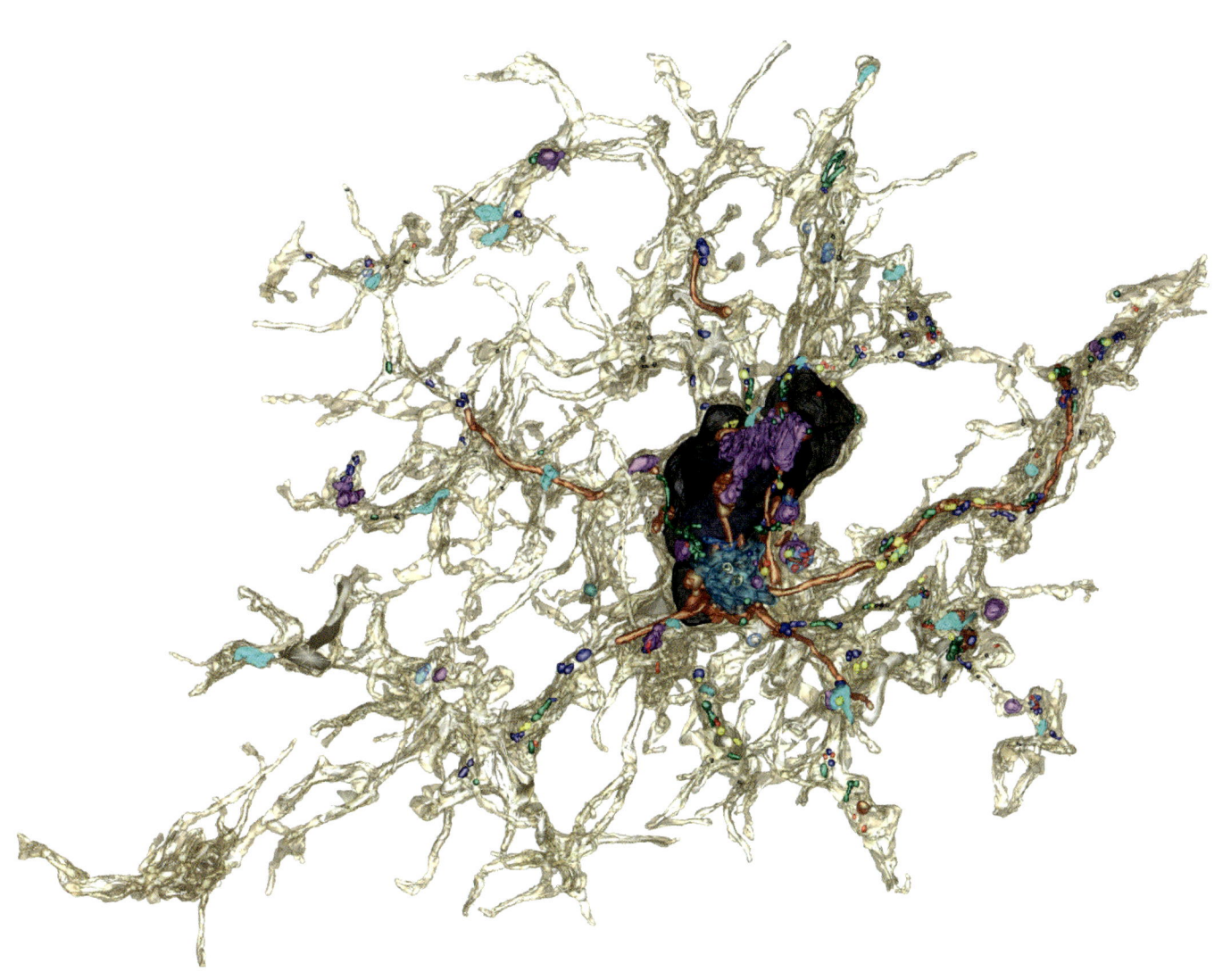

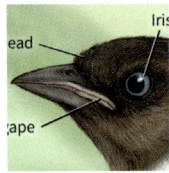

Alisa Brandt

Color Change in Maturing Red-Capped Cardinals, 2018

Digital illustration

Department of Art as Applied to Medicine, Johns Hopkins University School of Medicine
Baltimore, Maryland, United States

This poster communicates the typical progression of color changes observed in red-capped cardinals as they mature from fledgling to adult. The feathers of the head transform from brown to red. The eye color also changes from blue to brown to bright orange. The presented timeline summarizes researcher observations of 25 birds at the National Aquarium, Baltimore, Maryland.

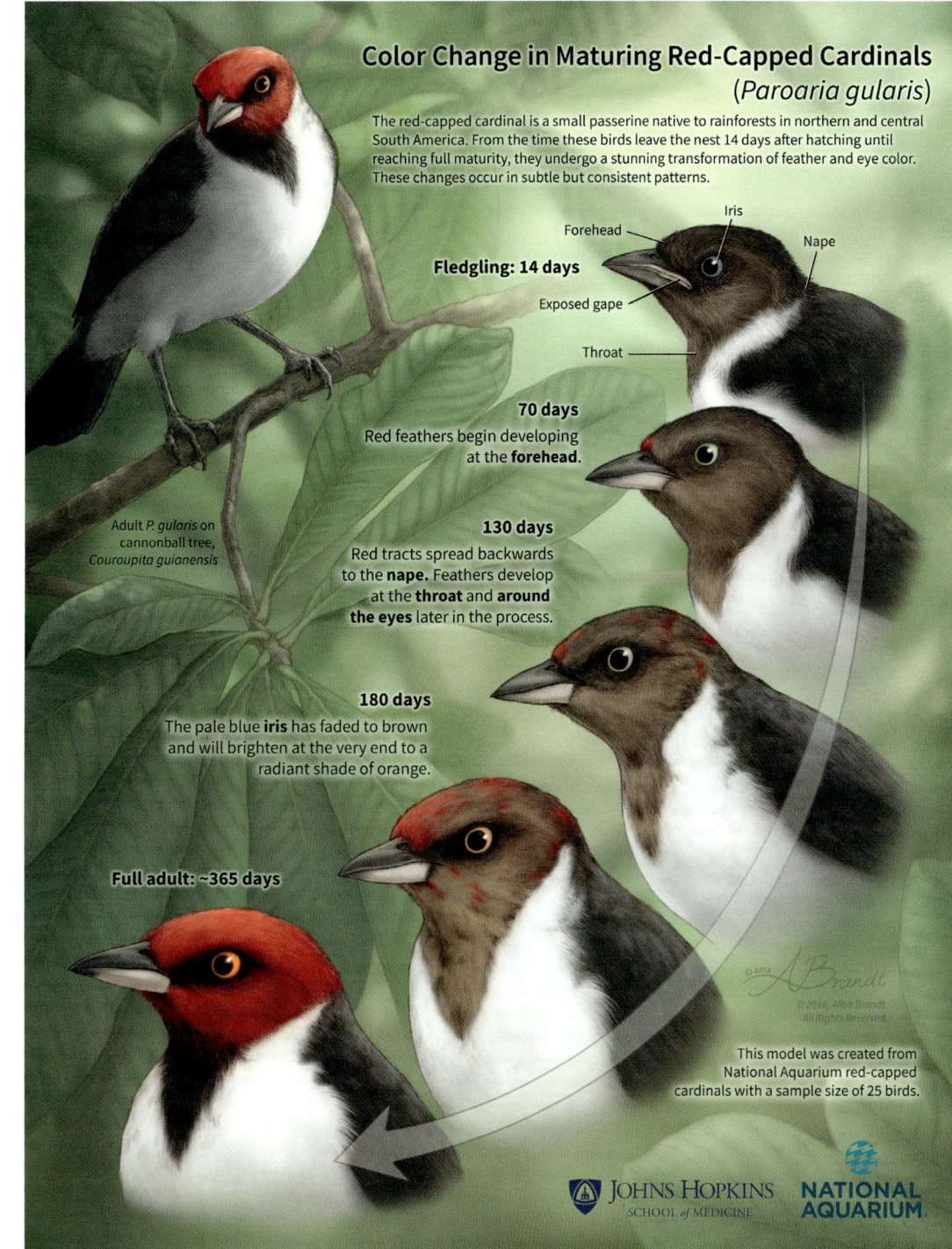

Color Change in Maturing Red-Capped Cardinals
(*Paroaria gularis*)

The red-capped cardinal is a small passerine native to rainforests in northern and central South America. From the time these birds leave the nest 14 days after hatching until reaching full maturity, they undergo a stunning transformation of feather and eye color. These changes occur in subtle but consistent patterns.

Adult *P. gularis* on cannonball tree, *Couroupita guianensis*

Fledgling: 14 days

Forehead

Iris

Nape

Exposed gape

Throat

70 days
Red feathers begin developing at the **forehead**.

130 days
Red tracts spread backwards to the **nape.** Feathers develop at the **throat** and **around the eyes** later in the process.

180 days
The pale blue **iris** has faded to brown and will brighten at the very end to a radiant shade of orange.

Full adult: ~365 days

This model was created from National Aquarium red-capped cardinals with a sample size of 25 birds.

JOHNS HOPKINS
SCHOOL *of* MEDICINE

NATIONAL AQUARIUM

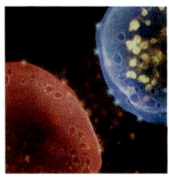

Allison Bruce

T Cells Fighting Cancer, 2019

Digital illustration

A. K. Bruce Design
Brisbane, California, United States

Through a variety of mechanisms, cytotoxic T cells (blue) are able to distinguish cancer cells (red) from non-cancer cells by specific markers on their surfaces. The T cell, after recognizing a target cancer cell, delivers a mixture of toxins (yellow) to the cell. The chemical perforin punctures the cell membrane, and then granzyme induces apoptosis (cell death). The killer T cell then moves on, ready to fight again.

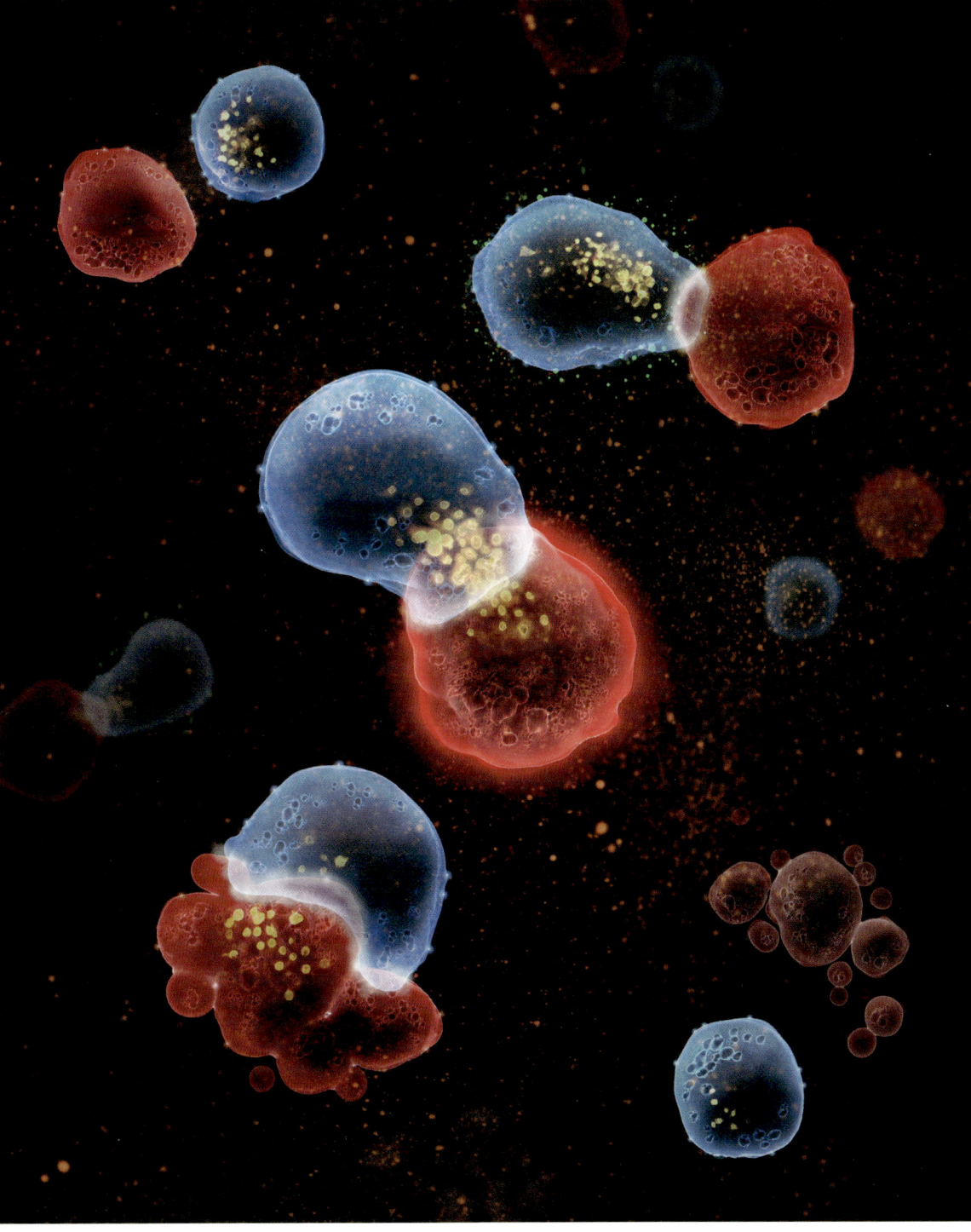

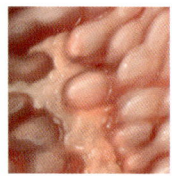

Todd Buck

Crohn's Disease, 2018

Digital illustration
Pixologic ZBrush, Luxion KeyShot, and Adobe Photoshop software

School of Art and Design, Northern Illinois University
DeKalb, Illinois, United States

This illustration highlights the digestive system using a partial cutaway of the ileocecal junction, revealing Crohn's disease. Thickening of the bowel wall and ulcers can be seen. Glowing areas throughout the intestine indicate additional areas of Crohn's disease. A unique characteristic of Crohn's is that it can affect any part of the digestive tract.

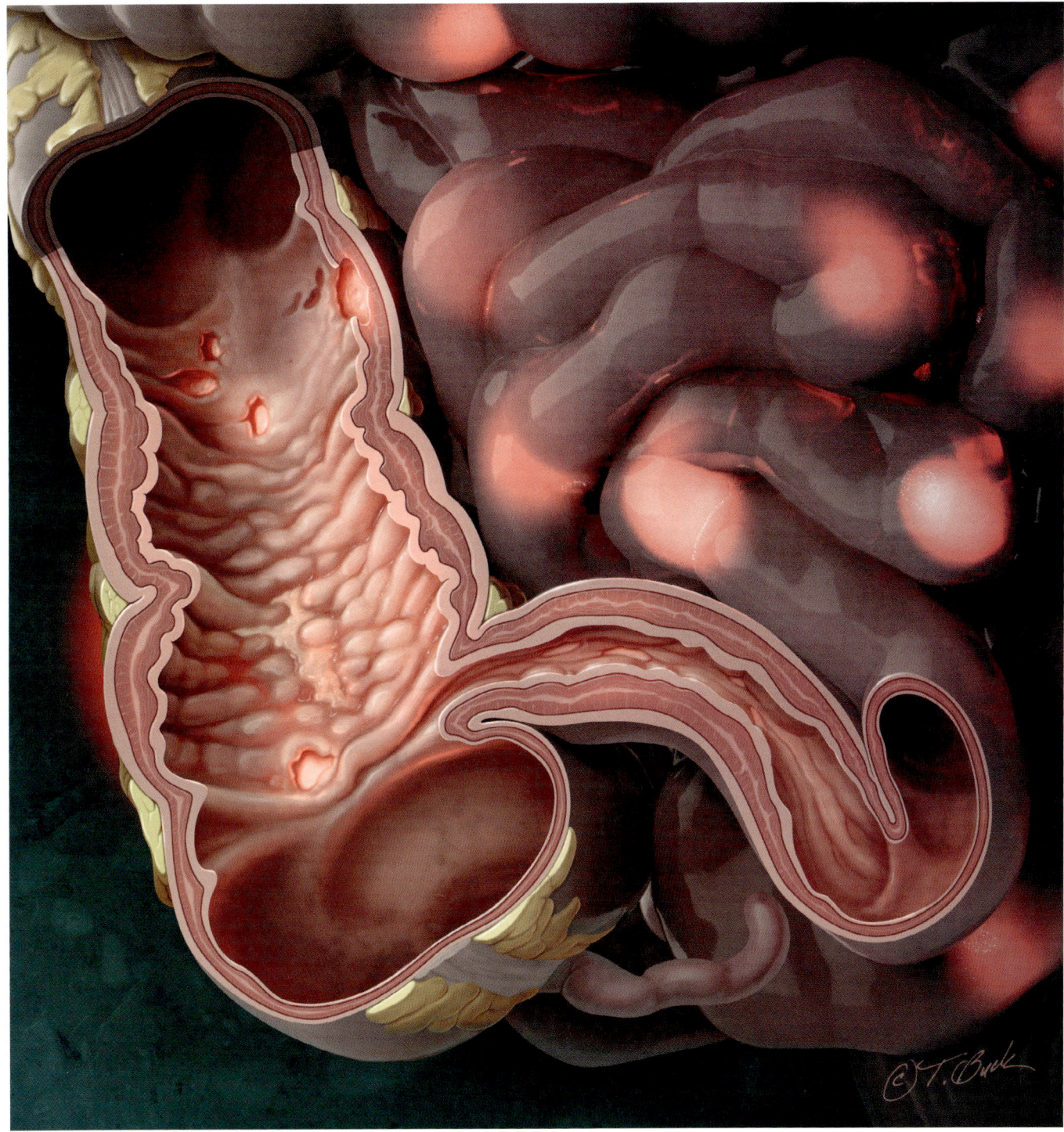

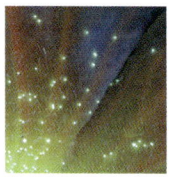

Craig Burrows

Cucumber Flower, 2017

Ultraviolet fluorescence photograph

Craig Burrows Photography
California, United States

This image was produced using ultraviolet-induced visible fluorescence. It features a cucumber flower. The image was digitally processed with the intent to retain authenticity while adding visual impact.

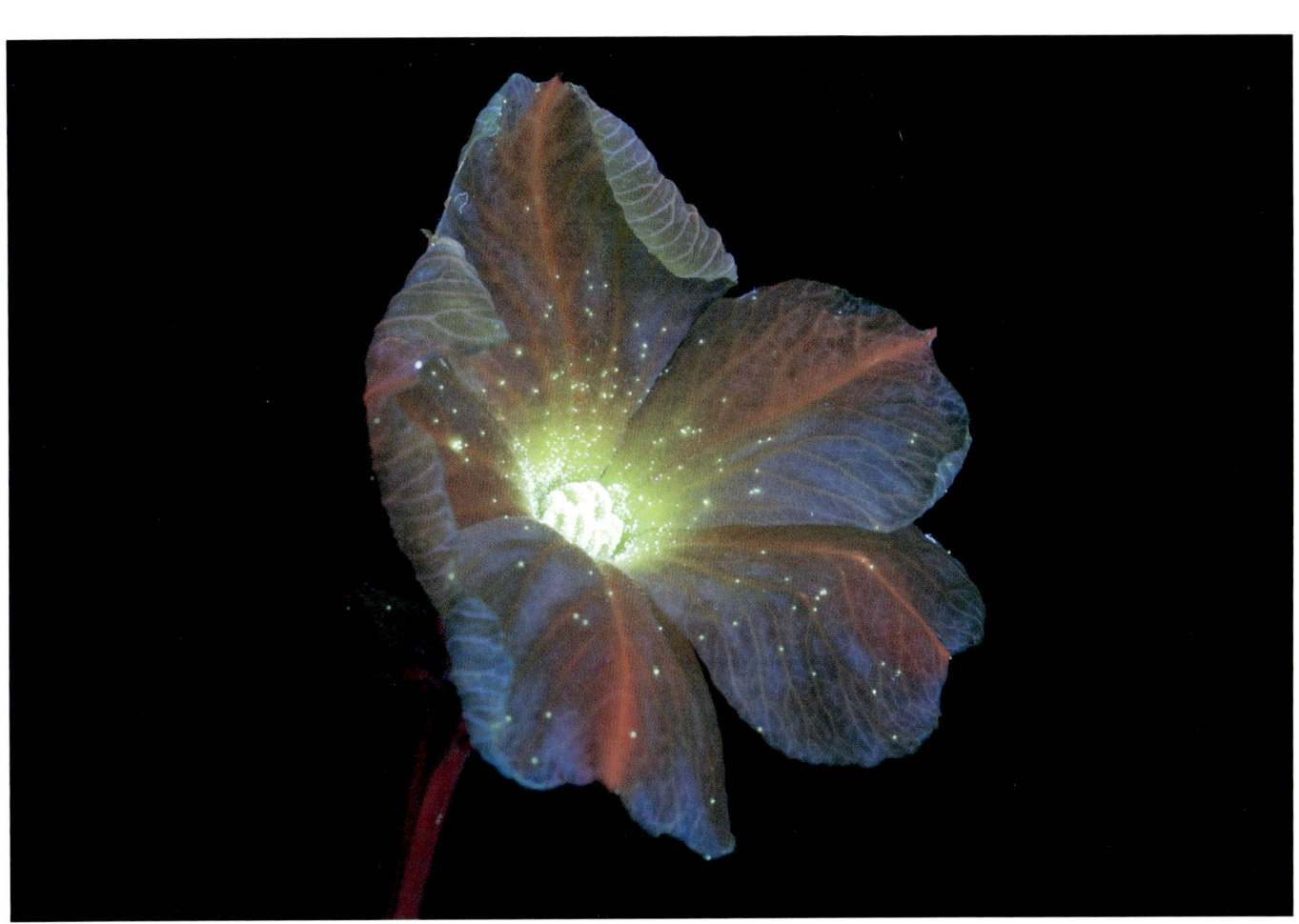

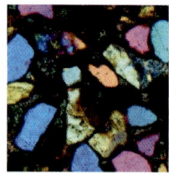

Bernardo Cesare

Dinosaur Bone, 2017

Polarized light photomicrograph; Zeiss Axioscope 40 POL polarized light microscope; 2.5x POL objective was used; polarizers at 90 degrees with a red tint plate in the optical pathway; Nikon D5500 DSLR camera

Geosciences Department, University of Padua, Padua, Italy

This photomicrograph features a 30-micron slice of a dinosaur bone collected in Utah, United States. The image shows the highly porous bone structure; the pores are filled with late chalcedony. The fossil reveals remnants of the bone tissue, and the black dots reveal the shape of former single bone cells. The larger void on the top left was filled with a silt-rich sediment composed of quartz angular clasts. The section of bone visible in the microscope was 5.3 millimeters.

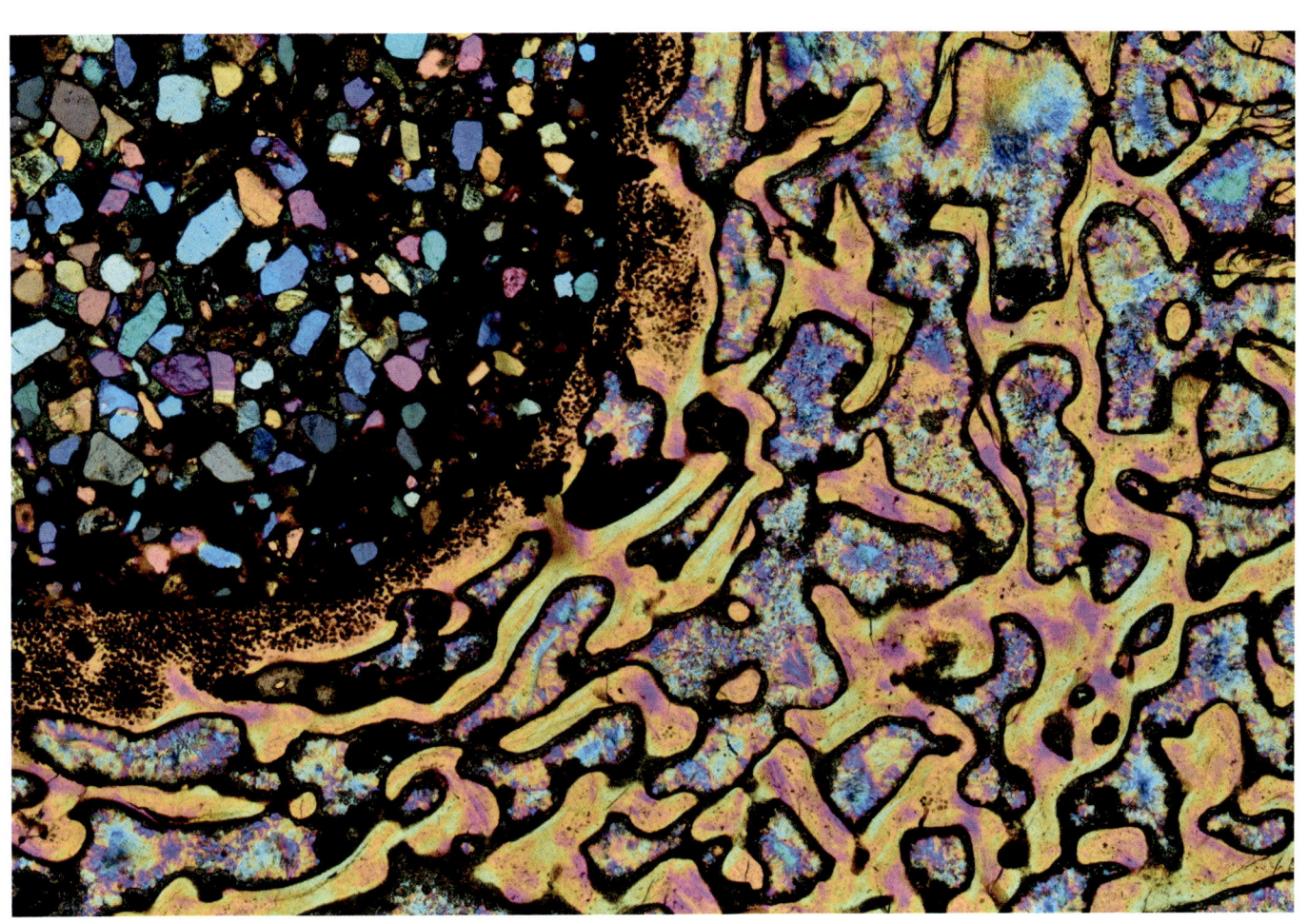

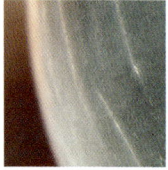

Angela Chappell

Wolverine Eye/Descemet's Membrane Folds, 2017

Ophthalmic sclerotic scatter slit lamp photograph; Haag-Streit PBQ900 photo slit lamp

Ophthalmology Department, Flinders Medical Centre, Bedford Park, South Australia, Australia

---

This external eye photograph was captured using sclerotic scatter lighting. A controlled, decentered slit beam is directed to the corneoscleral junction or limbus, scattering light through the cornea or front window structure of the eye. The linear corneal abnormalities revealed are folds in a deep layer of the cornea which is called Descemet's membrane. These can be caused by birth trauma, including forceps injury of the eye, or other eye trauma later in life. In this case the clarity of the cornea was adversely affected such that the patient was later given a Descemet's stripping endothelial keratoplasty or DSEK corneal transplant to restore clear vision.

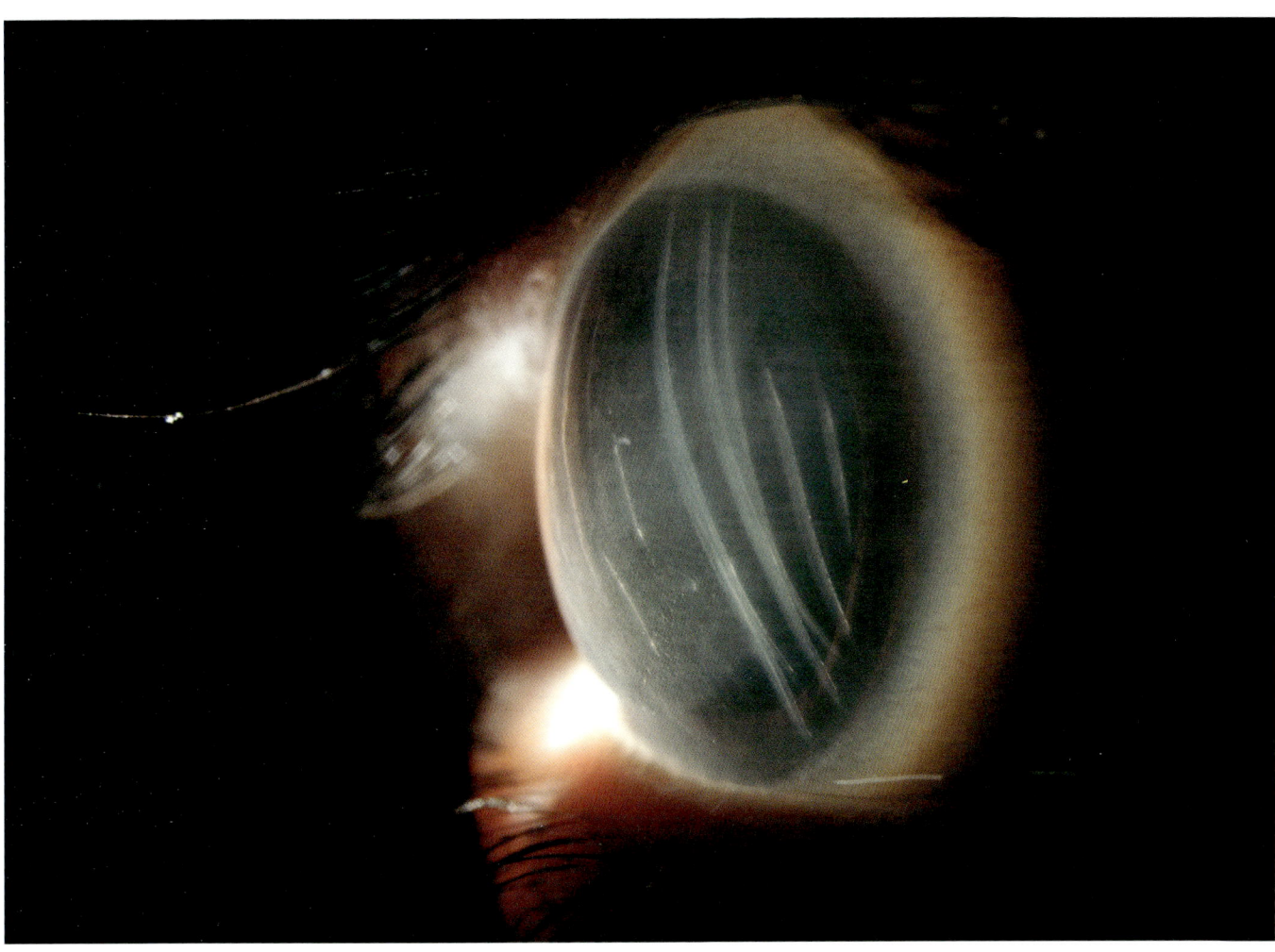

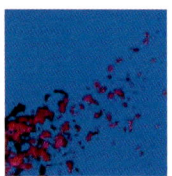

Ashley Crichton

Lipstick Being Shot by a Bullet, 2018

High-speed photograph; DSLR camera with 100mm lens; Arduino circuit with infrared sensors and trigger; image processed with Adobe Photoshop

Rochester Institute of Technology, Rochester, New York, United States

---

This picture features the results of a high-speed photographic system used to capture the impact of a bullet milliseconds after passing through a tube of lipstick. Before reaching the lipstick tube, the bullet passed in front of infrared sensors, which triggered a high-speed electronic flash. The platform used to support the subject has been removed.

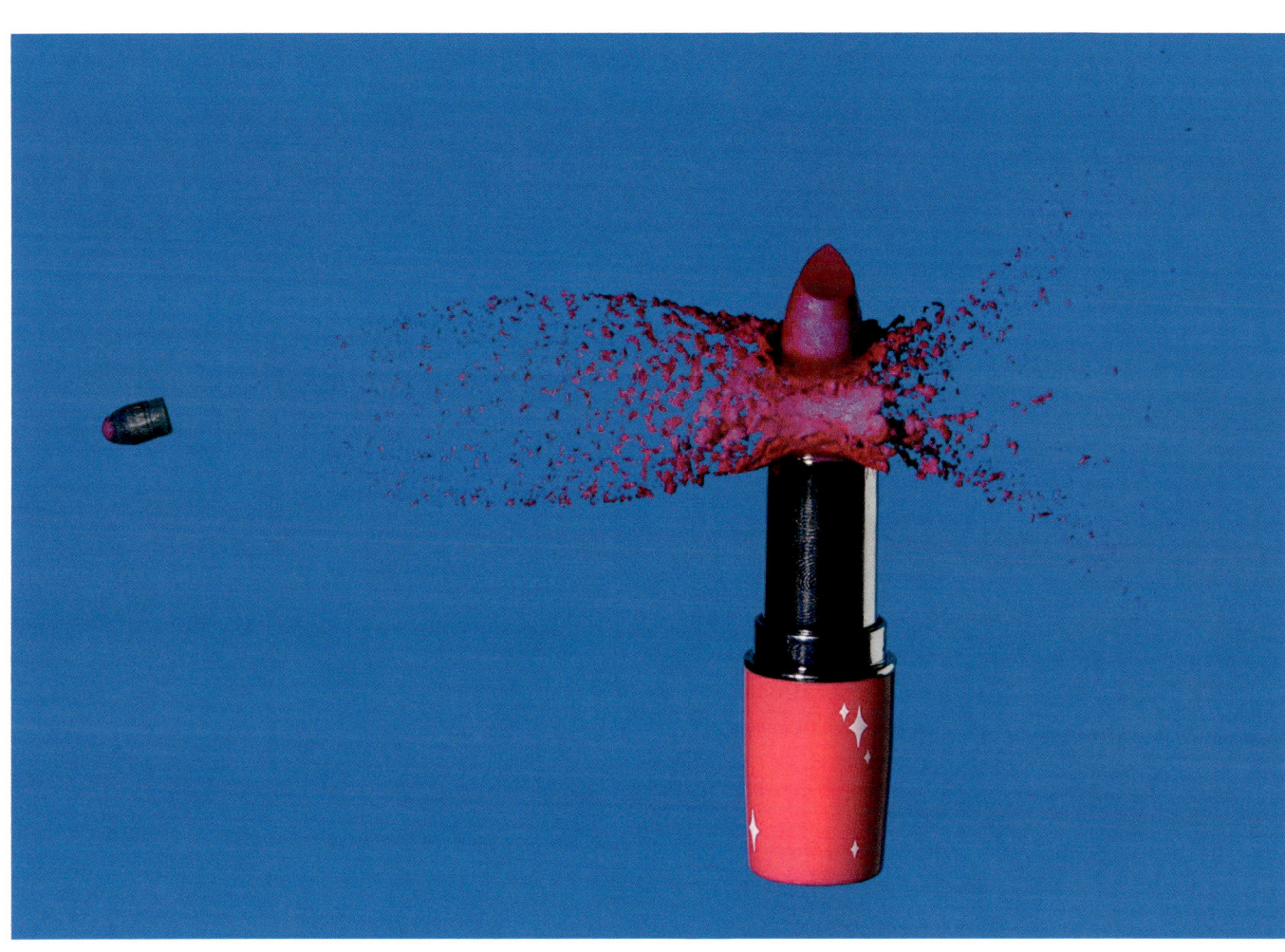

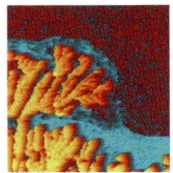

Hans U. Danzebrink

Flow in Colors, 2018

Composite photomicrograph; area approximately 3x3 millimeters; Zeiss Axiophot2 equipped with EC Epiplan 5x/0.13 HD objective; Axiocam; white light illumination, dark-field contrast, and post-capture coloring; a composite of multiple images stitched together

Physikalisch-Technische Bundesanstalt, Braunschweig, Germany

This image is part of a study in which a droplet of a liquid suspension of nanoparticles (PMMA, 190 nanometers in diameter) was placed onto a silicon surface and dried. This created a circular pattern sharing different particle densities. Nanoparticles are among the most controversial materials in science today. They could revolutionize drug delivery and enhance medical imaging, but they also provoke concerns about unknown influences to health and the environment. The imaging technique combines optical microscopy and scanning probe techniques—atomic force microscopes—that bridge the micro- and nanoscales.

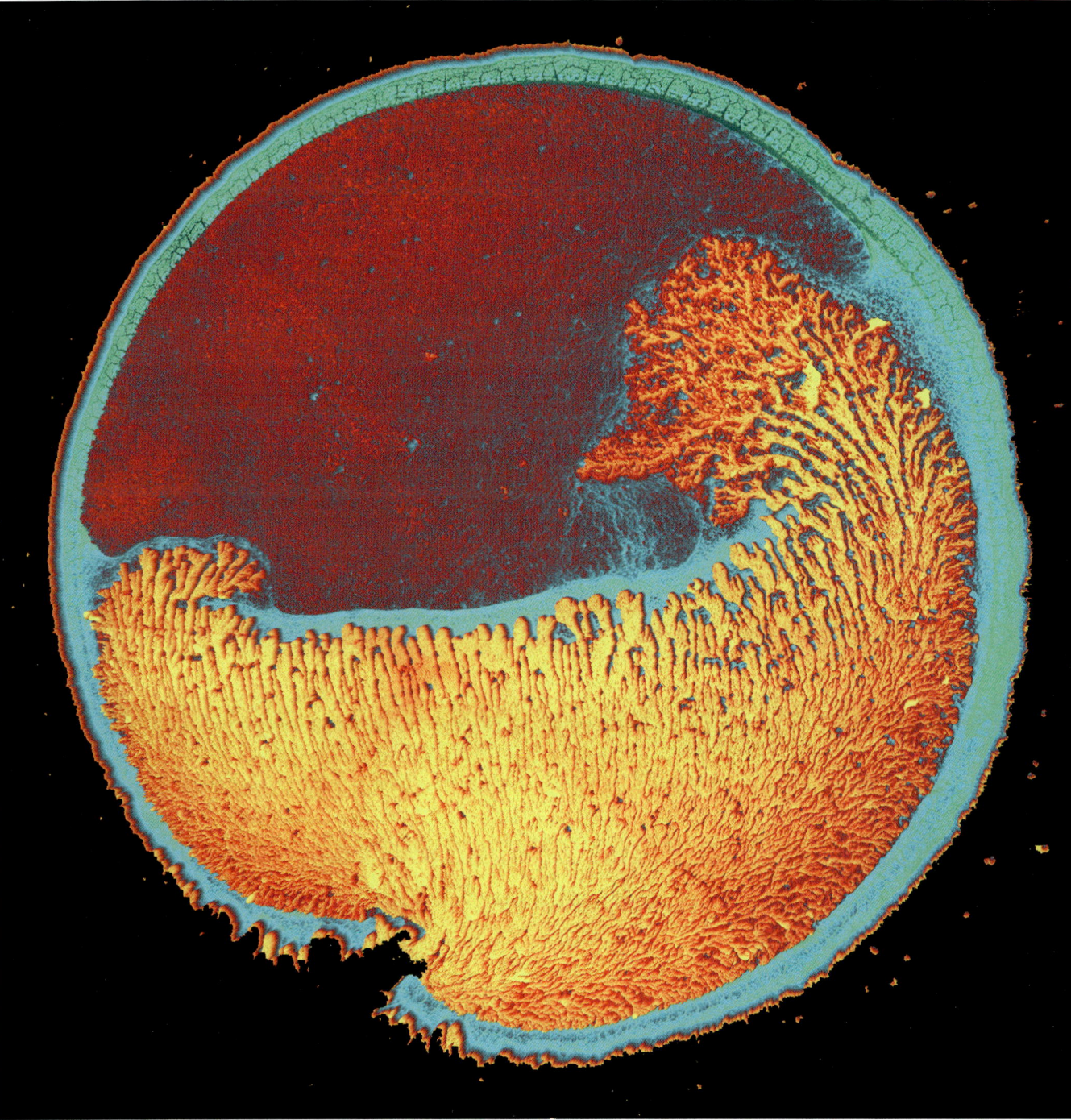

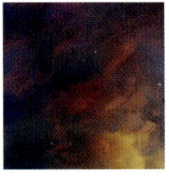

Joseph DePasquale

Lagoon Nebula — Messier 8, 2018

Astrophotograph

Space Telescope Science Institute, Johns Hopkins University, Baltimore, Maryland, United States

---

This colorful image, taken by NASA's Hubble Space Telescope, gives a breathtaking view of the universe's extraordinary tapestry of stellar birth and destruction. At the center of the photo, a monster young star, 200,000 times brighter than our Sun, is blasting powerful ultraviolet radiation and hurricane-like stellar winds, carving out a fantasy landscape of ridges, cavities, and mountains of gas and dust. This mayhem is all happening at the heart of the Lagoon Nebula, a vast stellar nursery located 4,000 light-years away and visible in binoculars simply as a smudge of light with a bright core. The clouds may look majestic and peaceful, but they are in a constant state of flux due to the surrounding torrent of searing radiation and high-speed particles from stellar winds. The Hubble view shows off the nebula's 3D structure. Dust pushed away from the core reveals the glowing oxygen gas (blue) behind the blown-out cavity. The central star's brilliant light illuminates the top of the cavity (yellow). The reddish hue that dominates part of the region is glowing nitrogen. The dark purple areas represent a mixture of hydrogen, oxygen, and nitrogen. The image shows a region of the nebula measuring about 4 light-years across.

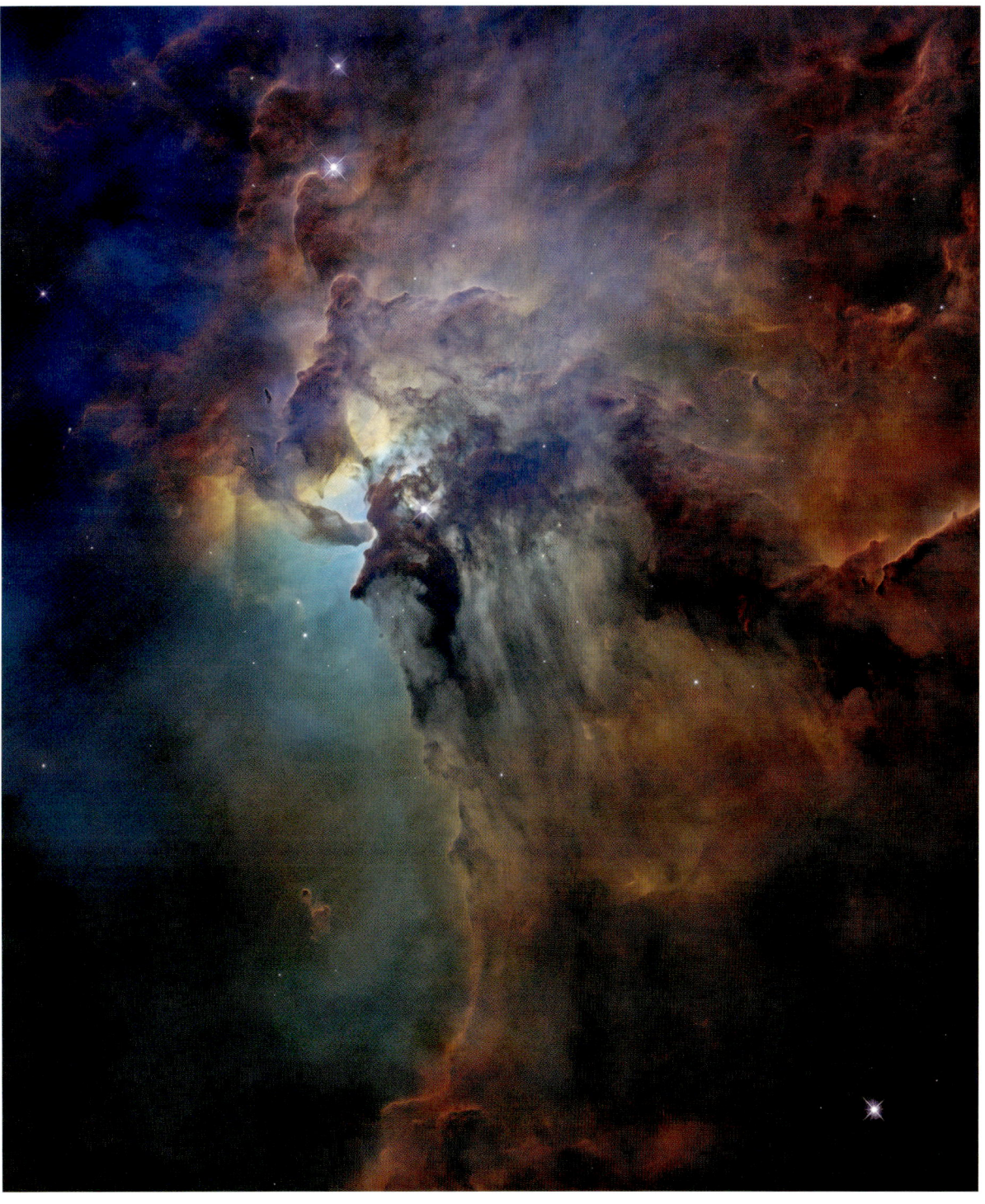

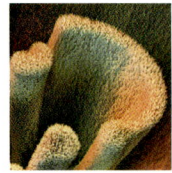

Stefan Diller

Self-assembling Hierarchical Microstructures, 2019

Scanning electron photomicrograph; TESCAN MIRA3 field emission scanning electron microscope with four-channel multi-detector image system, developed by Point Electronic in Halle, Germany, that colorizes an image as it is formed

Würzburg, Germany

The micrograph features carbonate-silica microstructures grown in a dynamic reaction-diffusion system. This allows for precise sculpting of a great variety of elementary shapes by diffusion of carbon dioxide in a solution of barium chloride and sodium metasilicate. Samples were prepared at AMOLF Institute, Amsterdam, Netherlands, by Lukas Helmbrecht and Wim L. Noorduin.

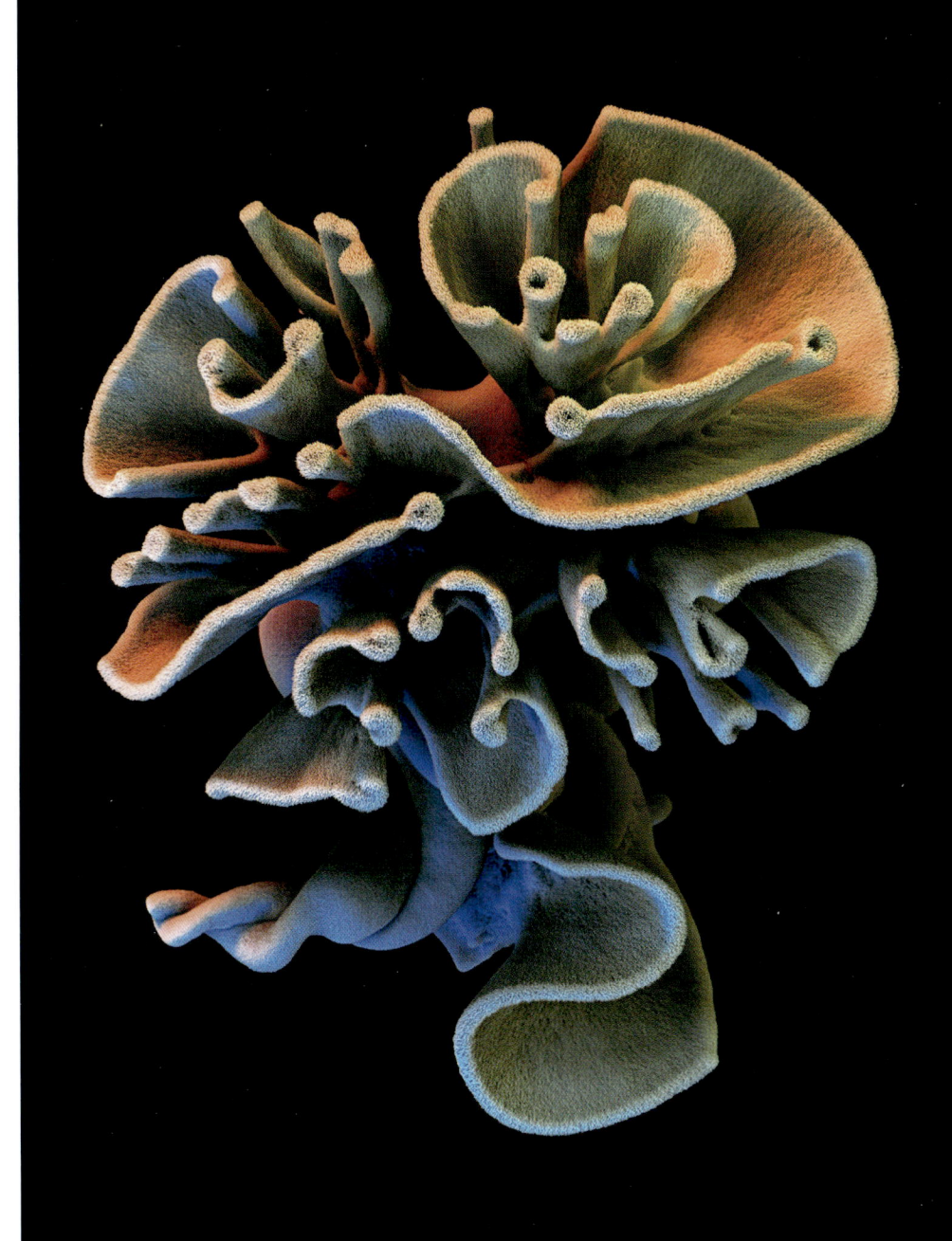

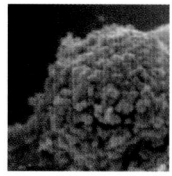

Stefan Diller

Cellular Flybys, 2018

Scanning electron microscope video montage; TESCAN MIRA3 field emission scanning electron microscope; SmarAct Oldenburg to-the-nanometer, micro-degree controllable eight-axes piezo stage for specimen movement; four-channel multi-detector image system, developed by Point Electronic in Halle, Germany, that colorized the image as it was formed; nanoflight.creator control software; 1 second of video approximates 1 hour of scanning

Würzburg, Germany

This video features three nanoflight sequences on and around genetically engineered cell structures. First shown are very tiny (600-nanometer diameter) "minimal genome" cells developed at the J. Craig Venter Institute. The cell line is SYN3A. The second sequence shows genetically engineered T cells that fight lymphoblastic leukemia; the cells are from the Clinical Cell and Vaccine Production Facility at the University of Pennsylvania. The therapy, now named KYMRIAH by Novartis, had been the first CAR (chimeric antigen receptor) T cell therapy approved by the FDA; it was approved in 2018. The final sequence shows organoids made by CPO Berlin-Buch. CPO's approach to "Precision Oncology and Personalized Therapy Prediction" is to develop cell model structures to test various combinations of chemotherapy treatments.

https://vimeo.com/313015303/8f42b22337

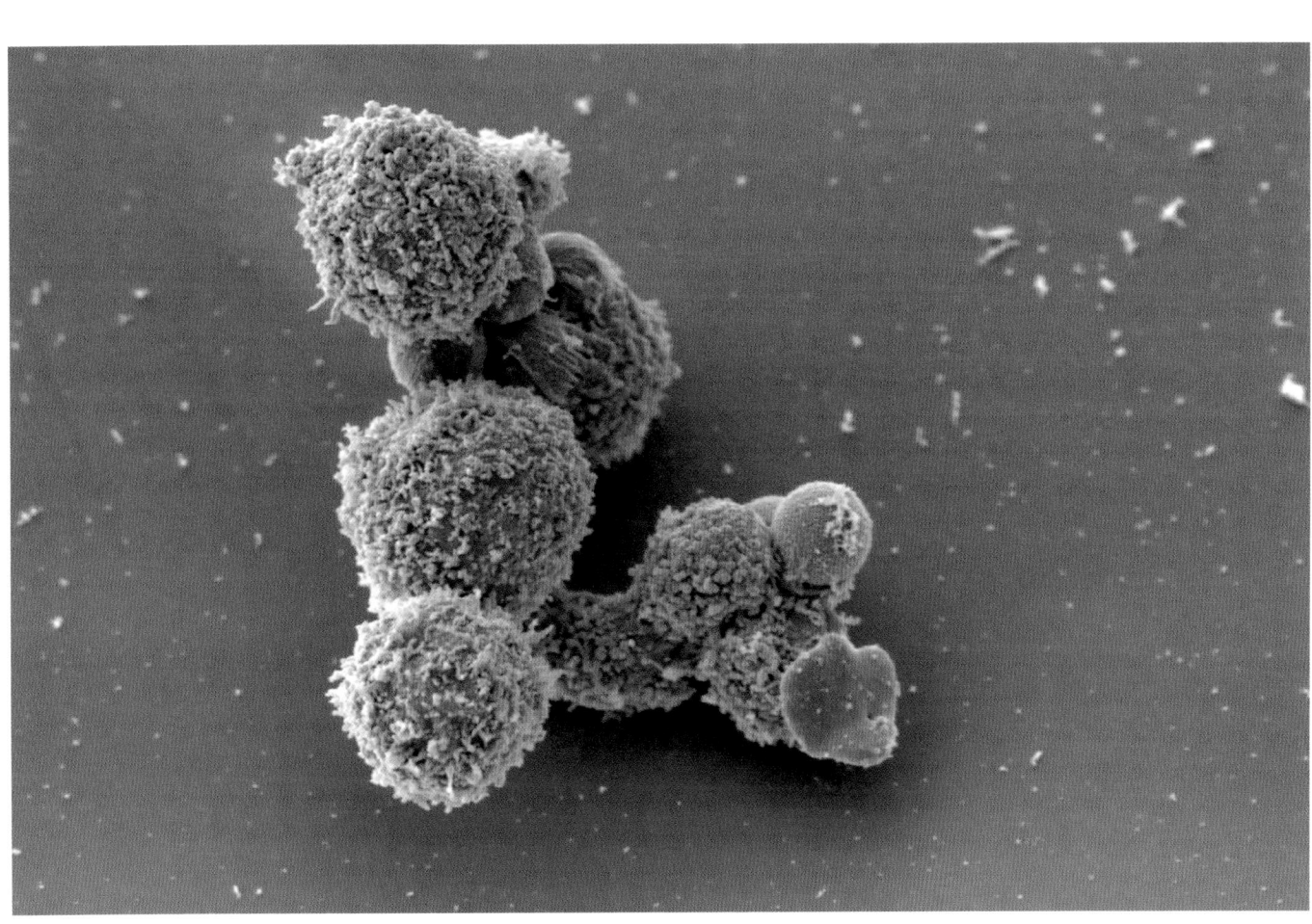

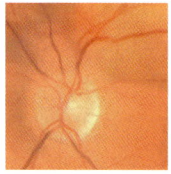

Joss Dimock

Worm Tracks in a Retina, 2018

Retinal fundus photograph; 30 millimeters wide x 27 millimeters high; Topcon 50 EX fundus camera; 30 images taken at 50-degree views were stitched together using Adobe Photoshop; overlapping edges were erased and some were distorted where blood vessels did not match up perfectly, but the actual worm track was not distorted in any way; composite image received a small amount of sharpening

Melbourne Health, Melbourne, Victoria, Australia

This is a composite retinal fundus photograph of a patient with worm tracks showing peripheral chorioretinal changes with pigment dispersion and focal areas of atrophy. The image was taken for clinical reasons.

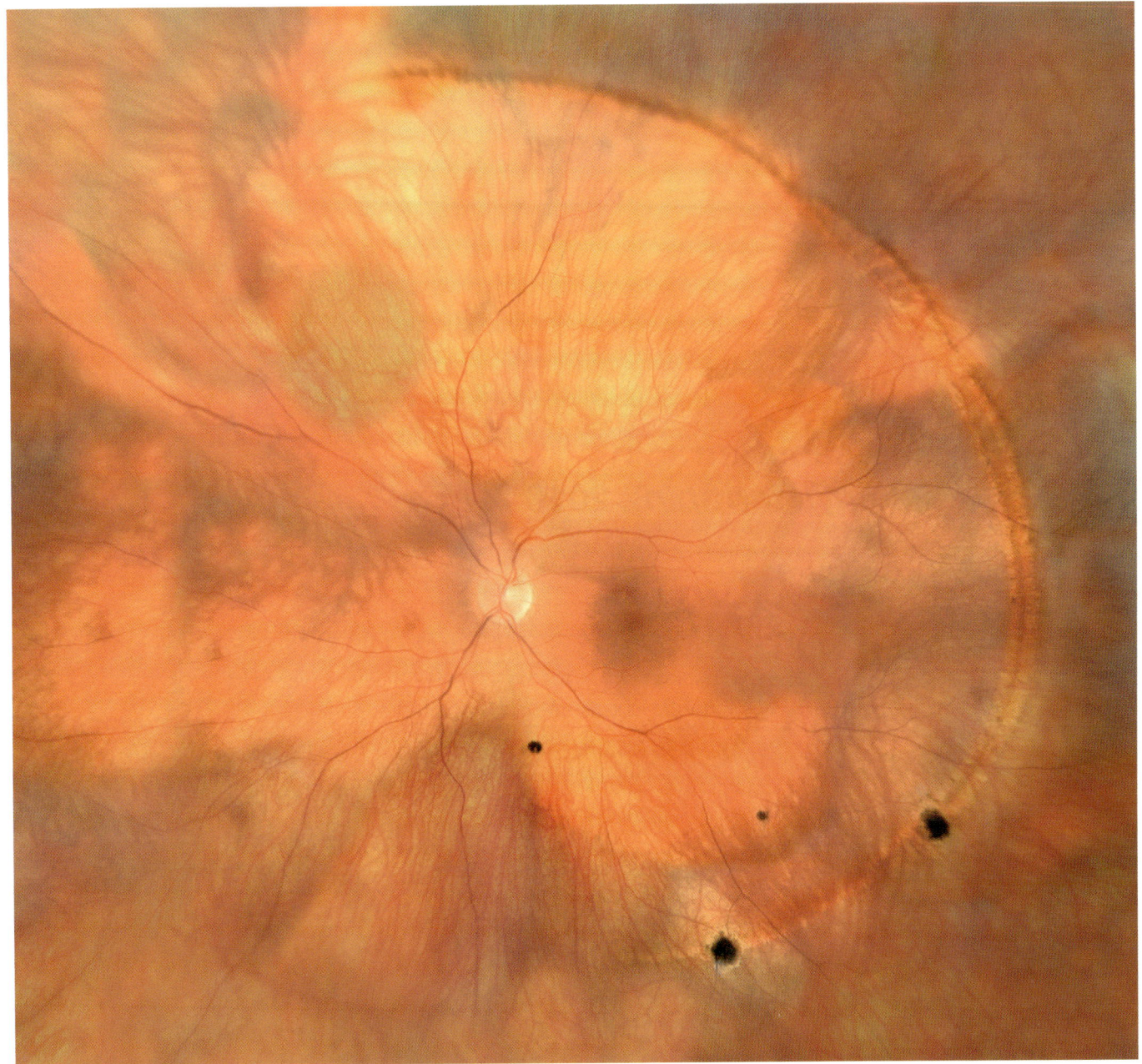

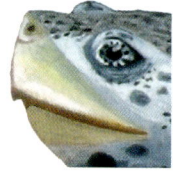

Emily A. Dustman

Diamondback Terrapin (*Malaclemys terrapin*), 2016

Acrylic on board/digital reproduction

www.emilydustman.com, St. Louis, Missouri, United States

This illustration was part of a series of seven featuring turtles. It was created to visually represent the turtles found in Rhode Island for conservation and educational purposes.

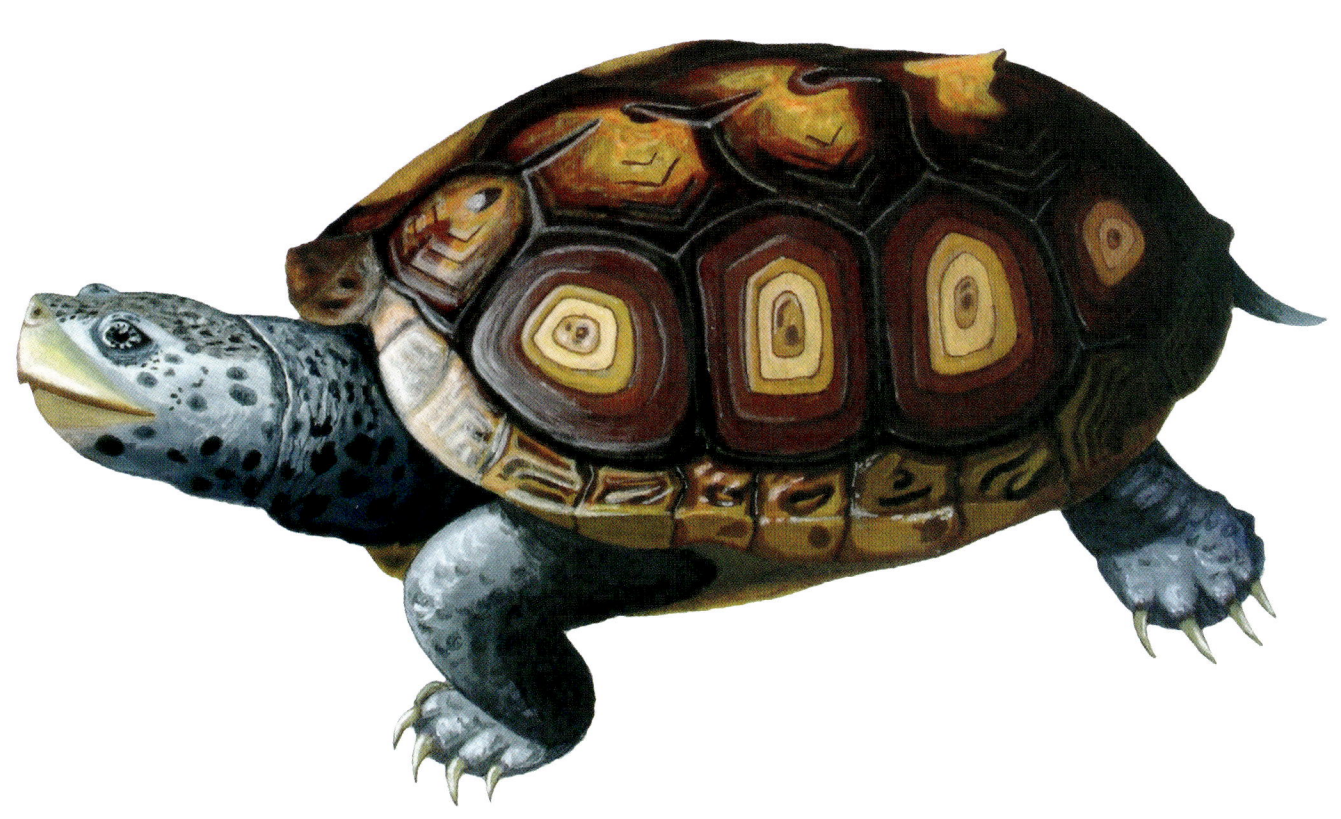

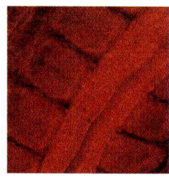

Lydia Dye

Chick Embryo at 48 Hours, 2018

Confocal photomicrograph; excitation energy 520–580 nanometers

Rochester Institute of Technology, Rochester, New York, United States

This photomicrograph features a chick embryo. The sample was prepared 48 hours after fertilization. The specimen was approximately 3 millimeters from top to bottom.

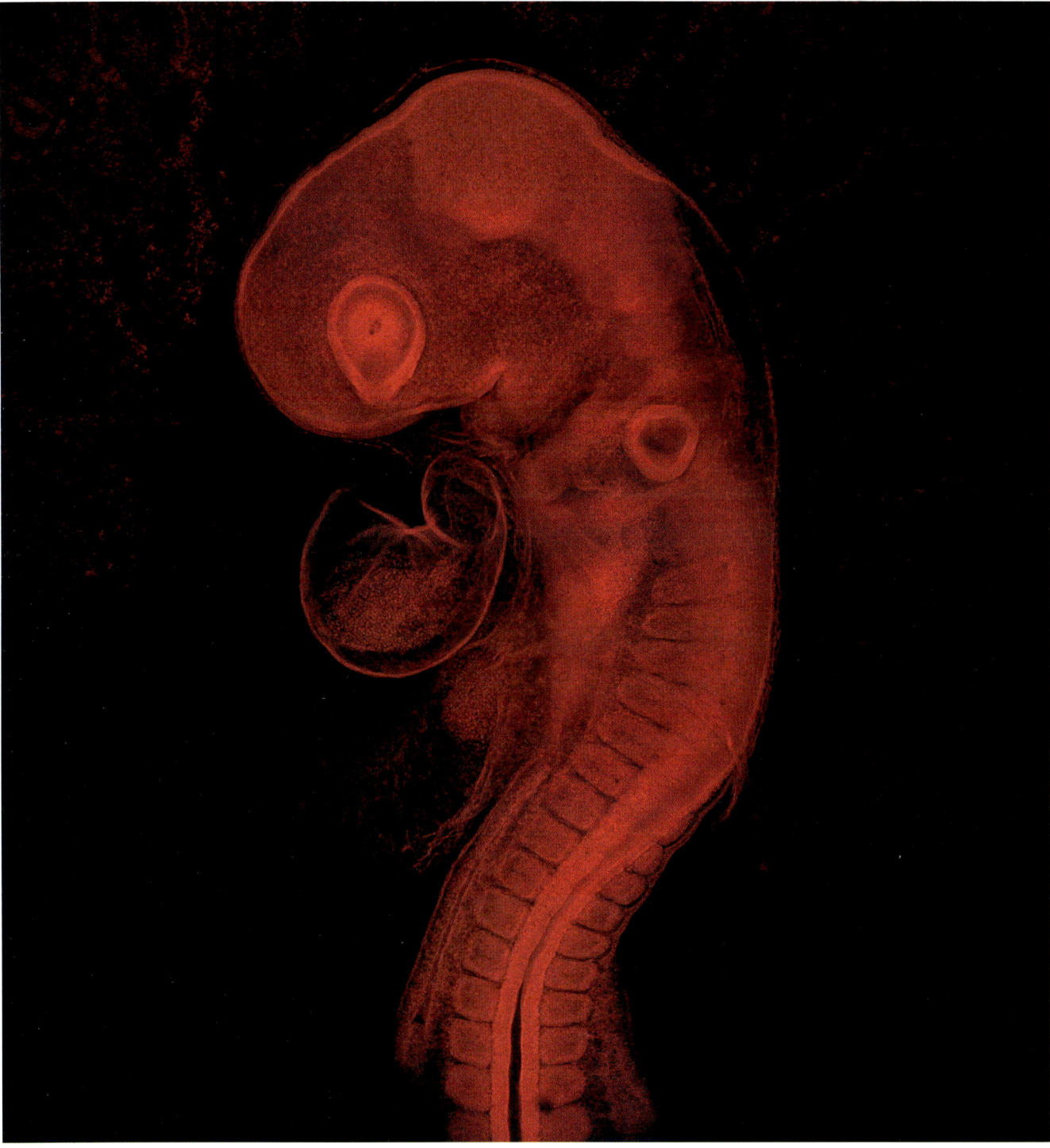

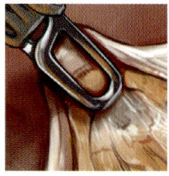

Hannah Bryce Ely

Incising the Periureteral Space during Robot-assisted Radical Cystectomy, 2019

Digital illustration; sketched by hand using surgical video footage and Adobe Photoshop

ATLAS Studios, Roswell Park Comprehensive Cancer Center, Buffalo, New York, United States

This image shows the first step of a robot-assisted radical cystectomy. Featured is the process of locating the ureter and then incising the periureteral space. It was drawn for inclusion in a surgical atlas used to train robotic surgeons on new techniques and procedures.

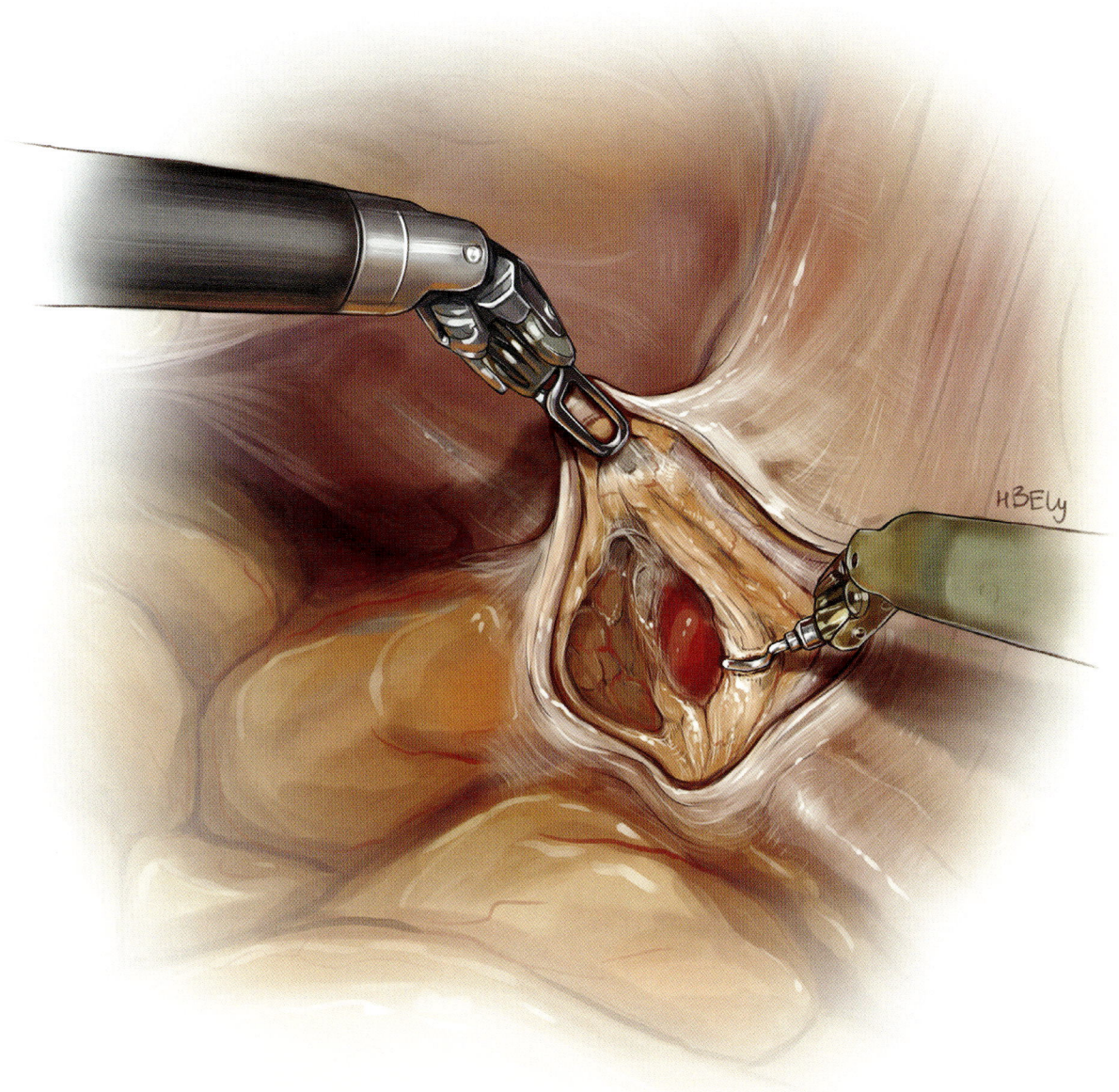

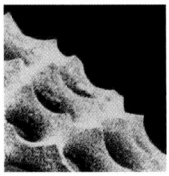

Nathan Ely

Radiolaria, 2018

Scanning electron photomicrograph; cyanotype; digital reproduction

The State University of New York at Buffalo, Buffalo, New York, United States

---

This work operates at the intersection of scientific and historic photographic processes. Its origins are grounded in interdisciplinary research using an electron microscope required for the production of carefully made sublime representations of nature. Final prints are created using a historic photographic process known as cyanotype, which produces a characteristic Prussian blue color. Incorporating handcrafted printing techniques places the image further outside of its ordinary taxonomy as an object of science and emphasizes aesthetic qualities, as well as the physicality of sample.

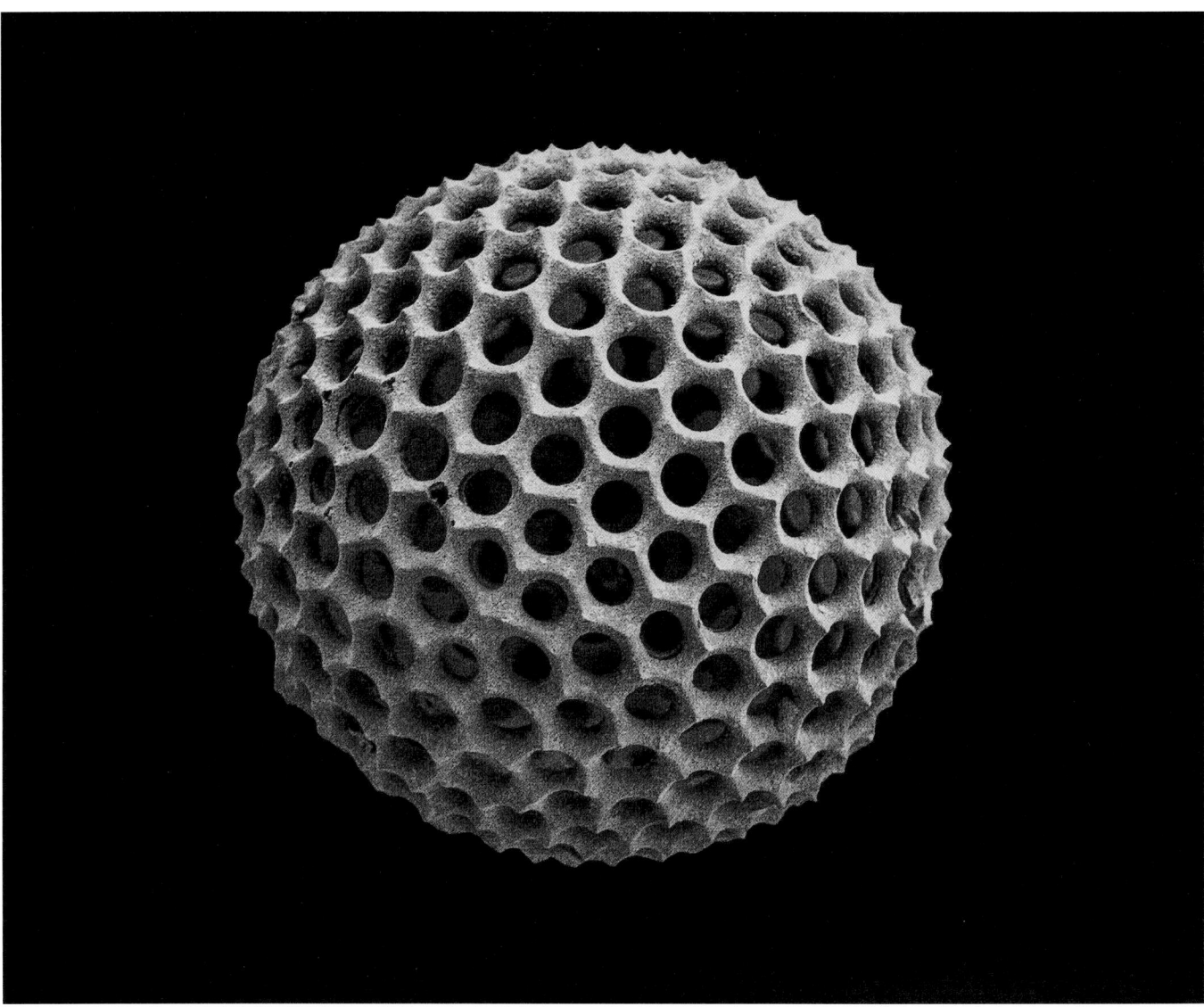

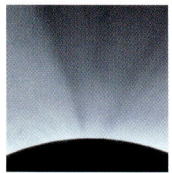

Blake Estes

Solar Eclipse, 2017

Astrophotograph; SkyWatcher Esprit 150ED triplet telescope; Celestron CGE Pro computerized tracking mount; Sony A7R II DSLR camera, and HDR combination software

Mount Wilson Observatory, Mount Wilson, California; and OPT, Carlsbad, California, United States

---

This photograph shows the structures of the solar corona, the outermost part of the Sun's atmosphere.

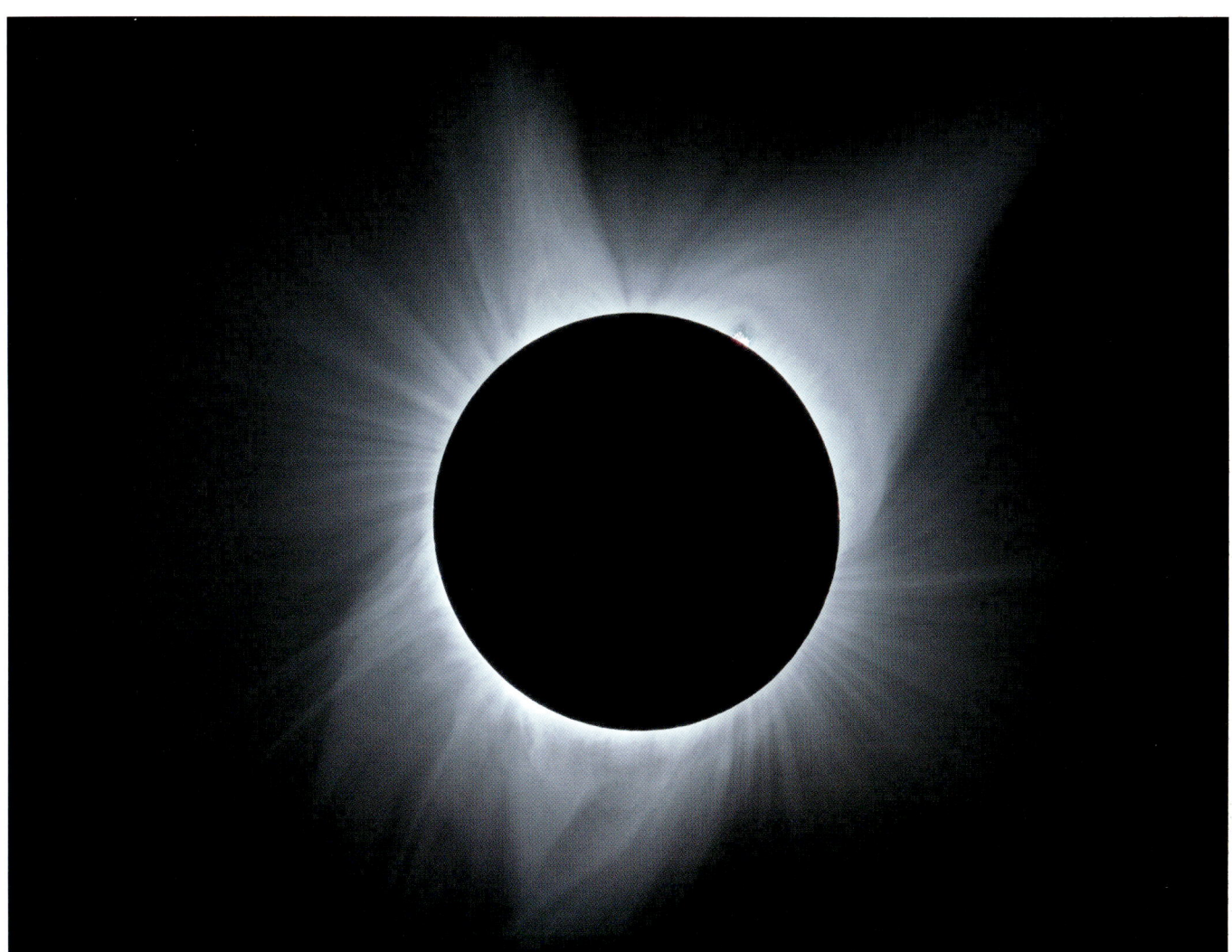

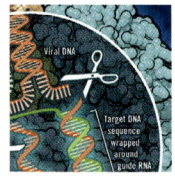

Jennifer E. Fairman

Juror Selection Award

Snip vs. Shred—Understanding CRISPR-Cas Systems (Cas9 vs. Cascade/Cas3), 2015

Digital illustration; Protein Data Bank data; Adobe Illustrator and Adobe Photoshop

Johns Hopkins University School of Medicine, Baltimore, Maryland, United States

---

This illustration depicts two CRISPR-Cas systems, comparing a scissor-snipping Cas9 complex and a shredder-like Cascade/Cas3 complex. The illustration conceptually highlights the differences between their structures and functions. Both complexes are genetically engineered tools based on one of several naturally occurring bacterial immune systems that fight bacteriophages by targeting viral DNA sequences. Key differences are that the Cas9 is a single protein, while Cascade/Cas3 is a complex of multiple proteins. Cas9 acts as a dual antibody-enzyme, while Cascade/Cas3 acts sequentially as an antibody-enzyme. Cas9 targets viral DNA when it is still formed as a double helix with a hairpin of bacterial guide-RNA, while Cascade/Cas3 targets viral DNA as it unwinds and binds with bacterial guide-RNA in a flat, ladder-like configuration. Cas9 precisely snips viral DNA, like molecular scissors, cleaving individual base pairs, while Cas3 shreds large portions of viral DNA.

Briefings

SNIP VS. SHRED

While CRISPR-Cas9 genome editing gets all the headlines, its cousin may revolutionize the fight against bad bacteria.

BY ALEXANDER GELFAND

THE POWERFUL GENOME-EDITING TECHNOLOGY known as CRISPR-Cas made headlines this year— partly because many leading biologists called for a moratorium last March against using it to modify the genomes of human embryos, only to discover in April that Chinese scientists had already done just that.

But CRISPR-Cas is more than a genetic engineering tool with profound ethical implications. In fact, the tool itself is a modified version of one of several types of naturally occurring bacterial immune systems that fight bacteriophages (viruses that infect bacteria). The particular system that researchers have adapted for gene-editing is a relatively rare and simple one called CRISPR-Cas9. Scott Bailey, PhD, associate professor in Biochemistry and Molecular Biology, recently described the atomic structure of a far more common, and far more complicated, CRISPR-Cas system called CRISPR-Cascade—one with profound implications of its own.

Bacteria use CRISPR-Cas systems to store the genetic signatures of phages that have previously infected them. These viral mug shots appear in host DNA as stretches of viral DNA separated by short, repeated sequences. (CRISPR stands for "clustered, regularly interspaced, short palindromic repeats.") When a phage invades, CRISPR-Cas compares phage DNA to its archive of previous invaders. If a match is found, Cas9 cuts the invading DNA like a pair of molecular scissors, while Cascade employs Cas3 to shred the viral DNA.

Using synthetic RNA, scientists can program CRISPR-Cas9 to target specific genes, allowing them to disrupt, delete or replace DNA more quickly, easily and cheaply than ever before. And whereas making changes to multiple genes at the same time was once extremely difficult and inefficient, CRISPR-Cas9 makes it simple. Its reliability and ease of use have already revolutionized genomic research, and could one day lead to clinical applications such as gene therapy.

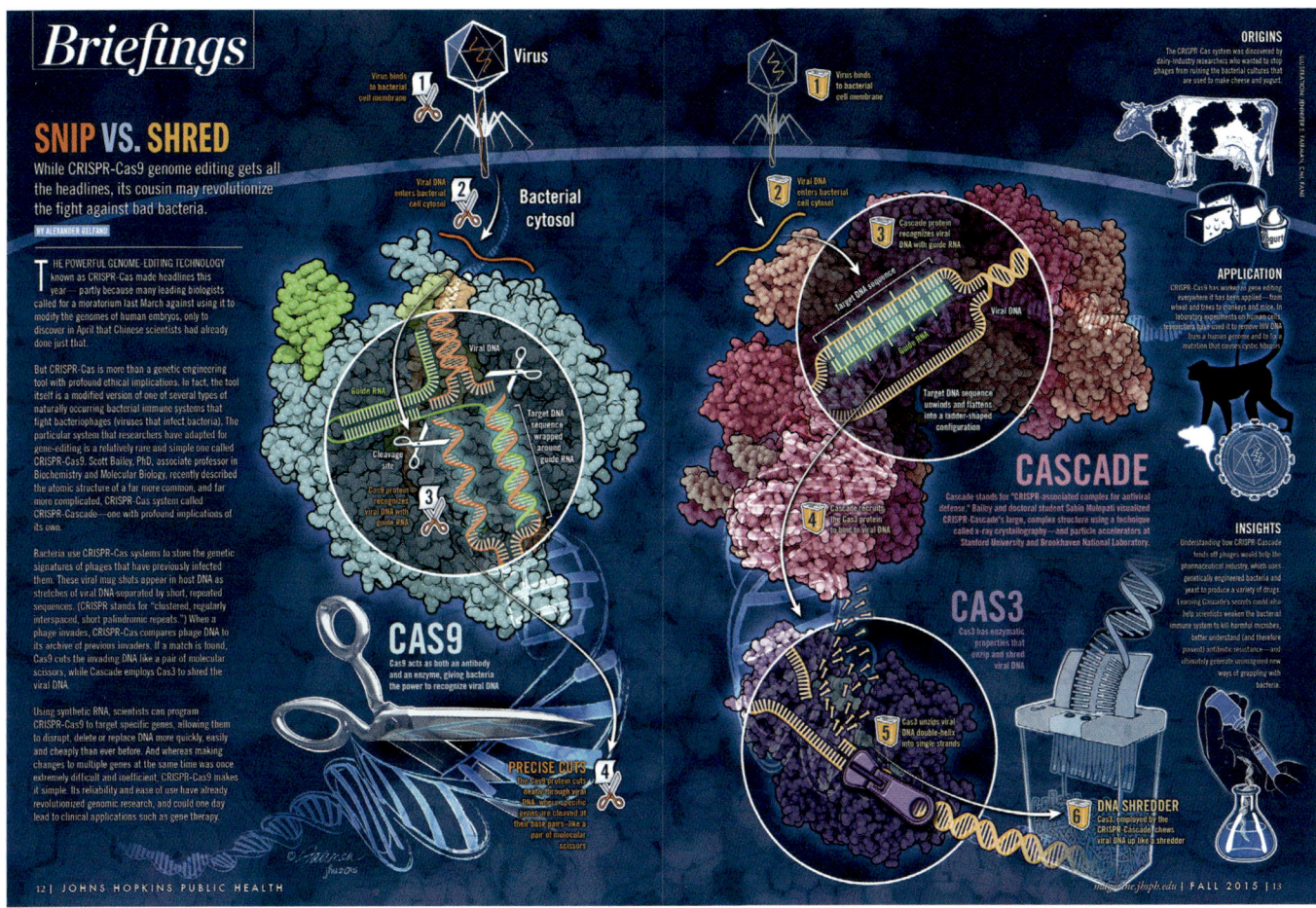

Virus

1 Virus binds to bacterial cell membrane

2 Viral DNA enters bacterial cell cytosol

Bacterial cytosol

Viral DNA

Guide RNA

Target DNA sequence wrapped around guide RNA

Cleavage site

3 Cas9 protein recognizes viral DNA with guide RNA

CAS9

Cas9 acts as both an antibody and an enzyme, giving bacteria the power to recognize viral DNA

PRECISE CUTS
4 The Cas9 protein cuts neatly through viral DNA, where specific genes are cleaved at their base pairs—like a pair of molecular scissors

1 Virus binds to bacterial cell membrane

2 Viral DNA enters bacterial cell cytosol

3 Cascade protein recognizes viral DNA with guide RNA

Target DNA sequence

Viral DNA

Guide RNA

Target DNA sequence unwinds and flattens into a ladder-shaped configuration

4 Cascade recruits the Cas3 protein to bind to viral DNA

CASCADE

Cascade stands for "CRISPR-associated complex for antiviral defense." Bailey and doctoral student Sabin Mulepati visualized CRISPR-Cascade's large, complex structure using a technique called x-ray crystallography—and particle accelerators at Stanford University and Brookhaven National Laboratory.

CAS3
Cas3 has enzymatic properties that unzip and shred viral DNA

5 Cas3 unzips viral DNA double-helix into single strands

DNA SHREDDER
6 Cas3, employed by the CRISPR-Cascade, chews viral DNA up like a shredder

ORIGINS
The CRISPR-Cas system was discovered by dairy-industry researchers who wanted to stop phages from ruining the bacterial cultures that are used to make cheese and yogurt.

APPLICATION
CRISPR-Cas9 has worked as gene editing everywhere it has been applied—from wheat and trees to monkeys and mice. In laboratory experiments on human cells, researchers have used it to remove HIV DNA from a human genome and to fix a mutation that causes cystic fibrosis.

INSIGHTS
Understanding how CRISPR-Cascade fends off invaders would help the pharmaceutical industry, which uses genetically engineered bacteria and yeast to produce a variety of drugs. Learning Cascade's secrets could also help scientists weaken the bacterial immune system to kill harmful microbes, better understand (and therefore prevent) antibiotic resistance—and ultimately generate unimagined new ways of grappling with bacteria.

ILLUSTRATION: JENNIFER E. FAIRMAN, CMI, FAMI

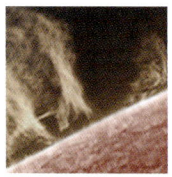

Alan Friedman

Massive Solar Prominence, 2017

Astrophotograph; small telescope; narrowband hydrogen-alpha filter

Buffalo, New York, United States

This photograph shows a close-up of a large solar prominence at the edge of the Sun.

http://www.avertedimagination.com/img_pages/whoa_again.html

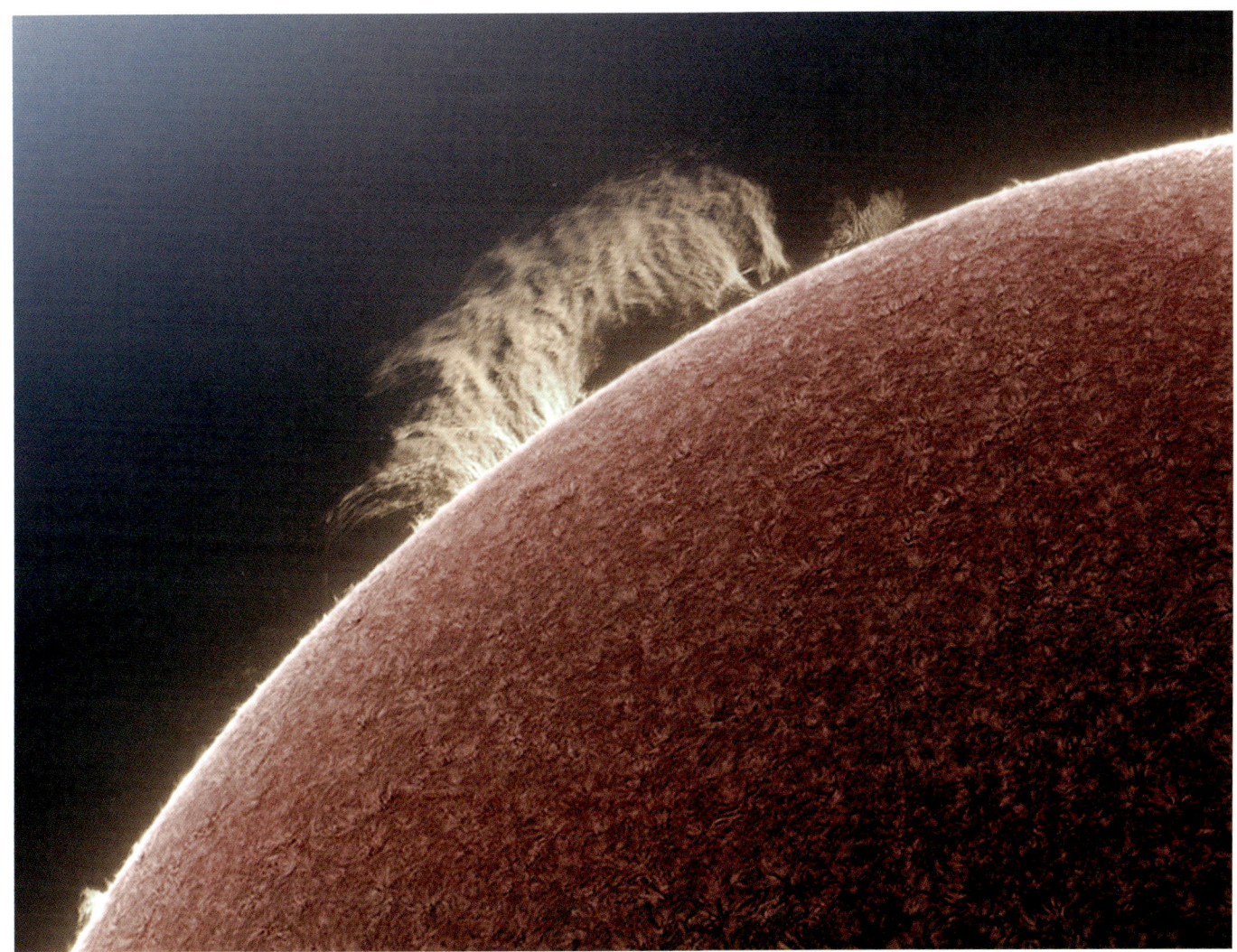

Alan Friedman

Chromosphere, 2016

Astrophotograph; small telescope; narrowband filter

Buffalo, New York, United States

This photograph features a full disk portrait of the Sun photographed using hydrogen-alpha light.

http://www.avertedimagination.com/img_pages/chromosphere_color.html

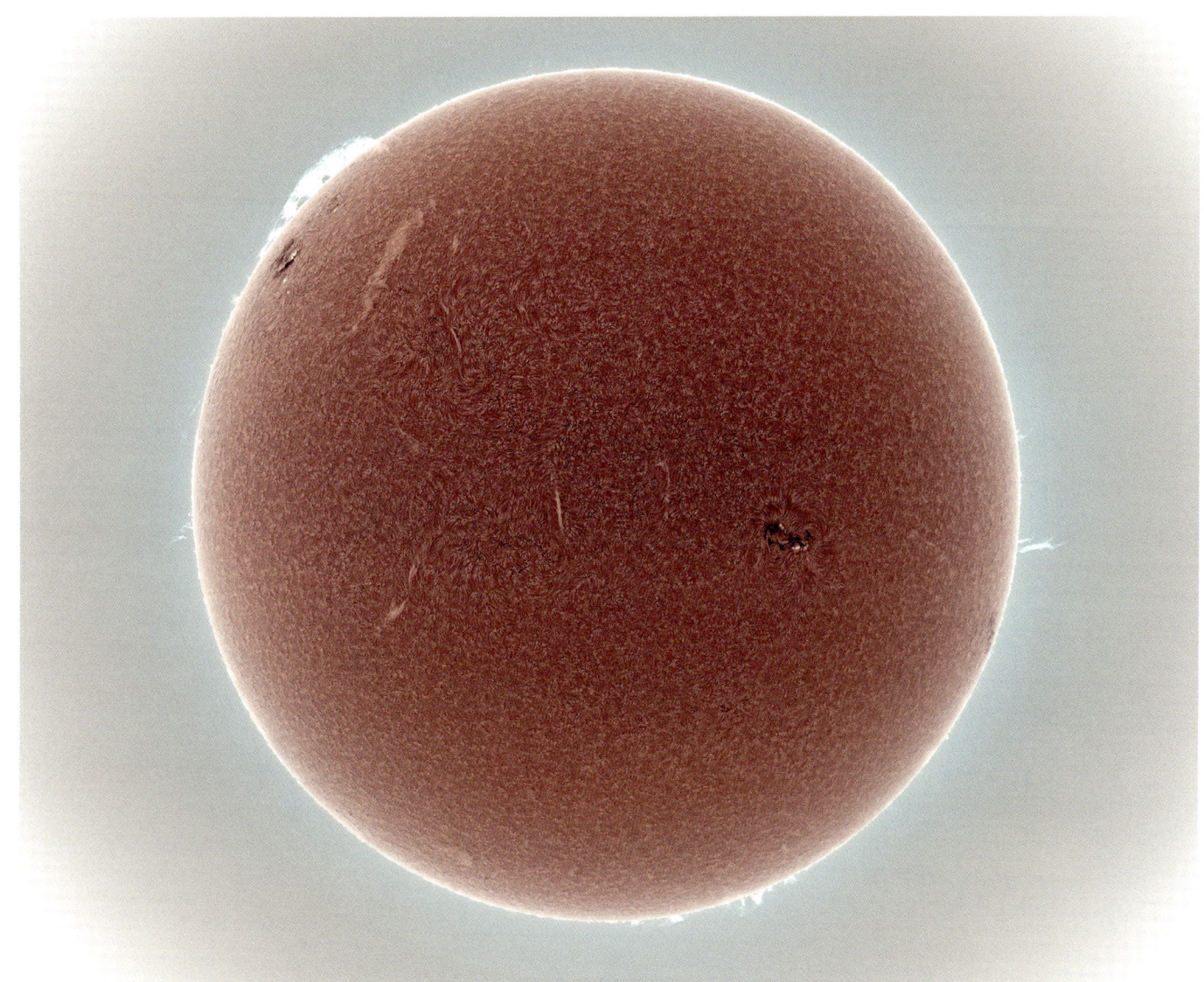

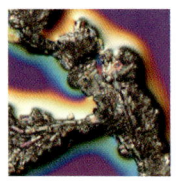

Karl Gaff

Branching Creatine, 2018

Photomicrograph; Olympus BX51 DIC microscope; capture magnification ~x150

Dublin, Ireland

Here we see a close-up of creatine crystals. Initially forming a heterogeneous mixture, solute particles consisting of creatine crystals were suspended in a bulk solvent of water. The crystals, jittering about in the molecular storm of Brownian motion, undergo random walks, colliding and sticking to other crystals like tiny magnets. Over time, these clusters grow in size, eventually forming the branched fractal structure seen here, called a Brownian tree.

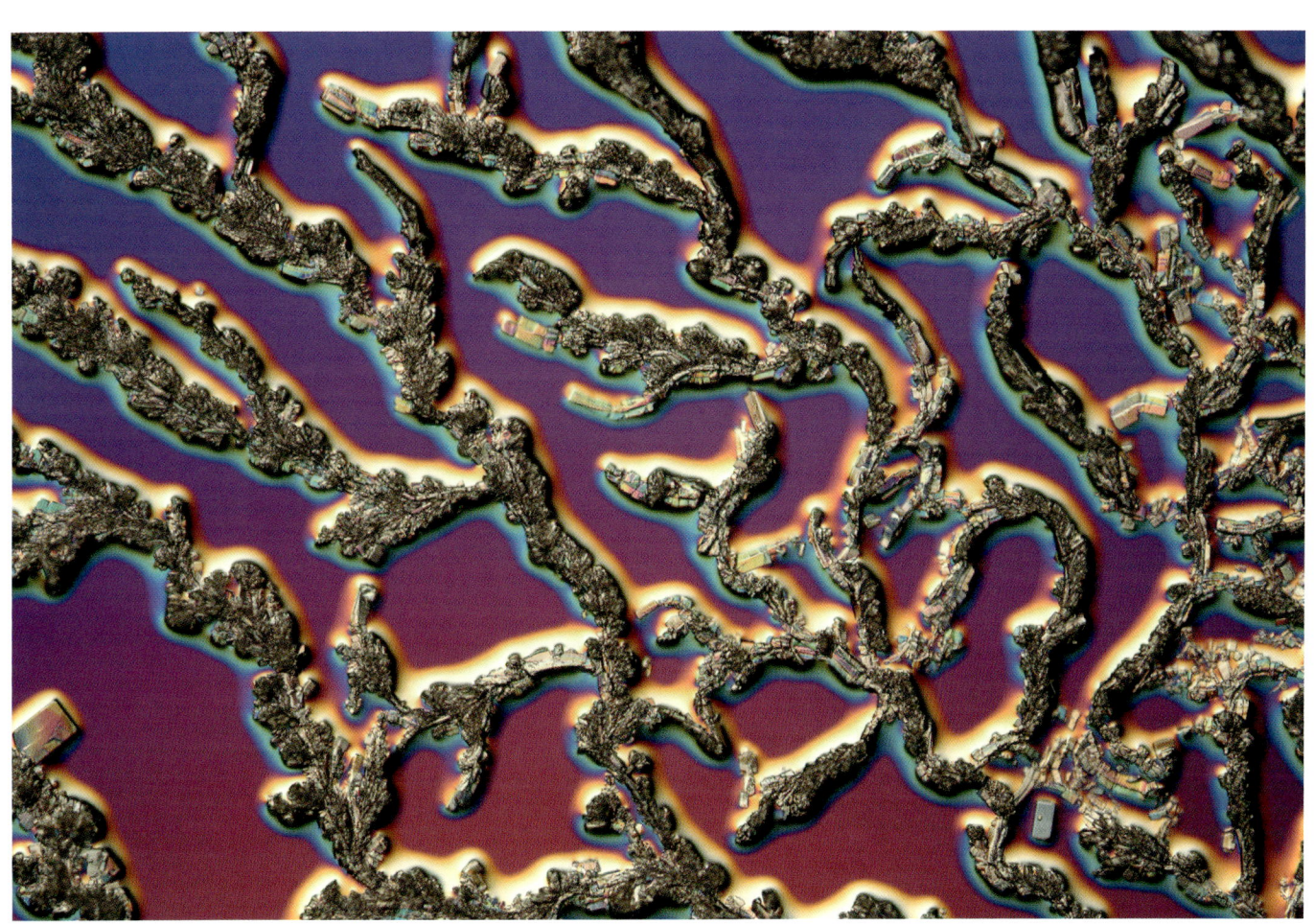

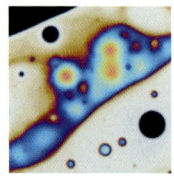

Karl Gaff

Thin Film Cosmicscape, 2018

Photomicrograph; Olympus BX51 DIC microscope; capture magnification ~x150;
the image displays thin film interference

Dublin, Ireland

When two fluids of different surface tensions are mixed, a complex interplay of fluid dynamics unfolds. In this case, the fluid is a mixture of dishwashing liquid and water. By introducing some sugar into the mixture, the lifetime of the soap film can be extended, while the continuous film breaks up into islands, as seen here. The islands are lipid globules floating on a thin film; because the film is too thin to support the interference of light, it appears as black as space. The islands and continuous lipid film produce dazzling interference colors because their film thickness is on the same order of magnitude as the wavelength of light. Variations in color are a result of the modulations in the thickness of the film. The film is thickest in the lower right of the image and gradually thins out diagonally toward the upper left, before decreasing to only several nanometers, where it becomes jet black.

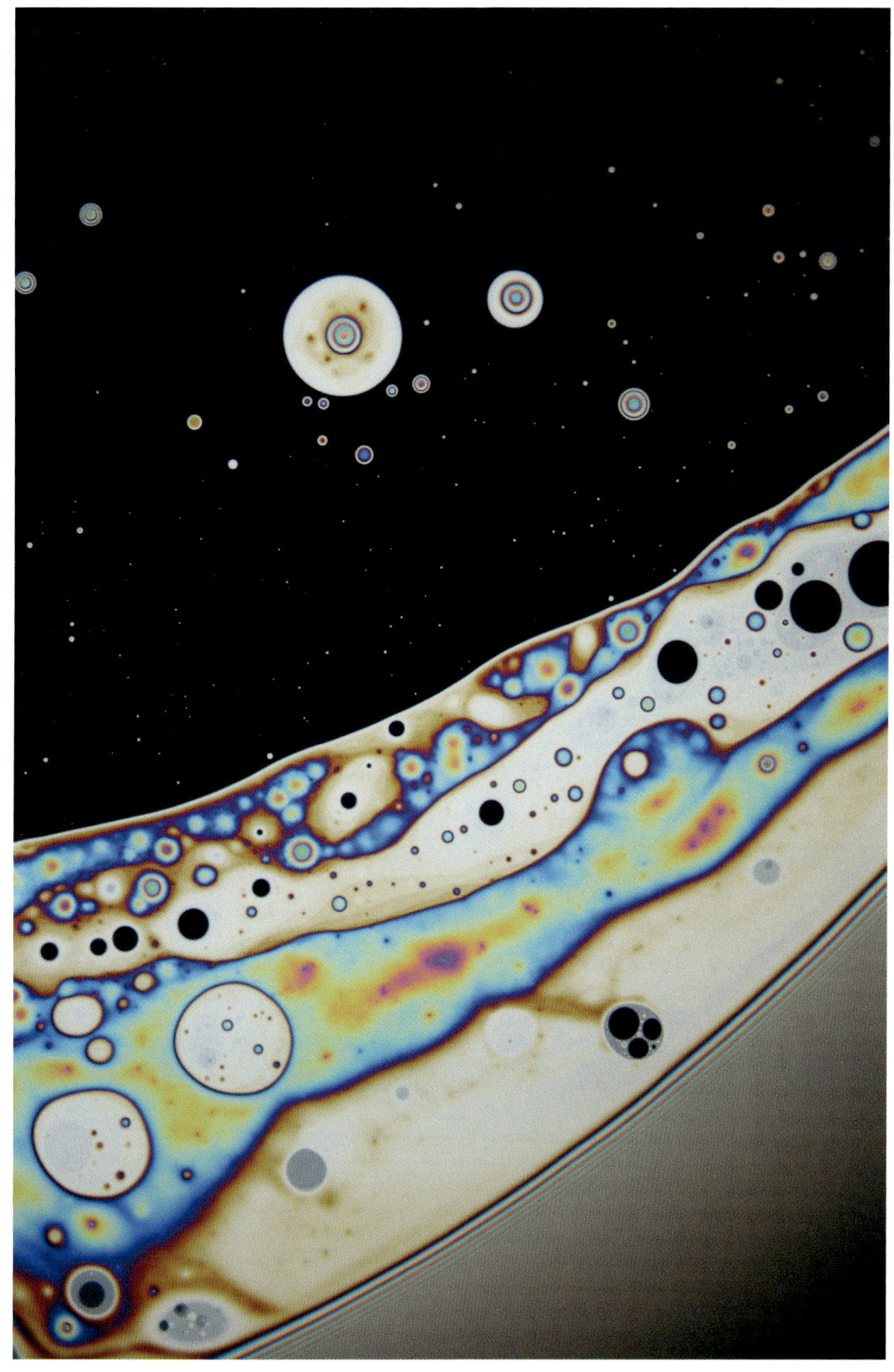

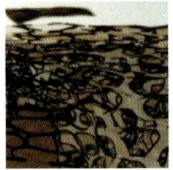

Casey Garr

How Tattoos Work, 2018

Multimedia animation; Autodesk 3ds Max; Adobe After Effects; Adobe Media Encoder; Adobe Photoshop; Adobe Illustrator

University of Illinois at Chicago, Chicago, Illinois, United States

---

This animation describes the science behind tattoos. While many people have tattoos, it is not commonly known how the body reacts to and retains tattoo ink. This animation was created to share that information in a fun, informative manner. The style of the piece was inspired by traditional American tattoos, also known as Sailor Jerry tattoos, which gained popularity during the World War II era. Thus, the entire animation takes on the look and feel of a film from that time period.

https://vimeo.com/312977195/9d04ee1244

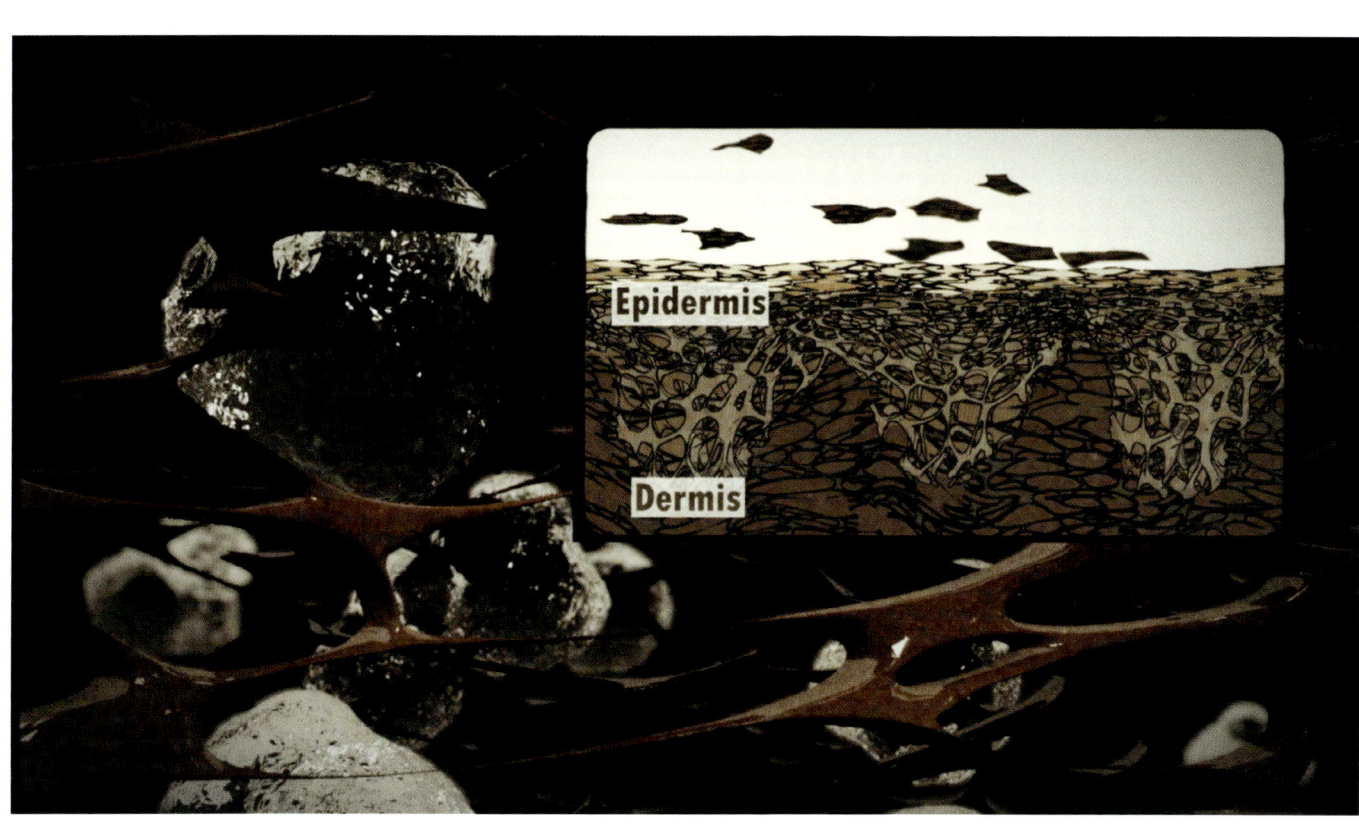

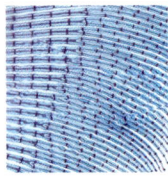

Michael Chaise Gilbert

Dasyatis sabina, Atlantic Stingray, 2018

Computational scientific photograph; Canon EOS Rebel T3 DSLR camera; Canon EF-S 18–55mm lens f/3.5–5.6 macro lens; a composite of numerous images that were focus stacked and stitched together; images were taken from five overlapping sections of various heights

University of Massachusetts Amherst, Amherst, Massachusetts, United States

---

This image shows a cleared and stained Atlantic stingray. This specimen was stained using traditional processes. The staining shows the calcified structures as purple and the cartilage as blue. The staining technique enzymatically removes cells to leave behind collagen. Once immersed in glycerin, the tissues appear transparent and reveal the stained skeleton. The specimen was 11.8 centimeters left to right.

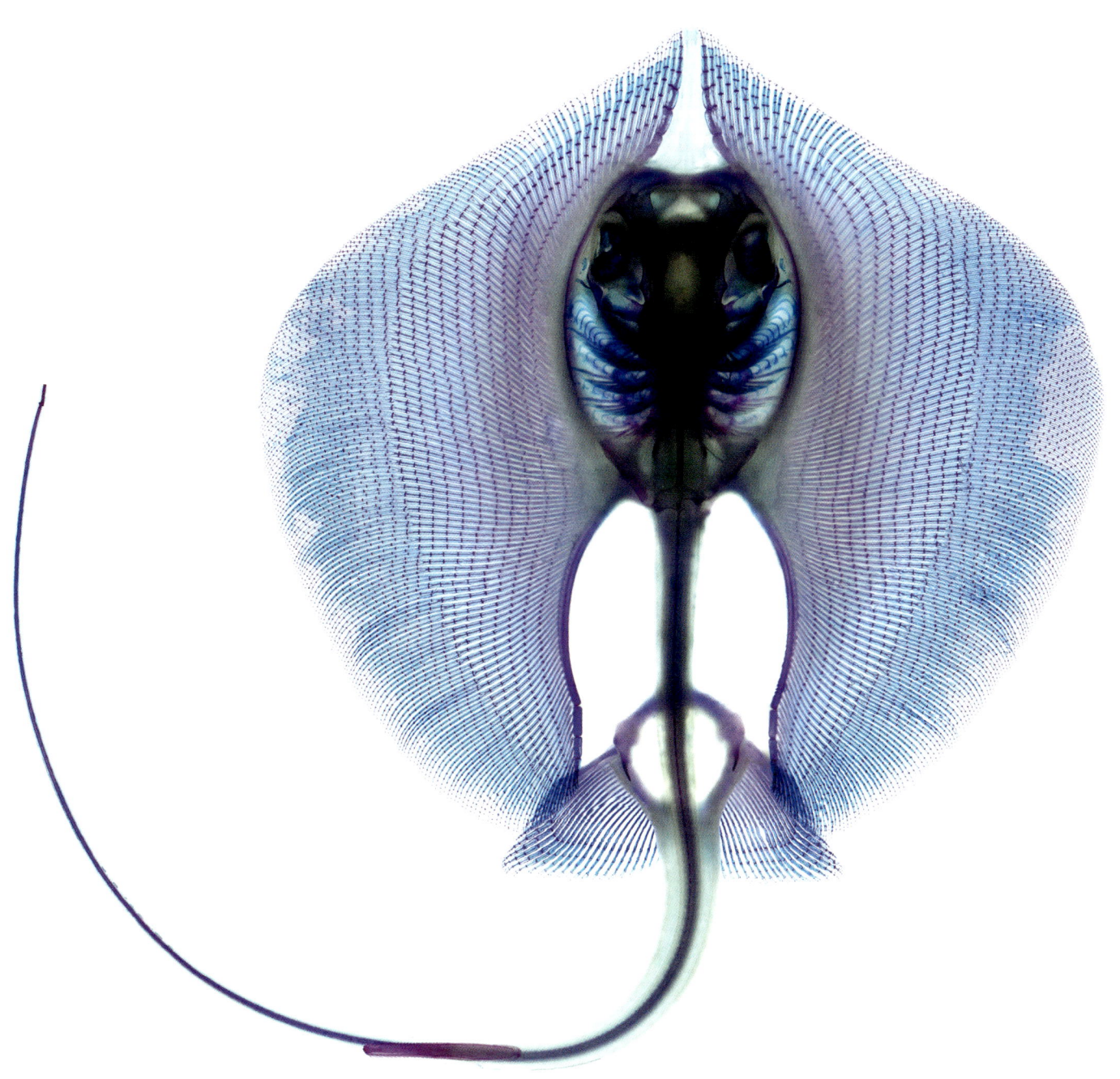

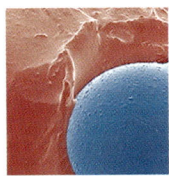

Steve Gschmeissner

Quantum Tunneling Composite, 2018

Scanning electron photomicrograph; capture magnification ~x615; image colored using Adobe Photoshop

Bedford, England, United Kingdom

This photomicrograph was produced using a scanning electron microscope. It displays the appearance of the cut surface of a quantum tunneling composite (QTC) material that contains various metals. The metals are colored blue in this picture, and non-conducting elastomeric binders—used as pressure sensors— appear light red. In a QTC material and without the application of pressure, the conductive elements are separated at distances too far to conduct electricity. When pressure is applied, the elements migrate closer to one another, and electrons travel through the part of the material that acts as an insulator. This outcome is more evident than would be expected when examining classical (non-quantum) effects independently. Typical evidence of electrical resistance is demonstrated as a linear behavior. While the quantum tunneling behavior is greatly enhanced with decreasing distances, this outcome allows the resistance of the material to change significantly in its pressured and unpressured states. QTC materials are currently used to make membrane switches, such as those found in smartphones or in pressure sensors.

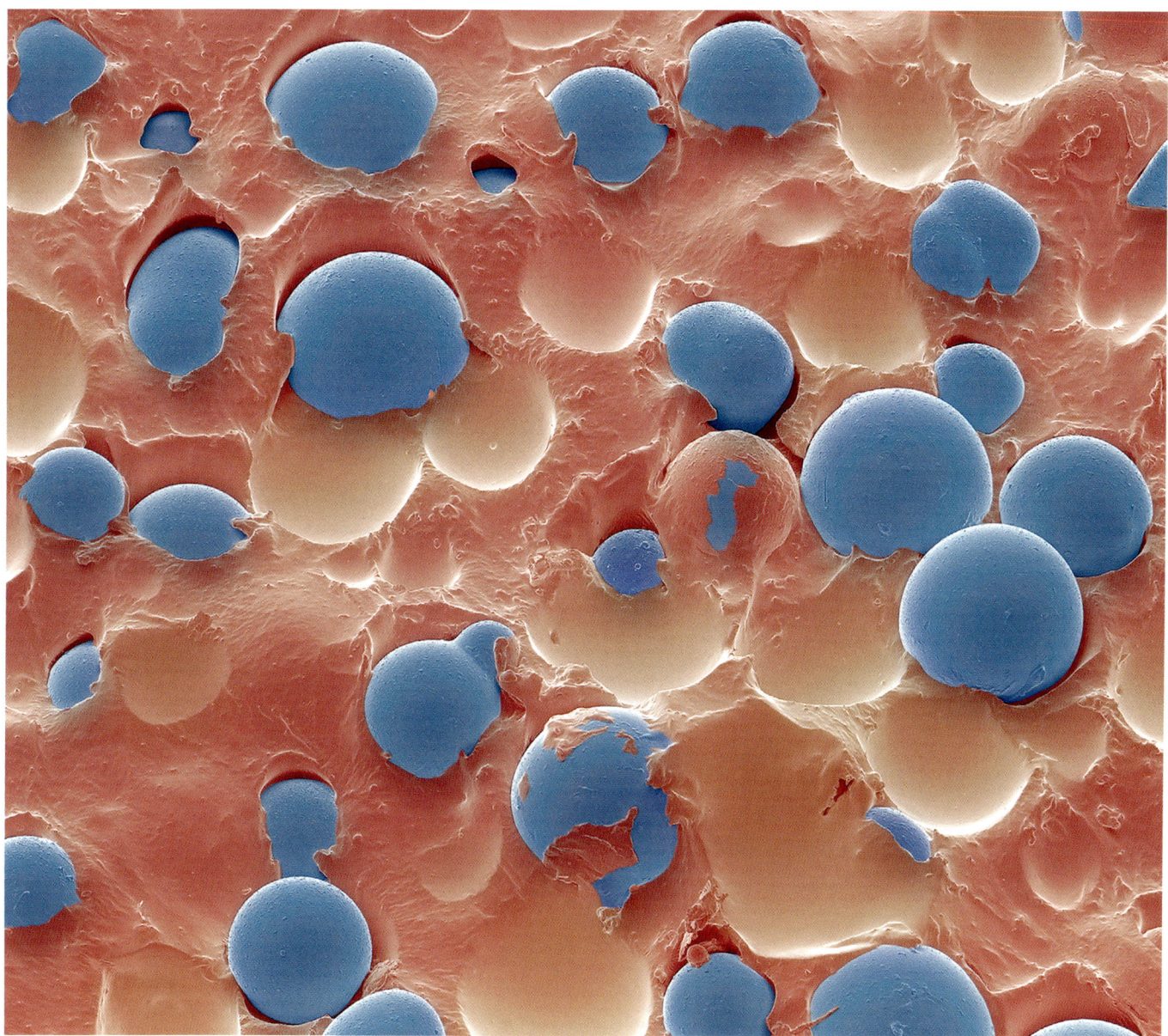

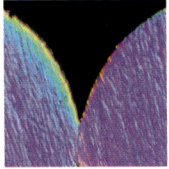

Gerd-A. Guenther

Bass Guitar String, 2017

Differential interference photomicrograph; Leica DMLB microscope with incident differential interference contrast illumination

Düsseldorf, Germany

This picture shares a longitudinal section through a 41 Hz bass guitar string. This steel-based string consists of a central wire with another steel wire wound closely around it. A short section of the guitar string was embedded in light curing resin and then grounded and diamond polished to match the middle of the longitudinal string. In material science, these sections are used to identify and show the inner composition of a given subject.

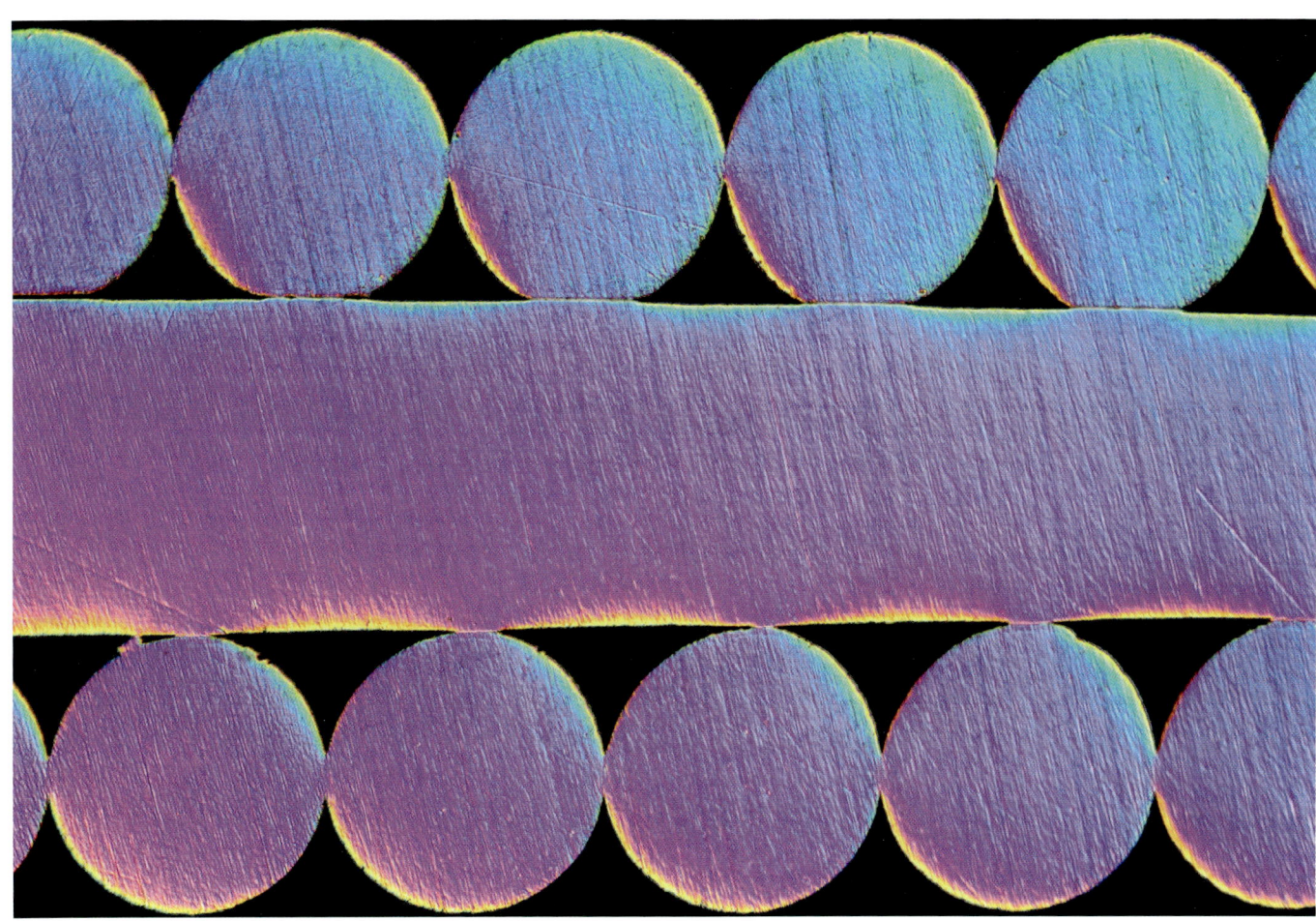

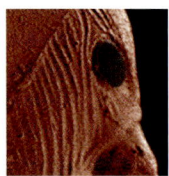

Hillary Guzik

Spider Beetle, *Gibbium psylloides,* 2018

Scanning electron photomicrograph; scanning electron microscope at 2 kV; a composite of four images stitched together; pseudo-colored with Adobe Photoshop

Albert Einstein College of Medicine, New York, New York, United States

---

This photomicrograph features the *Gibbium psylloides*, spider beetle. This beetle, from the Coleoptera order, is unique for its fused and glabrous elytra (wing cases). This beetle cannot fly, is quite small, and is often mistaken for a spider.

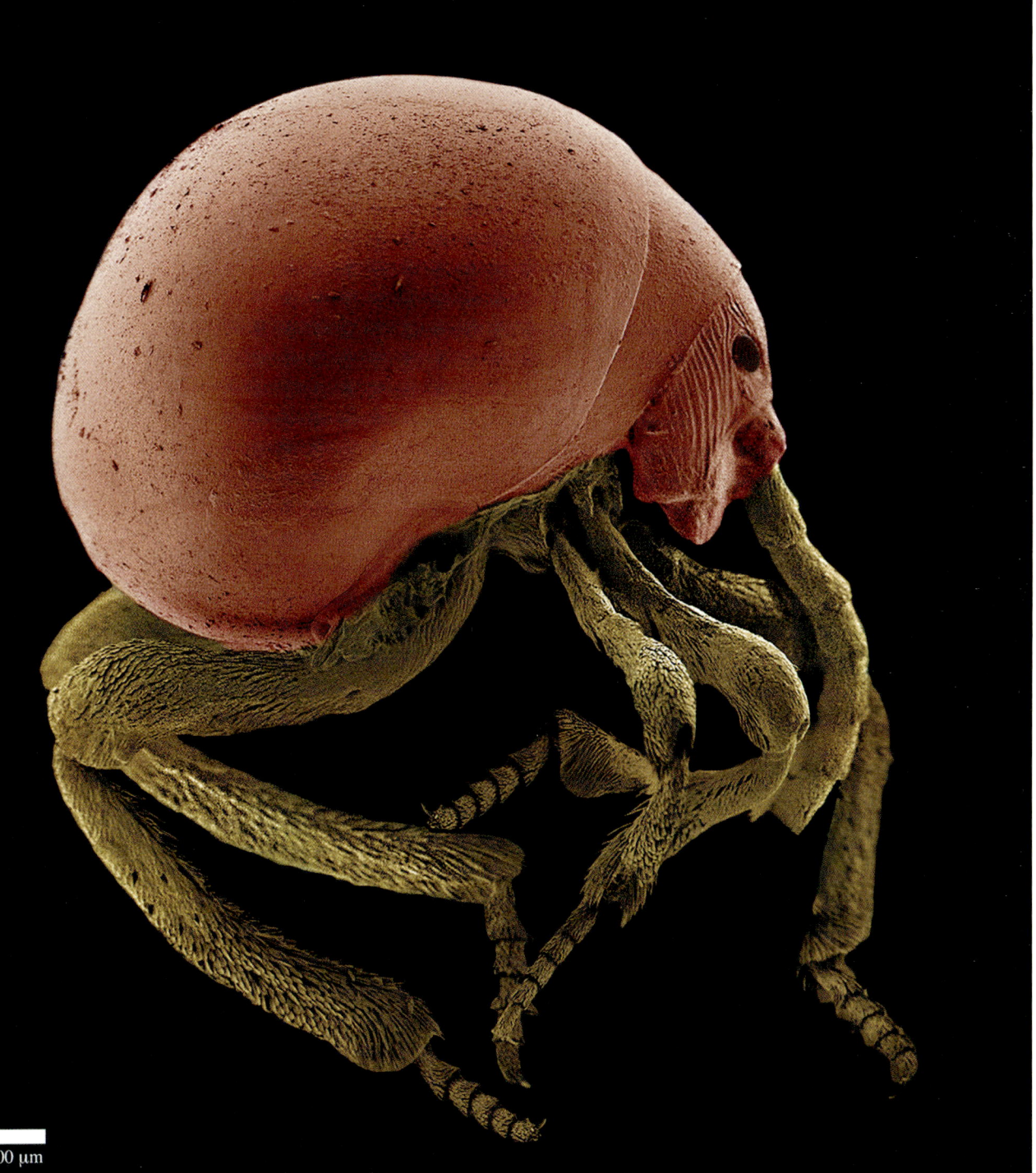

200 μm

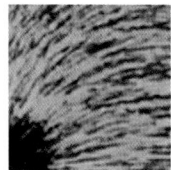

Raymond Hall

Iron Filing Field Detector, 2017

Video

Department of Physics, California State University, Fresno; Fresno, California, United States

@physicsfun

This video reveals the invisible: it shows the magnetic field lines around a dipole bar magnet. In the presence of a magnetic field, ferromagnetic materials (such as iron) temporarily become magnets. Here the iron filings become dipole magnets and link up and align like tiny compass needles to follow and reveal the magnetic field lines associated with the permanent magnet underneath. Viscous silicone oil temporarily keeps the iron particles suspended yet allows for rotation and repositioning under the influence of the magnetic field. This is used as a demonstration device for physics mapping of magnetic fields.

https://vimeo.com/313014257/d6f2d8b2f7

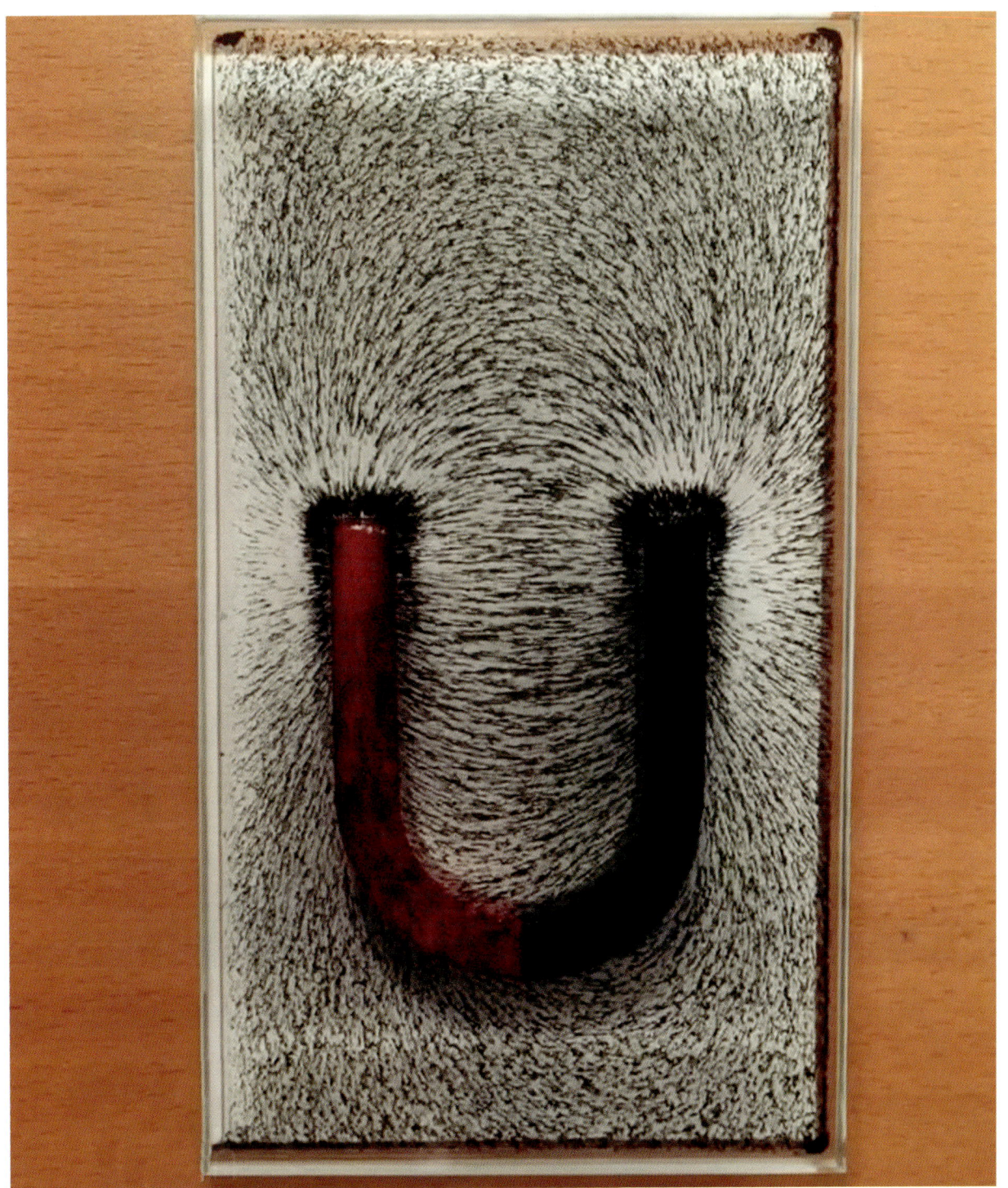

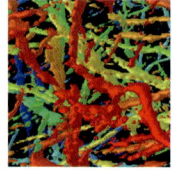

James E. Hayden

3D Collagen Matrix *in Vitro,* 2016

Photomicrograph; two-photon microscope; a composite of 200 stacked images or "slices" through material that is 200 microns thick

The Wistar Institute, Philadelphia, Pennsylvania, United States

---

A 3D collagen matrix is used in cancer research to support the growth of cell cultures for a more realistic representation of naturally growing tumors. The concentration of collagen is an important part of the extracellular matrix surrounding cancer cells and is partly responsible for the ease with which these cells can invade surrounding tissues. The collagen was visualized with second harmonic generation, a method that allows certain molecules, like collagen, to be seen without direct staining. A depth-coded color lookup table was added to the resulting black and white image to display thickness. Red is closest to the top of the tissue and blue is farthest away.

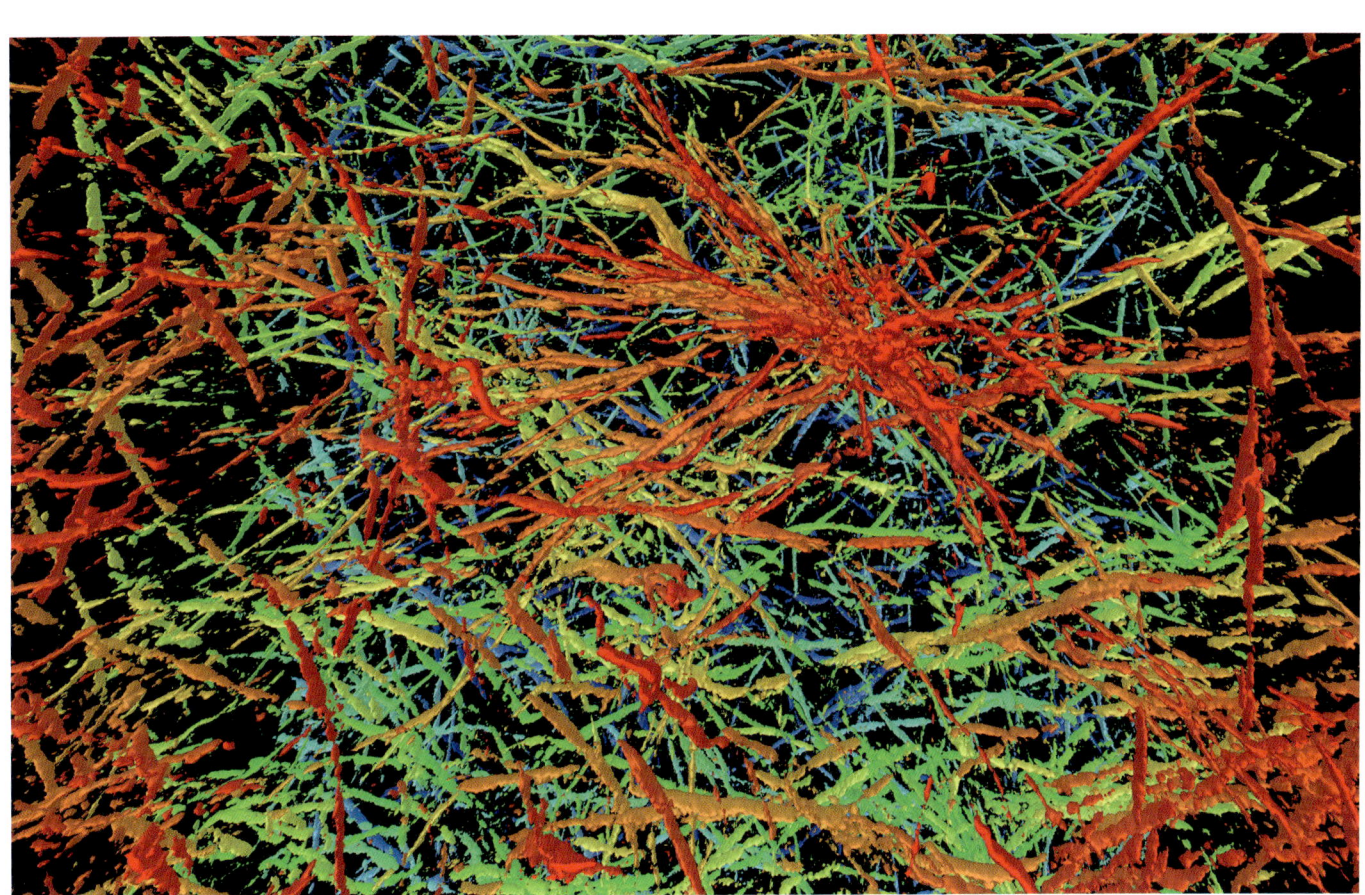

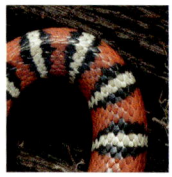

Charles Hedgcock

Knobloch's Mountain Kingsnake, *Lampropeltis knoblochi*, 2018

Close-up photograph; Nikon D7100 DSLR camera; 60mm Micro-NIKKOR lens; Vivitar 283 flash

GreaterGood.org, Tucson, Arizona, United States

This photograph features the documentation of species discovered during biological surveys into the remote Sky Islands of Northern Mexico by volunteer scientists working with GreaterGood.org. The snake was photographed in controlled conditions at the GreaterGood.org field camp, located at Arroyo La Presita, Mesa Tres Rios, Sonora, Mexico.

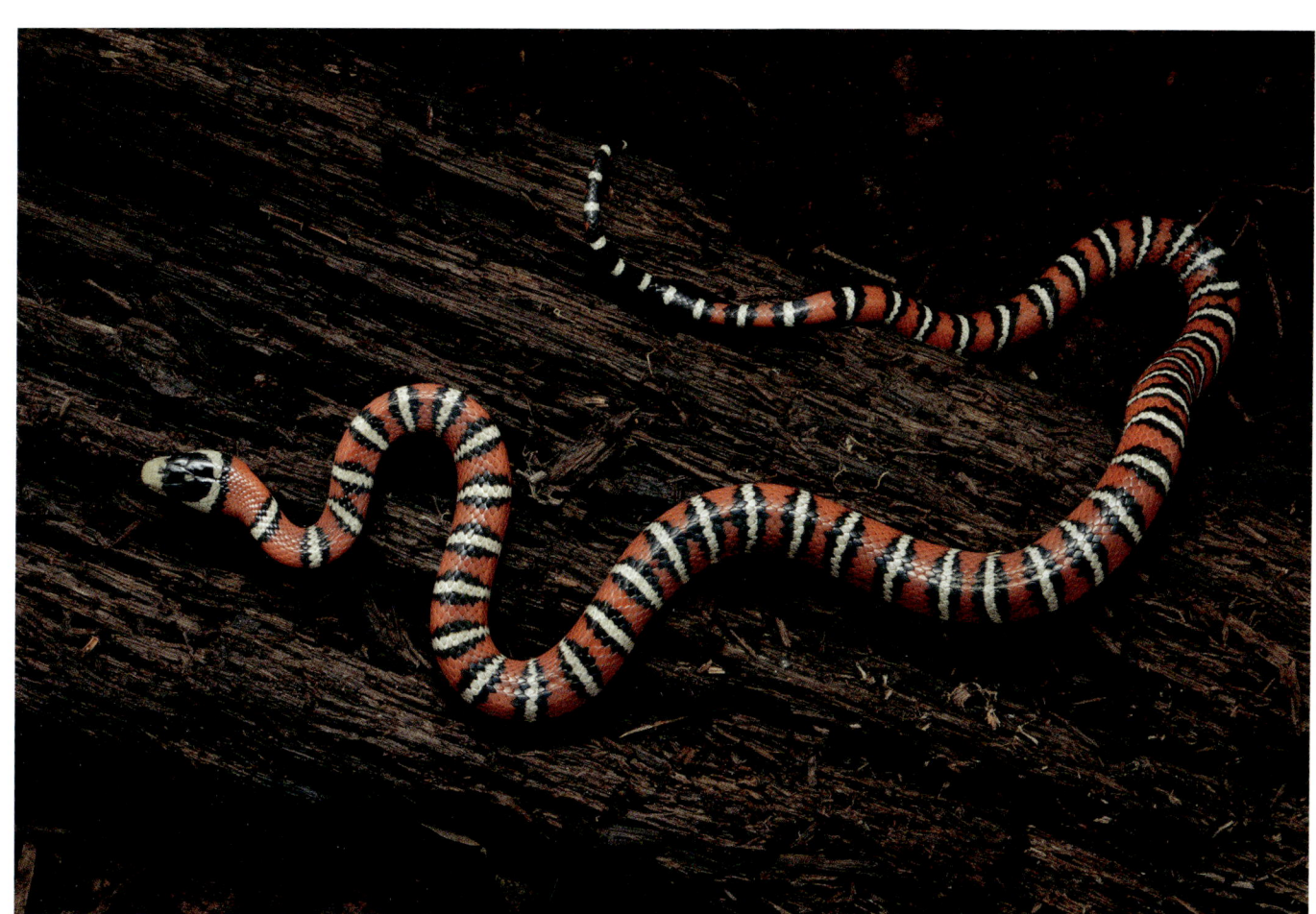

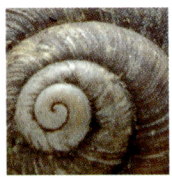

Charles Hedgcock

Land Snail, *Humboldtiana sp.*, 2018

Close-up photograph; Nikon D7100 DSLR camera; 60mm Micro-NIKKOR lens;
Vivitar 283 flash

GreaterGood.org, Tucson, Arizona, United States

This photograph features a possible new species of snail still not yet identified. This land snail is one of many new discoveries made during biological surveys into the remote Sky Islands of Northern Mexico by volunteer scientists working with GreaterGood.org. It was photographed in controlled conditions at the GreaterGood.org field camp, located at Arroyo La Presita, Mesa Tres Rios, Sonora, Mexico.

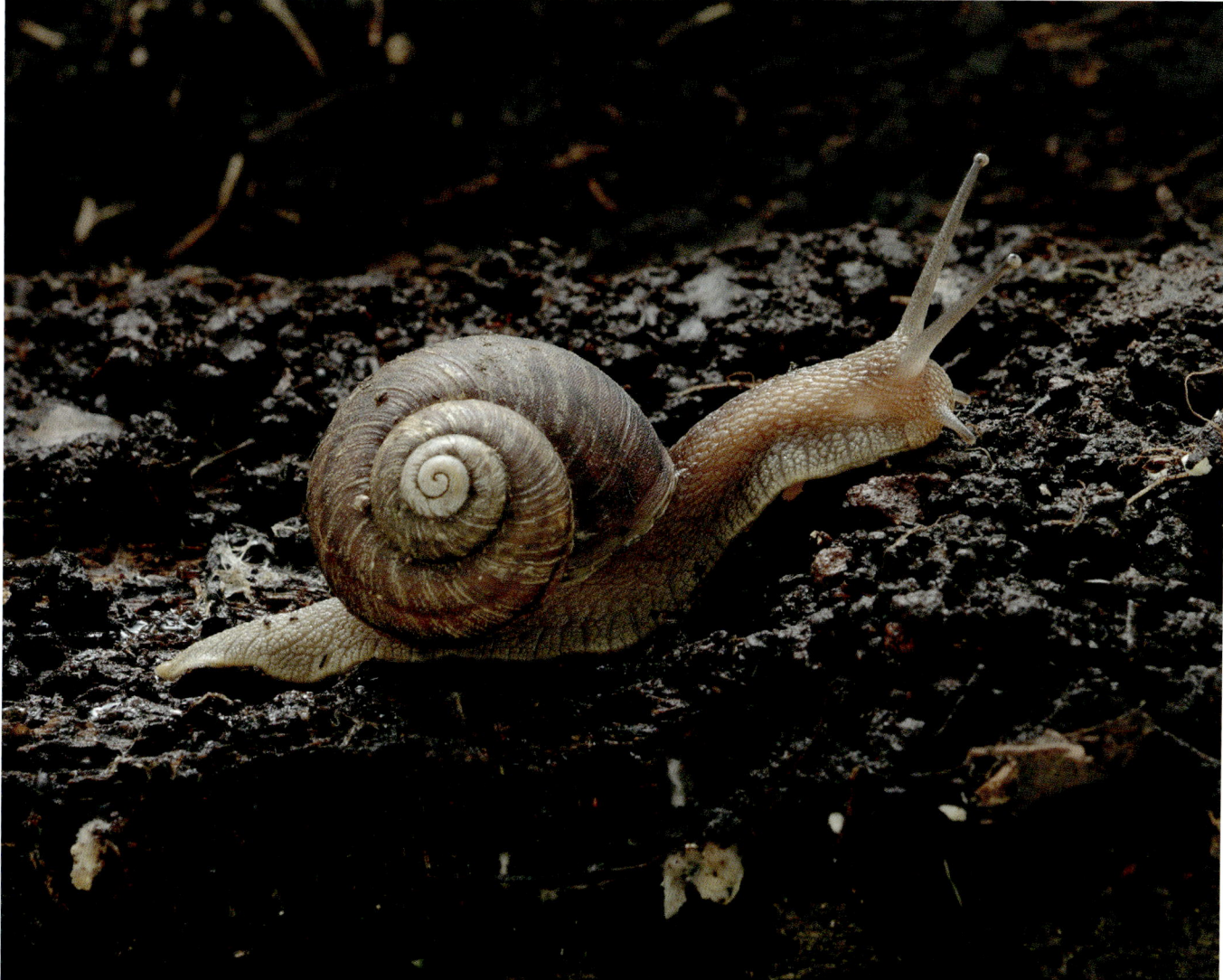

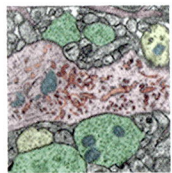

Marina Hesse and Joachim Lübke

Axon in the Human Brain, 2016

Transmission electron photomicrograph; Zeiss Libra 120 transmission electron microscope; colorized using image processing software

Jülich Research Center, Jülich, Germany

This photomicrograph features the axon initial segment of the human brain. Synapses colored green and dendrites colored yellow surround the axon (light red). The secretory pathway (dark red) is apparitional and transports cargo from the soma to the synaptic bouton inside the axon. An ultra-thin section (approximately 1 micron) of human biopsy tissue was processed for this investigation using a transmission electron microscope.

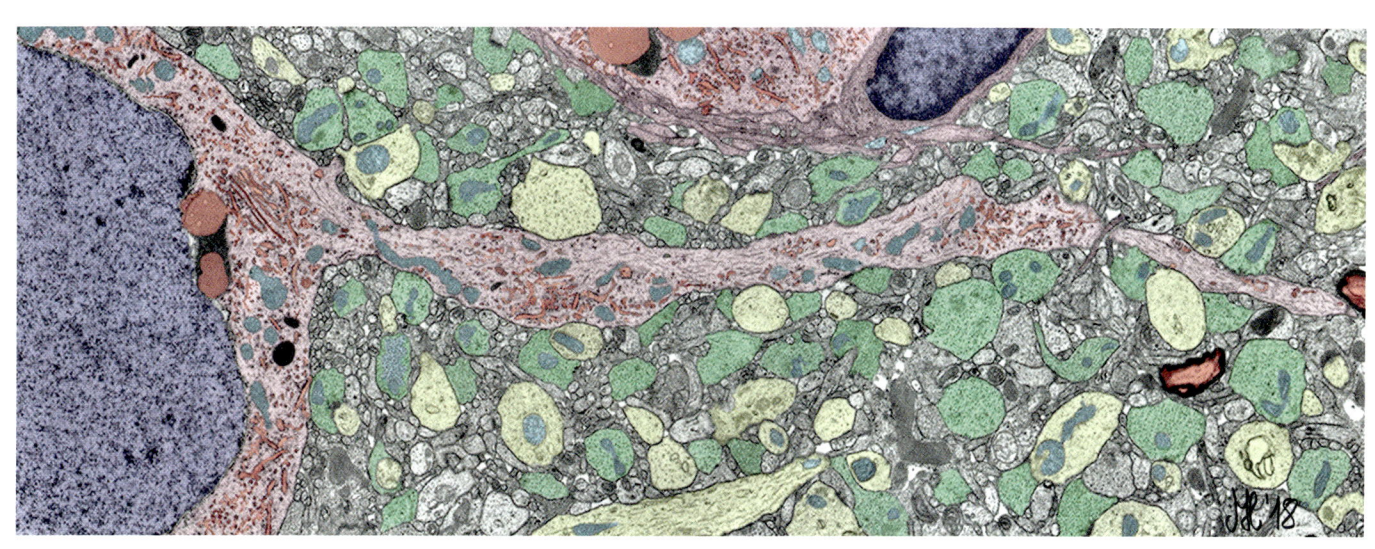

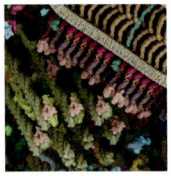

Evan Ingersoll and Gaël McGill

Cellular Landscape, 2015

Digital illustration; Digizyme's Molecular Maya custom software, Autodesk Maya,
and Foundry Modo used to import, model, rig, populate, and render all structural datasets

Digizyme Inc., Brookline, Massachusetts, United States

Created for Cell Signaling Technology, Inc., and inspired by the stunning art of
David Goodsell, this 3D rendering of a eukaryotic cell is modeled using X-ray,
nuclear magnetic resonance (NMR), and cryo-electron microscopy datasets
for all of its molecular actors. It is an attempt to recapitulate the myriad pathways involved in signal transduction, protein synthesis, endocytosis, vesicular
transport, cell-cell adhesion, apoptosis, and other processes. Although dilute
in its concentration relative to a real cell, this rendering is also an attempt to
visualize the great complexity and beauty of the cell's molecular choreography.
Interactive versions of parts of this landscape can be explored at
http://www.digizyme.com/cst_landscapes.html.

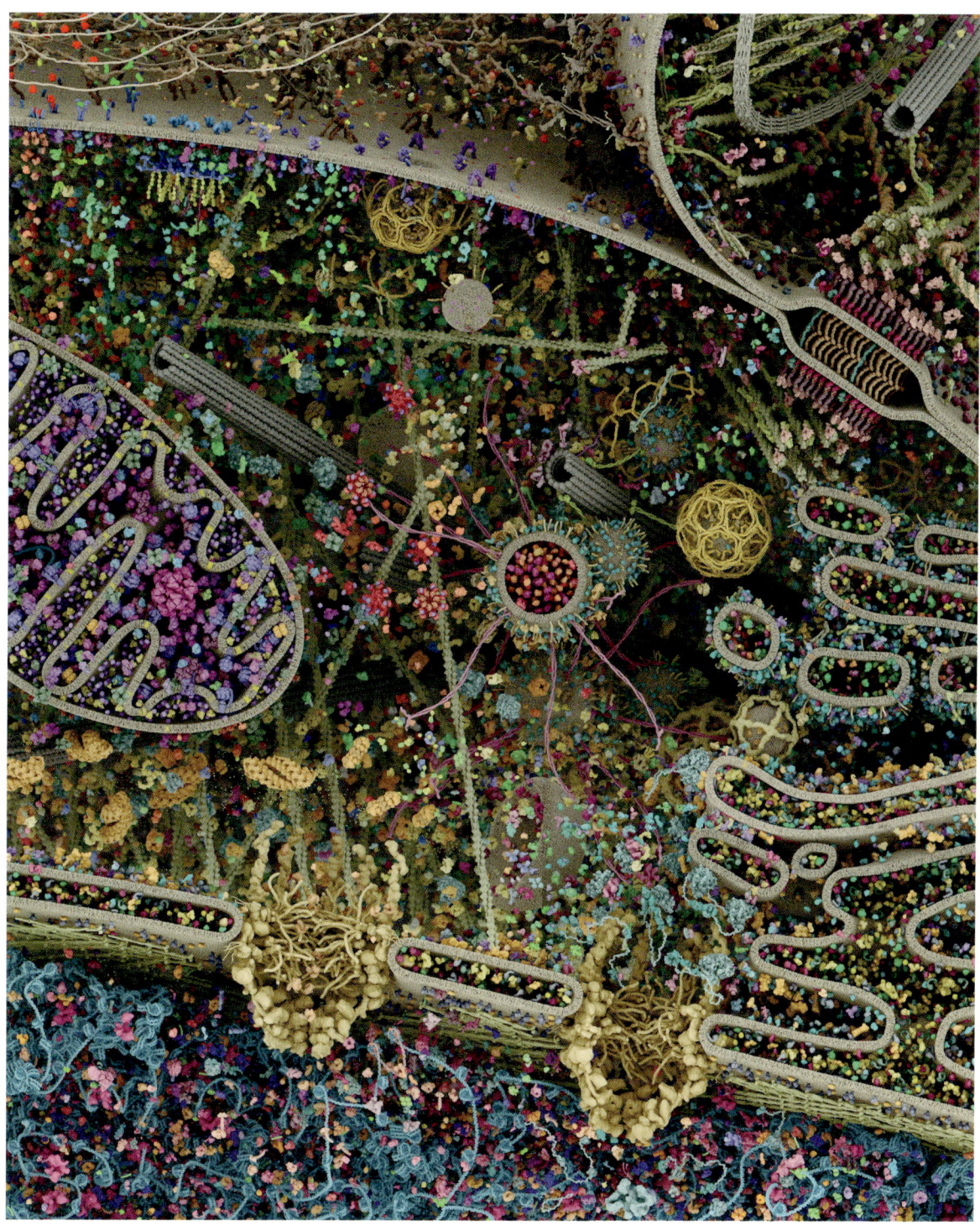

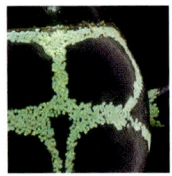

Kaleigh Jaron

Pachyrrhynchus reticulatus (Beetle), 2018

Close-up photograph; Canon 7D DSLR camera; Canon EF 100mm f/2.8L macro lens; computational photograph is a composite of 104 stacked images

Charlotte, North Carolina, United States

This photograph features the beetle *Pachyrrhynchus reticulatus*. The beetle was 1.3 centimeters. This beetle lives in Marinduque, Philippines.

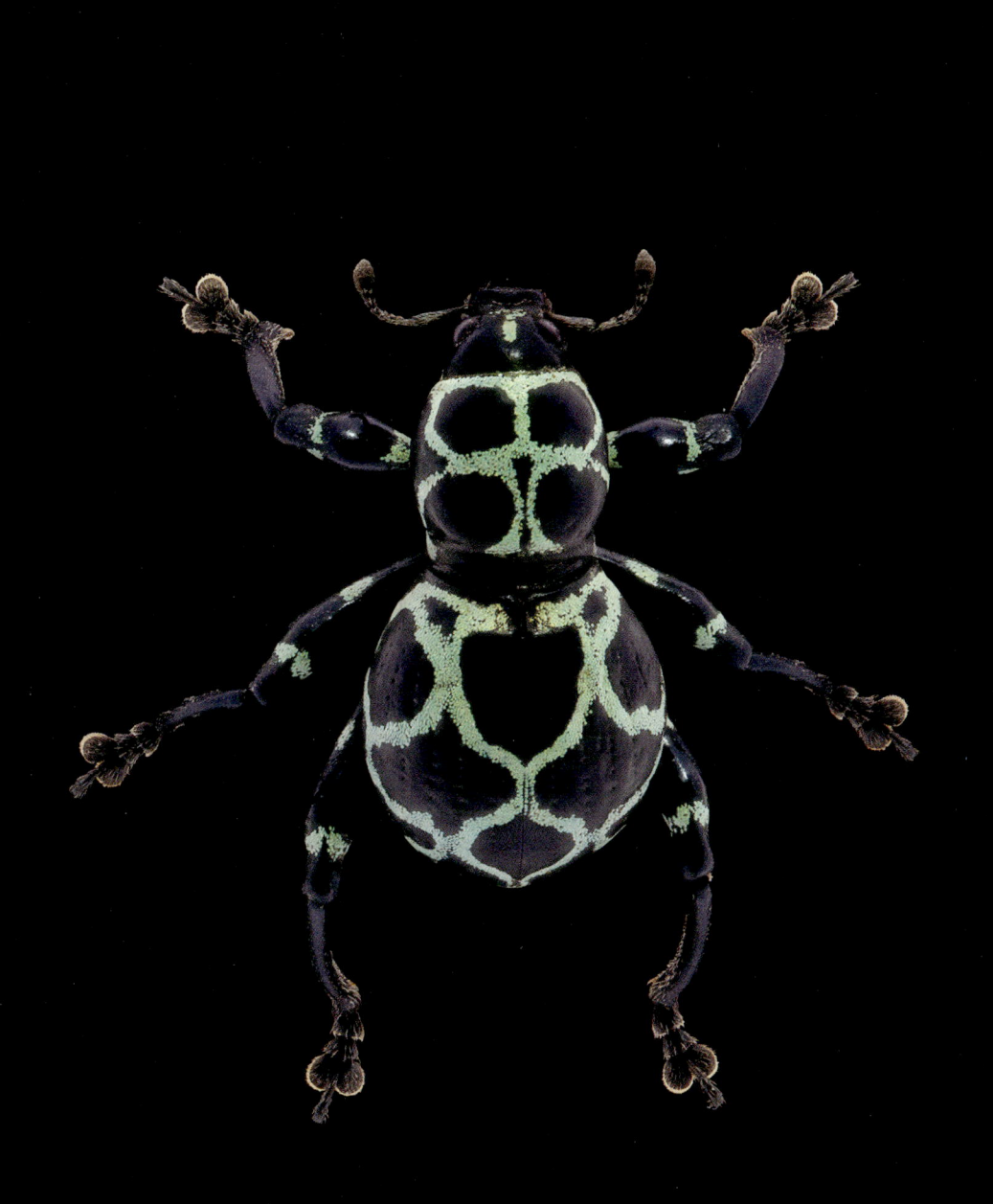

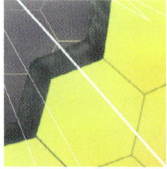

Ikumi Kayama

James Webb Space Telescope, 2017

Digital illustration; Graphite; Adobe Photoshop; Adobe Illustrator

Studio Kayama, LLC; Riverdale, Maryland, United States

The James Webb Space Telescope (JWST), scheduled to launch in 2021, is designed to take over the duties currently provided by the Hubble Space Telescope. The JWST has some key differences and improvements. First, the JWST's primary mirror is comprised of 18 hexagonal segments and is 6.5 meters (21 feet) across, compared to 2.4 meters (nearly 8 feet) for the Hubble's primary mirror. Second, because a mirror this large would be too heavy to launch into orbit if it were made of glass—as the Hubble is—the mirror segments are made from beryllium, which is both strong and light. Additionally, the mirror segments are coated in gold to better reflect infrared light because the JWST will make observations primarily in the lower frequency wavelengths of the electromagnetic spectrum (while the Hubble's telescope made observations in the ultraviolet and visible parts of the spectrum). This allows the JWST to "see" through space dust and observe very old and distant high redshift objects. In order to observe using such low wavelengths, the telescope needs to stay very cold; it contains five layers of heat-blocking sun shields. Unlike the Hubble, the JWST will not be positioned in Earth's orbit, but will be placed further away from the Earth, at the L2 Lagrangian point. This poster was designed to visualize the telescope basics and share JWST's project to better understand the origins of the universe.

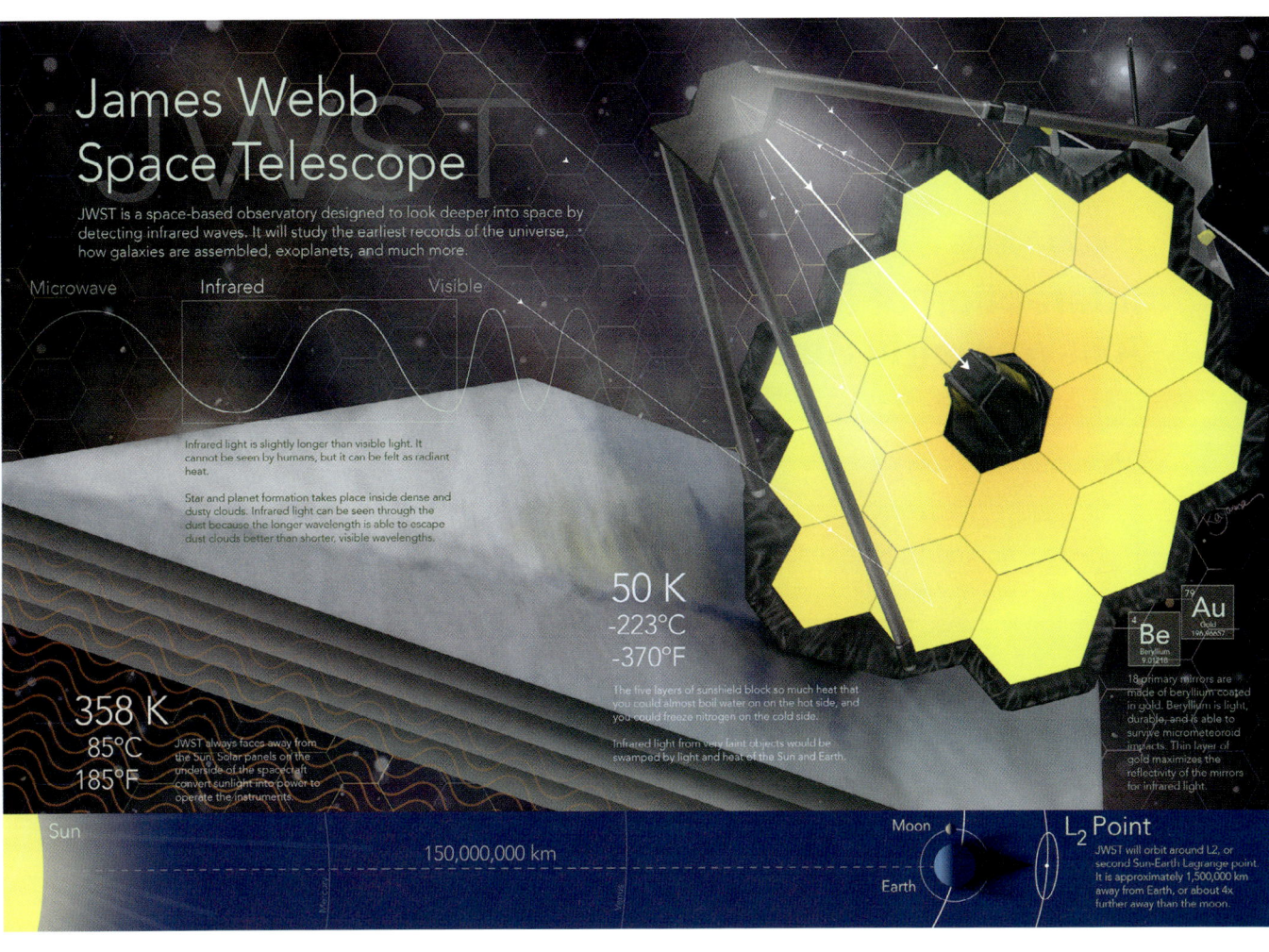

James Webb
Space Telescope

JWST is a space-based observatory designed to look deeper into space by detecting infrared waves. It will study the earliest records of the universe, how galaxies are assembled, exoplanets, and much more.

Microwave   Infrared   Visible

Infrared light is slightly longer than visible light. It cannot be seen by humans, but it can be felt as radiant heat.

Star and planet formation takes place inside dense and dusty clouds. Infrared light can be seen through the dust because the longer wavelength is able to escape dust clouds better than shorter, visible wavelengths.

50 K
-223°C
-370°F

The five layers of sunshield block so much heat that you could almost boil water on on the hot side, and you could freeze nitrogen on the cold side.

Infrared light from very faint objects would be swamped by light and heat of the Sun and Earth.

358 K
85°C
185°F

JWST always faces away from the Sun. Solar panels on the underside of the spacecraft convert sunlight into power to operate the instruments.

79 Au Gold 196.96657

4 Be Beryllium 9.01218

18 primary mirrors are made of beryllium coated in gold. Beryllium is light, durable, and is able to survive micrometeoroid impacts. Thin layer of gold maximizes the reflectivity of the mirrors for infrared light.

Sun

150,000,000 km

Moon

Earth

L₂ Point

JWST will orbit around L2, or second Sun-Earth Lagrange point. It is approximately 1,500,000 km away from Earth, or about 4x further away than the moon.

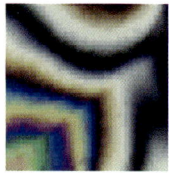

Harald Kleine, T.G. Etoh, and H. Olivier

Interaction of a Shock Wave with an Axisymmetric Structure, 2018

High-speed video; 330,000 fps; shock Mach number = 1.23

University of New South Wales, Canberra, Australian Capital Territories, Australia

This video recorded a time-resolved Mach-Zehnder interferometry visualization of a shock wave interacting with a complex structure. Three different tests were run. In the first test, monochrome interferometry with a laser light source was used. For the second and third tests, polychrome interferometry with different offset settings of the interferometer was used.

https://vimeo.com/312982699/fde2b3fe81

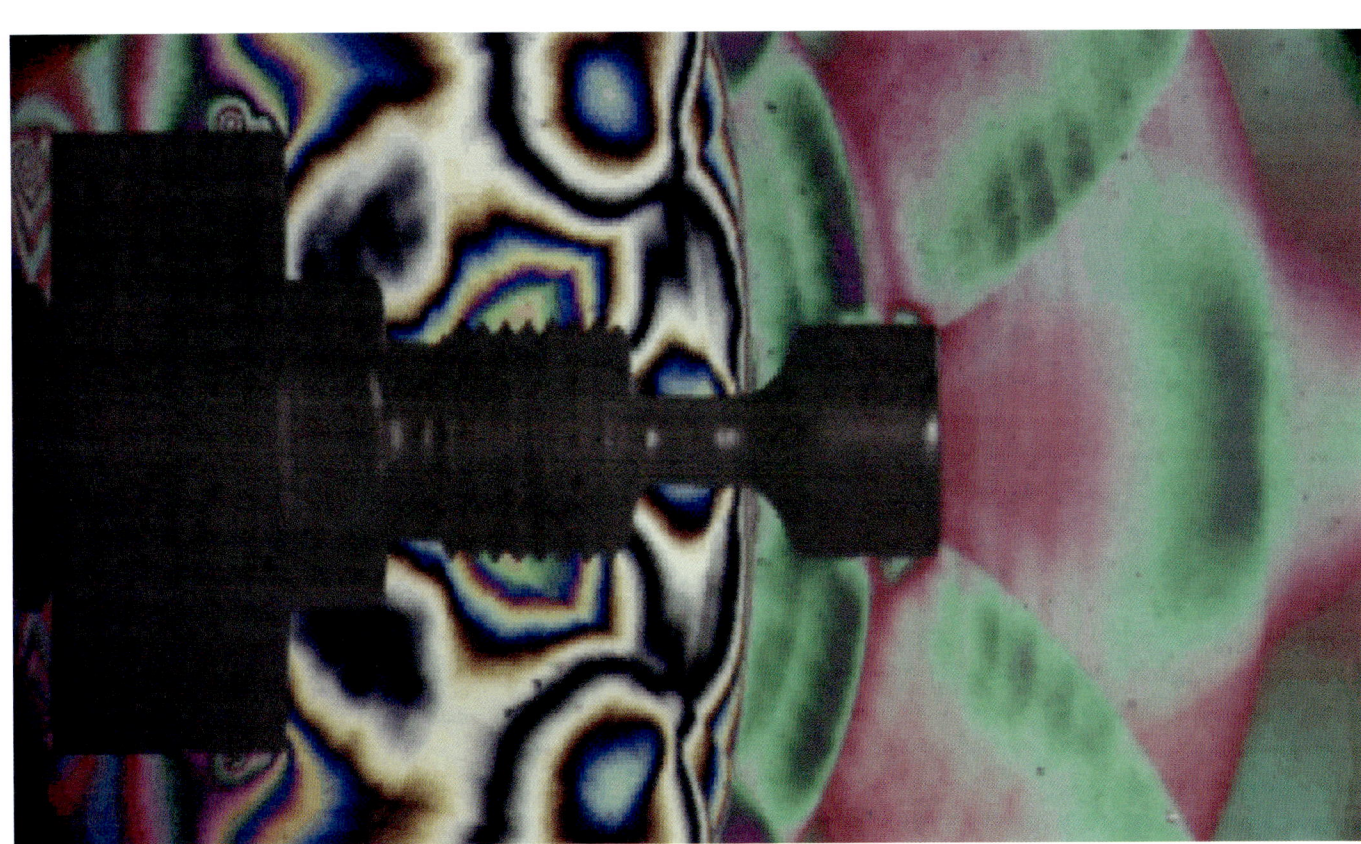

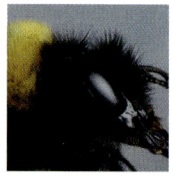

Heidi and Hans-Jürgen Koch

Marked Buff-tailed Bumblebee Drinking, 2016

Close-up photograph

Lifeform Photography, Goosefeld, Germany

This photograph features a marked buff-tailed bumblebee or large earth bumblebee, *Bombus terrestris*, drinking sugar liquid from a blossom dummy. The hand-made blossom dummy consists of blue foam rubber with orange-colored feathers and a piece of a pipette tip as a nectar tube. Researchers were exploring innate and learned blossom recognition in bumblebees. The basic research includes pollen signals, blossom recognition, and visual orientation of flower visitors. The work is part of the Institute of Sensory Ecology, Heinrich-Heine-University Düsseldorf, in Düsseldorf, Germany.

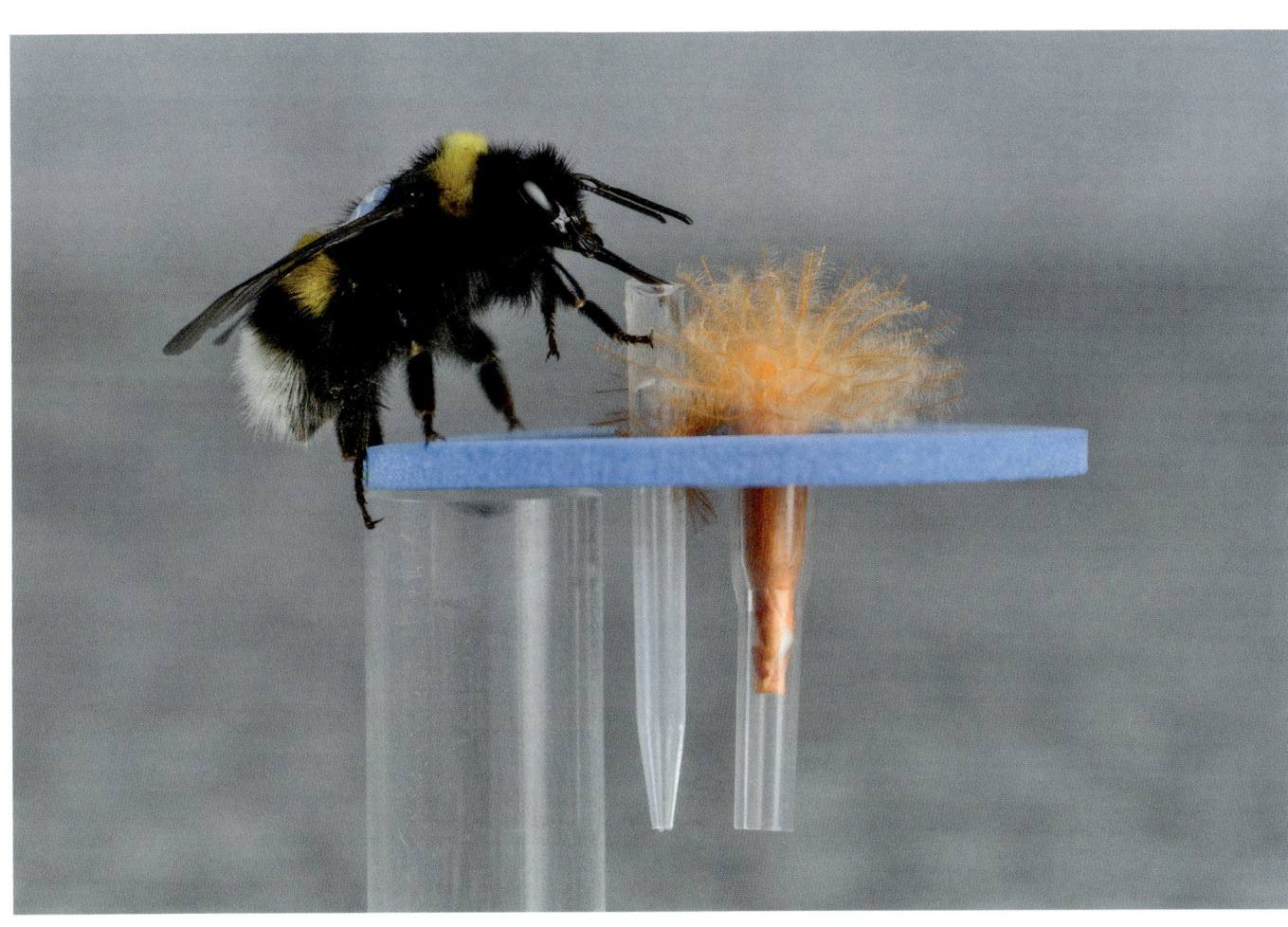

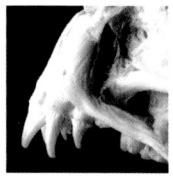

Heidi and Hans-Jürgen Koch

Atlantic Wolffish Skeleton, 2015

Photograph

Lifeform Photography, Goosefeld, Germany

This photograph features an Atlantic wolffish skeleton, *Anarhichas lupus*. The skull is about 28 centimeters long. This fish has a large head with fangs in the upper and lower jaws and has powerful molars. This fish feeds mainly on sea urchins, mussels, and crabs, crushing food with its powerful teeth. Because the Atlantic wolffish loses many teeth during its life, teeth grow again. It belongs to the order of the Perciformes and the family of the sea wolves (Anarhichadidae). It is a bony fish (Osteichthyes), and its skeleton is completely or partly ossified, in contrast to cartilaginous fishes (Chondrichthyes). It is a solitary fish that lives on the seabed, and its habitat is the North Sea, Barents Sea, West Atlantic, Baltic Sea, the waters around the British Isles, the Bay of Biscay, the coast of Norway, and southern Greenland. The skull was part of a collection at the Zoological Institute of the Christian-Albrechts-University Kiel, in Kiel, Germany, and was photographed for the project "The Inner Beauty of Fish."

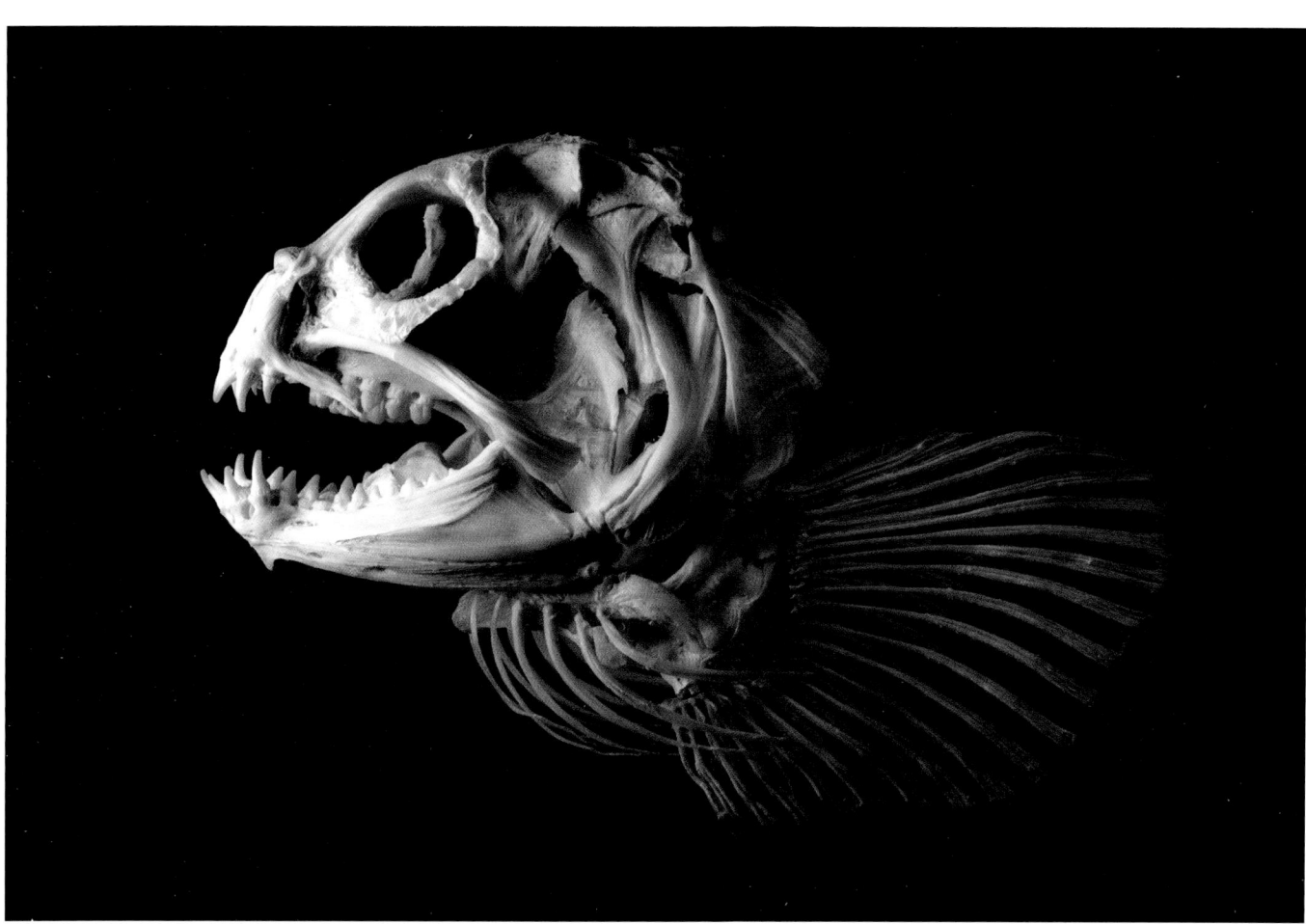

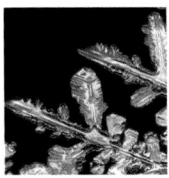

Don Komarechka

Snowflake, 2017

Composite photograph; a composite of multiple images that were focus stacked

Don Komarechka Photography, Barrie, Ontario, Canada

This snowflake was natural and not created in a lab. The images in the composite were shot outdoors in cold temperatures so that the snowflake did not melt.

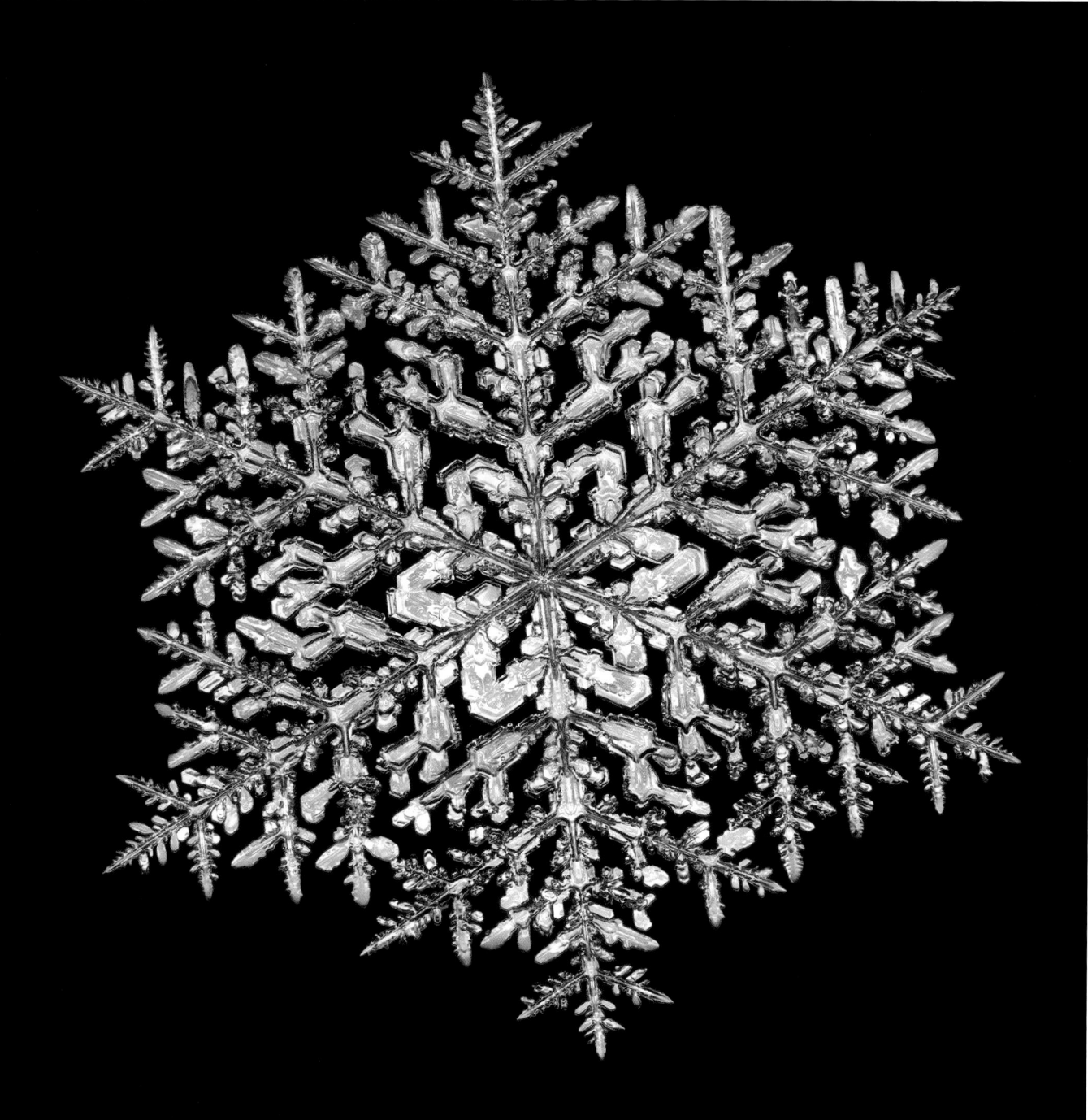

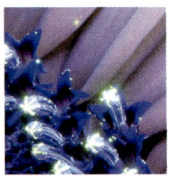

Don Komarechka

Sunflower Illuminated with UV Radiation, 2018

Ultraviolet fluorescence photograph

Don Komarechka Photography, Barrie, Ontario, Canada

The sunflower is illuminated with ultraviolet radiation, causing it to fluoresce.

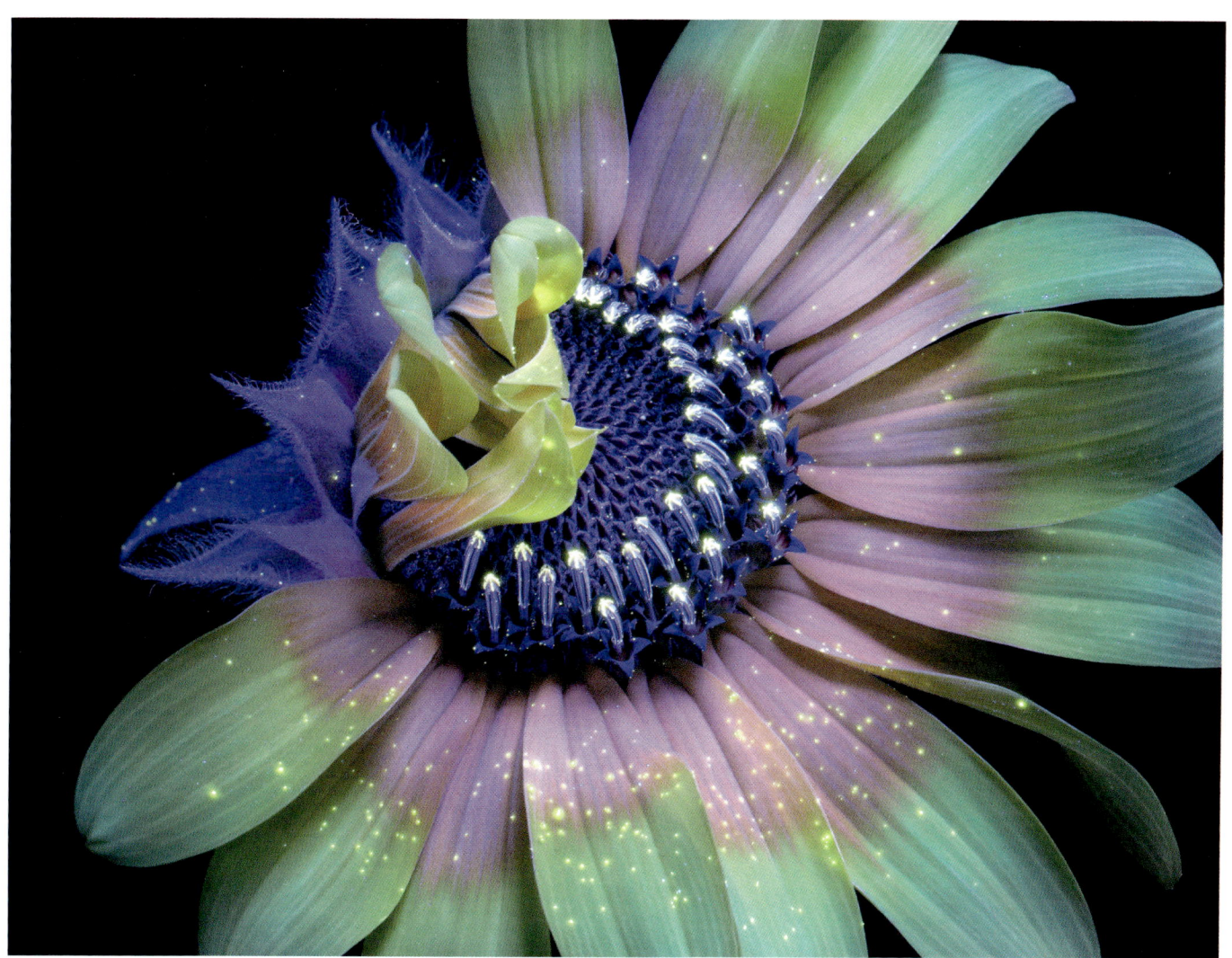

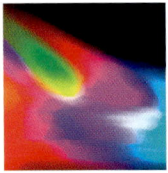

Eugene Kowaluk

Graxicon, 2015

Photograph; Nikon D800 DSLR camera; 70-180mm Micro-NIKKOR lens; lighting provided by six fiber optic modifiers; file processed with Adobe Photoshop

Optics and Imaging Sciences Group, Laboratory for Laser Energetics, University of Rochester, Rochester, New York, United States

---

In this image, brilliant colors illustrate the complex interaction between the diffractive and refractive axicons that constitute a Graxicon, a unique optical material developed by the Optics and Imaging Sciences Group at the Laboratory for Laser Energetics of the University of Rochester. The Graxicon can be designed to provide rapid focal-spot zooming to increase laser coupling to fusion targets or to provide a rapidly changing ring beam for a variety of laser applications.

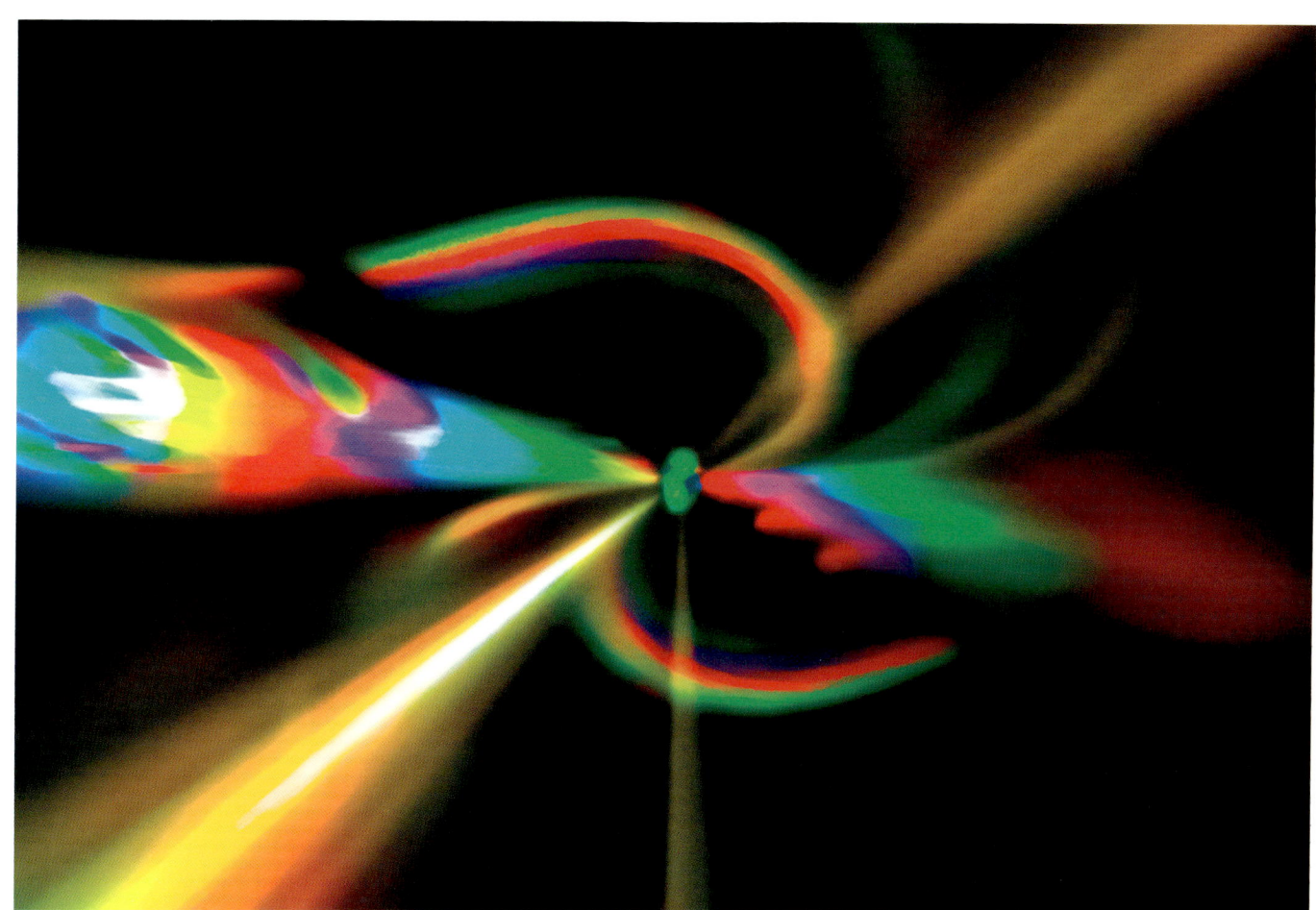

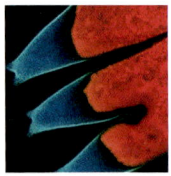

Håkan Kvarnström

Micrasterias in Double Illumination, 2018

Photomicrograph; differential interference contrast microscopy; fluorescence microscopy

Stockholm, Sweden

This photograph features a green alga called *Micrasterias*. It was illuminated using visible light as well as ultraviolet radiation. This method reveals different features and structures of the subject. The chlorophyll shines red under ultraviolet exposure.

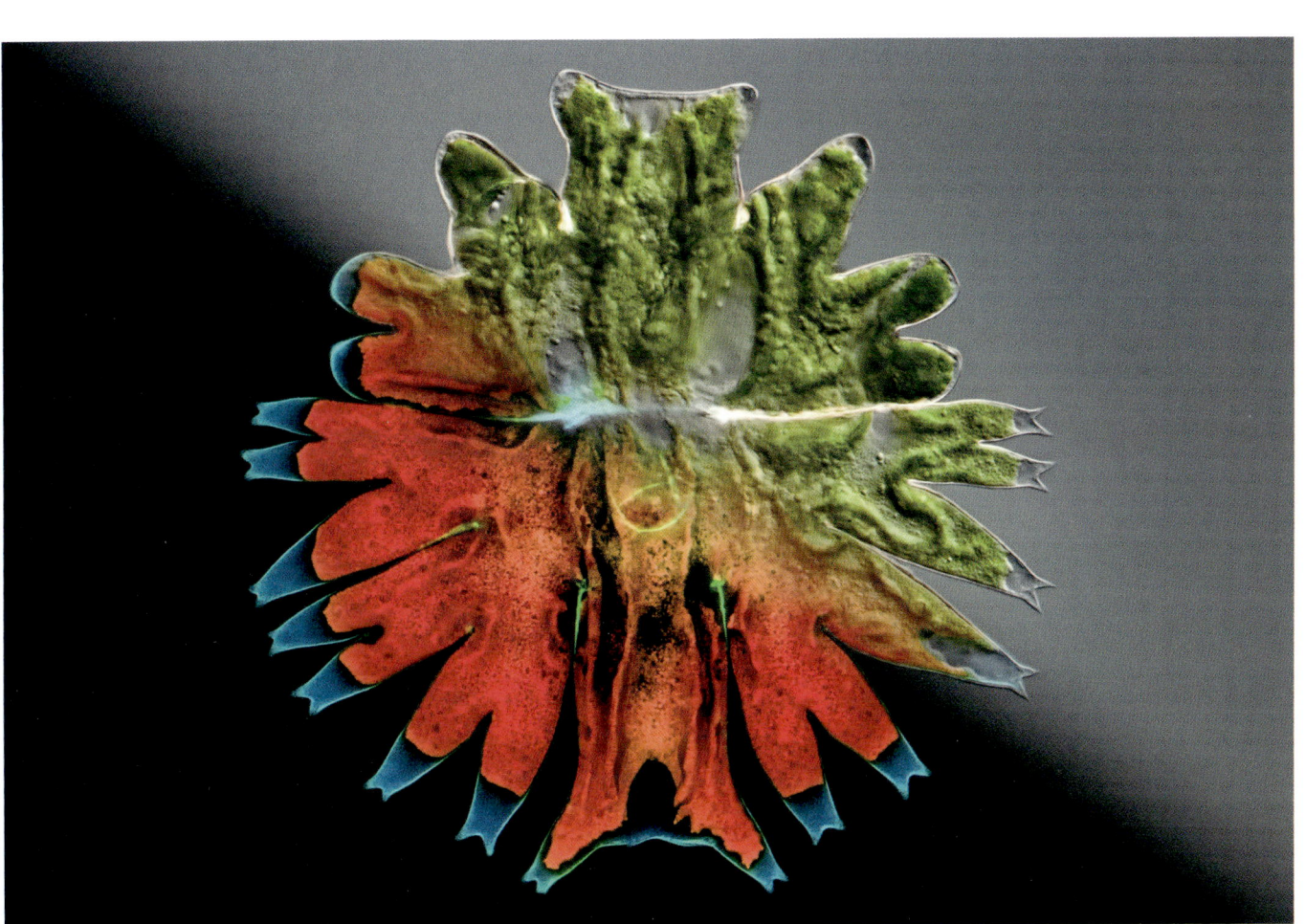

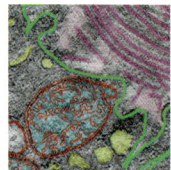

Christian Lamberz

Myotendinous Junction—Connection between Tendon and Muscle, 2018

Transmission electron micrography and tomography; JEOL JEM-2200FS transmission electron microscope at 200 kV

DZNE (German Center for Neurodegenerative Diseases) Bonn / University of Bonn, Bonn, Germany

This photomicrograph features the myotendinous junction, a region located at the muscle-tendon interface, which is essential for transmitting force between muscle and tendon. At this junction in humans, the sarcolemma invaginations form finger-like structures, which significantly increase the contact area between muscle and tendon. This image shows a piece of human muscle that was harvested and processed for transmission electron microscopy.

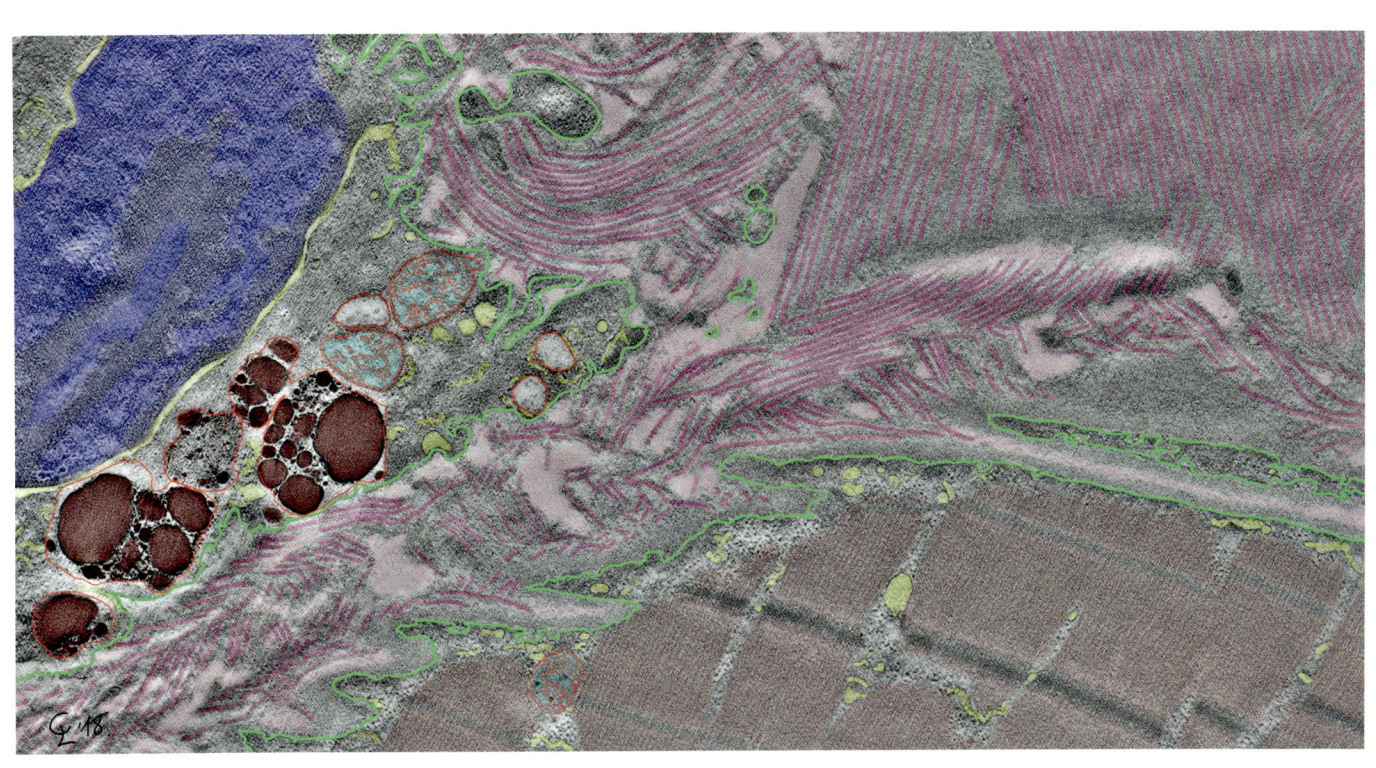

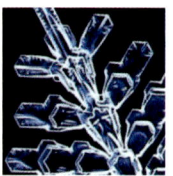

Kenneth Libbrecht

Designer Snow Crystal, 2015

Photomicrographic time-lapse video; custom snow-crystal growth chamber with built-in photomicroscope

California Institute of Technology, Pasadena, California, United States

---

A laboratory-created snow crystal is revealed, first growing and then evaporating away. A chamber was used to surround the crystal with fog droplets as it grew. Total elapsed time was 78 minutes. At its maximum size, the crystal measured 3.5 millimeters from tip to tip.

https://vimeo.com/312985344/3bde52ff44

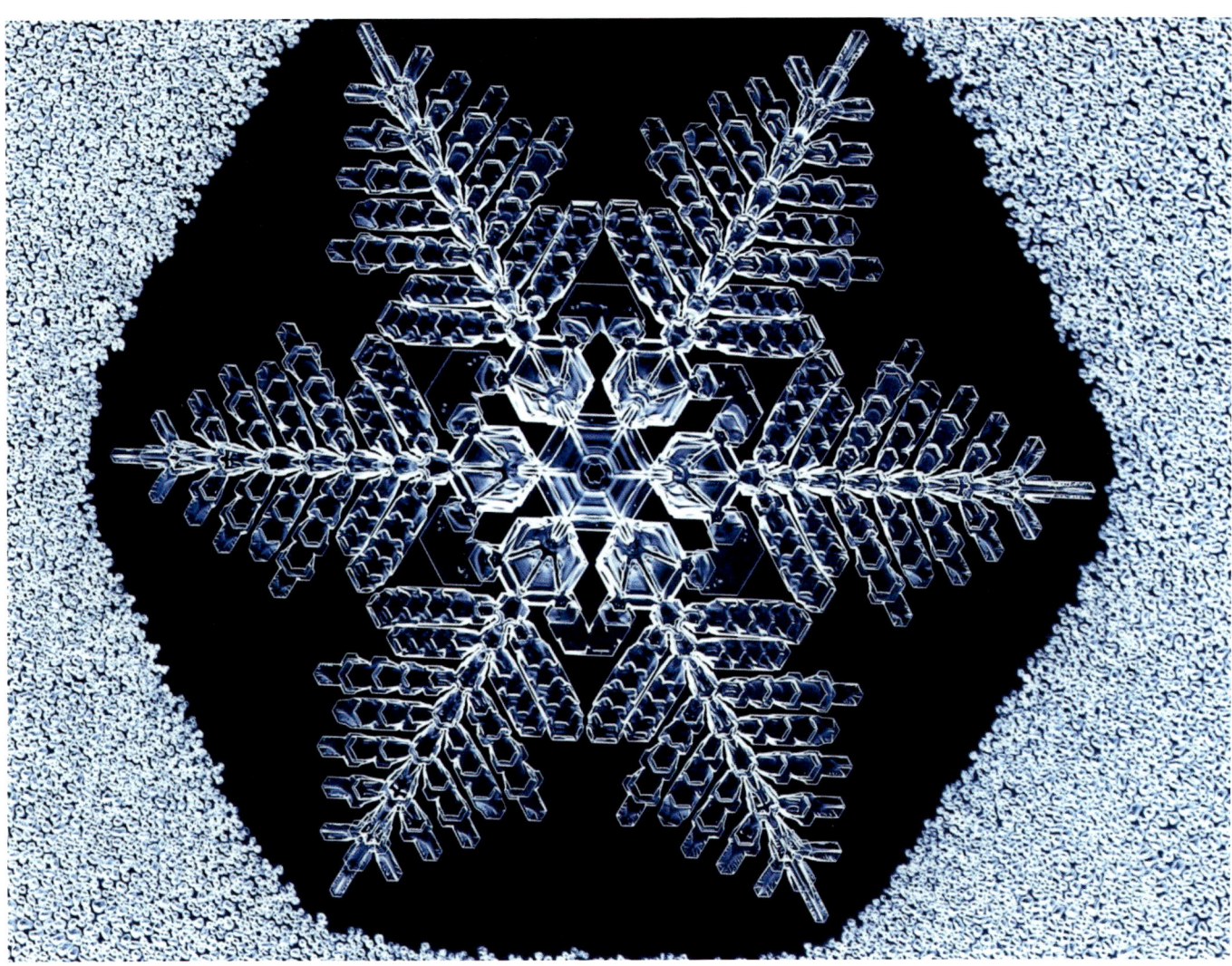

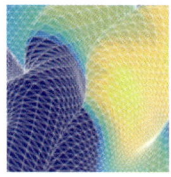

Dan Lloyd   **Juror Selection Award**

Listening between Your Ears:
Sonification and the Dynamic Brain, 2018

Multimedia animation

Trinity College, Hartford, Connecticut, United States

This video shares Independent Component Analysis that reveals brain activity.
This technique becomes especially useful when combined with data sonification.

https://vimeo.com/312979483/1e9c3bc076

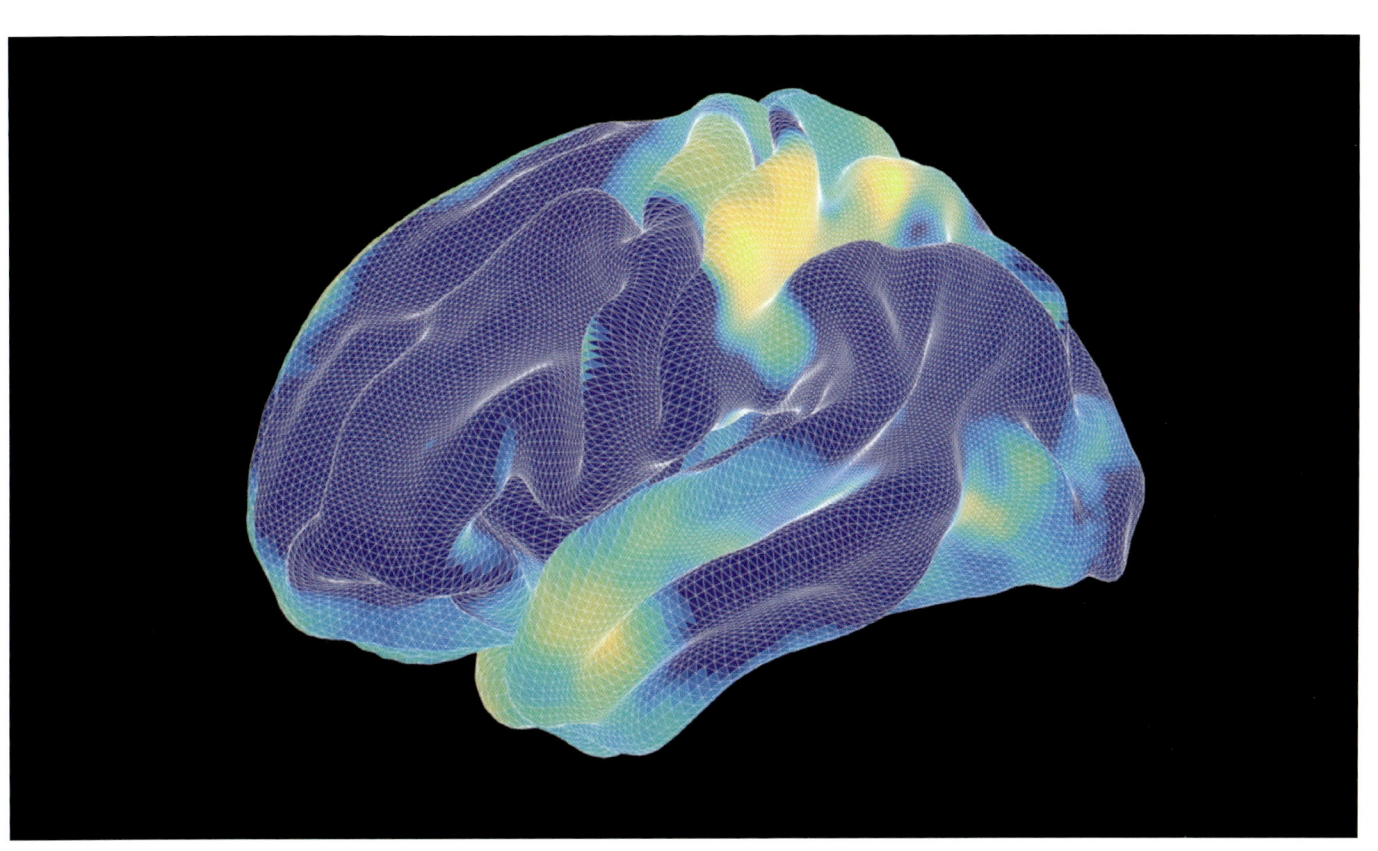

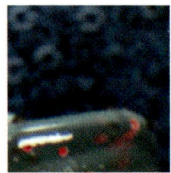

Zhaowen Luo

Metformin Promotes Anti-Tumor Immunity, 2018

Multimedia animation; Autodesk 3ds Max; Visual Molecular Dynamics computer program; Adobe After Effects

University of Illinois at Chicago, Chicago, Illinois, United States

---

This animation shares how metformin, a drug used for diabetes, could potentially be used for immunotherapy. Tumor cells can evade the immune system by overexpressing the protein PD-L1 (programmed death-ligand 1) to deactivate cytotoxic T cells. Metformin could cause PD-L1 to degrade in the endoplasmic reticulum instead of expressing on the cell surface.

https://vimeo.com/313015990/7631ffb948

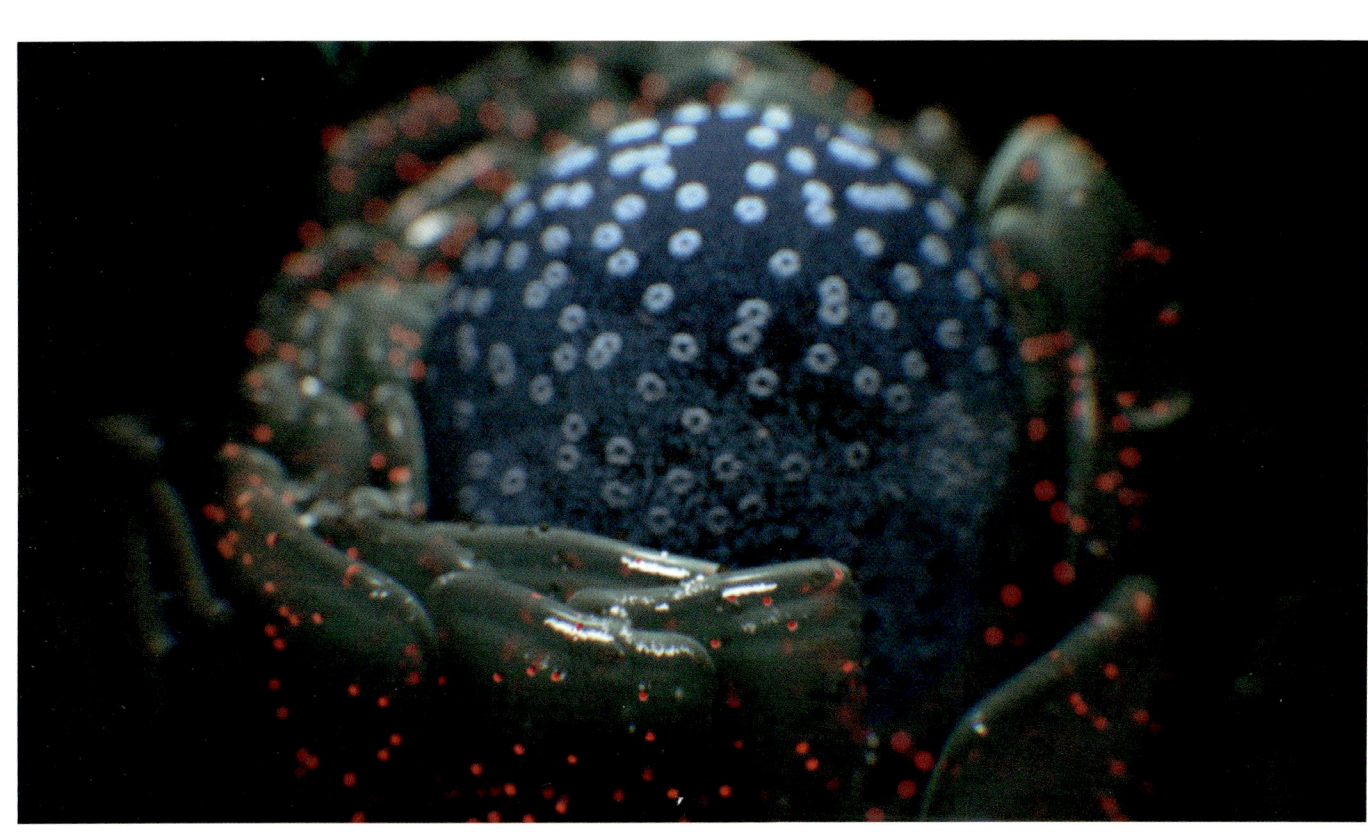

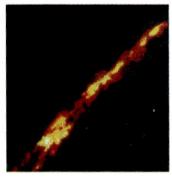

M. Apparition   **Juror Selection Award**

A Portion of the Universe/The Bright and Hallowed Sky 9-3-17-1, 2017

Chemically treated chromogenic-print; digital reproduction

New York, New York, United States

This is an image created from my imagination in my studio using corrosive chemicals on chromogenic papers that are exposed to the chemicals and processed conventionally. The reactions are quite variable. The resultant prints are then digitized and printed. Both the subject and the processes use controlled scientific methods.

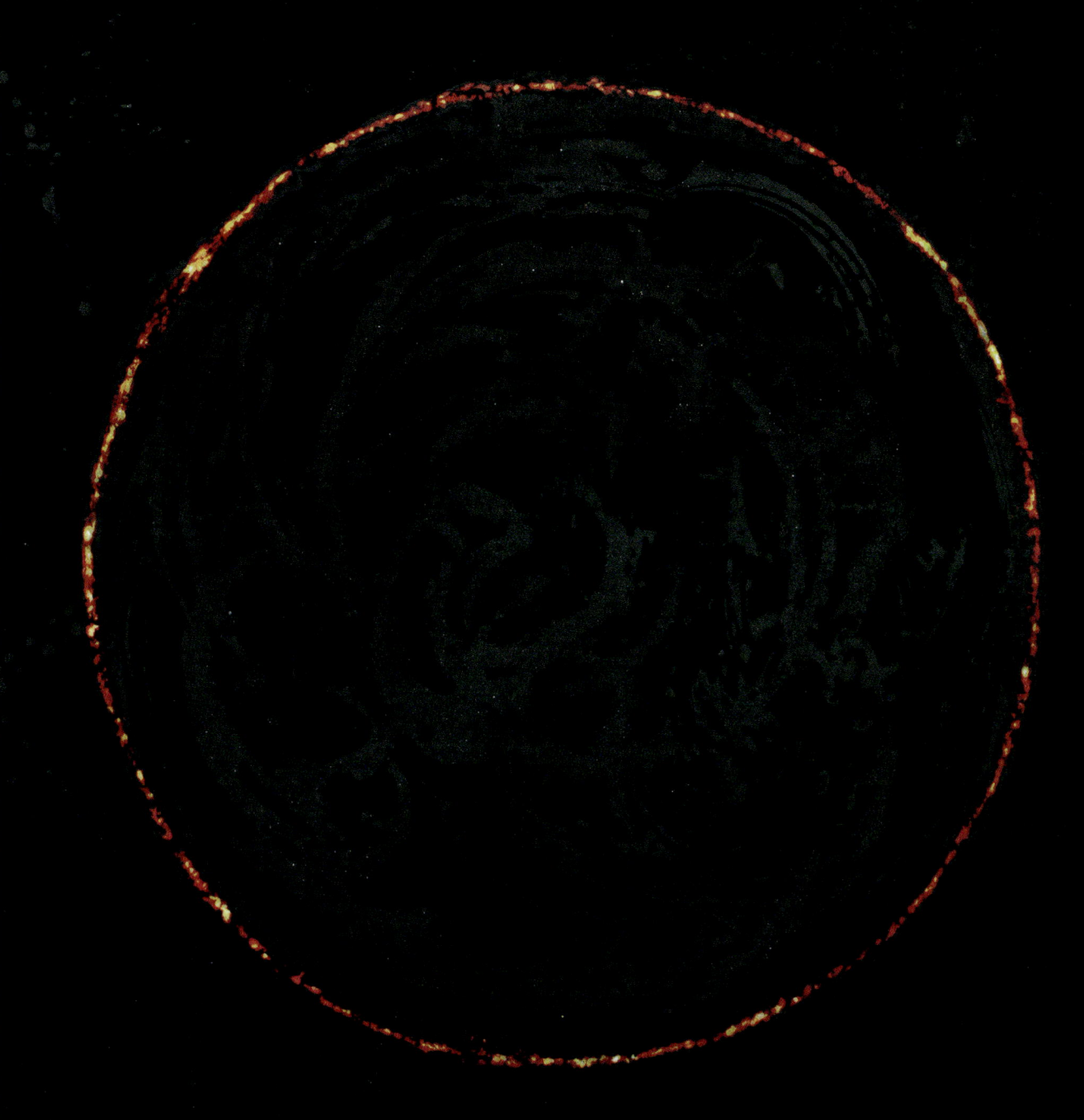

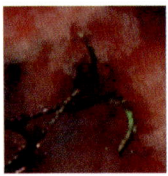

Marissa Masek

Nitrogen Triiodide Explosion, 2014

High-speed photograph; Canon 5D Mark II DSLR camera equipped with a Canon 24-70mm f/4L EF lens; tripod; short duration electronic flash; Arduino circuit with trigger

TissueVision, Boston, Massachusetts, United States

This image shows an explosion of nitrogen triiodide. To make this compound, solid iodide and ammonia are combined to create a slurry of nitrogen triiodide ammoniate. This slurry is stable due to the excess ammonia. As the slurry dries, the compound becomes very unstable. Any small disturbance or vibration will detonate it, turning it into the red gas seen in the image. The compound was touched with a peacock feather to trigger the explosion, and the sound of the explosion, which is quite loud, was used to trigger the flash. Special thanks to Dr. Scott Williams and Jason Faulring.

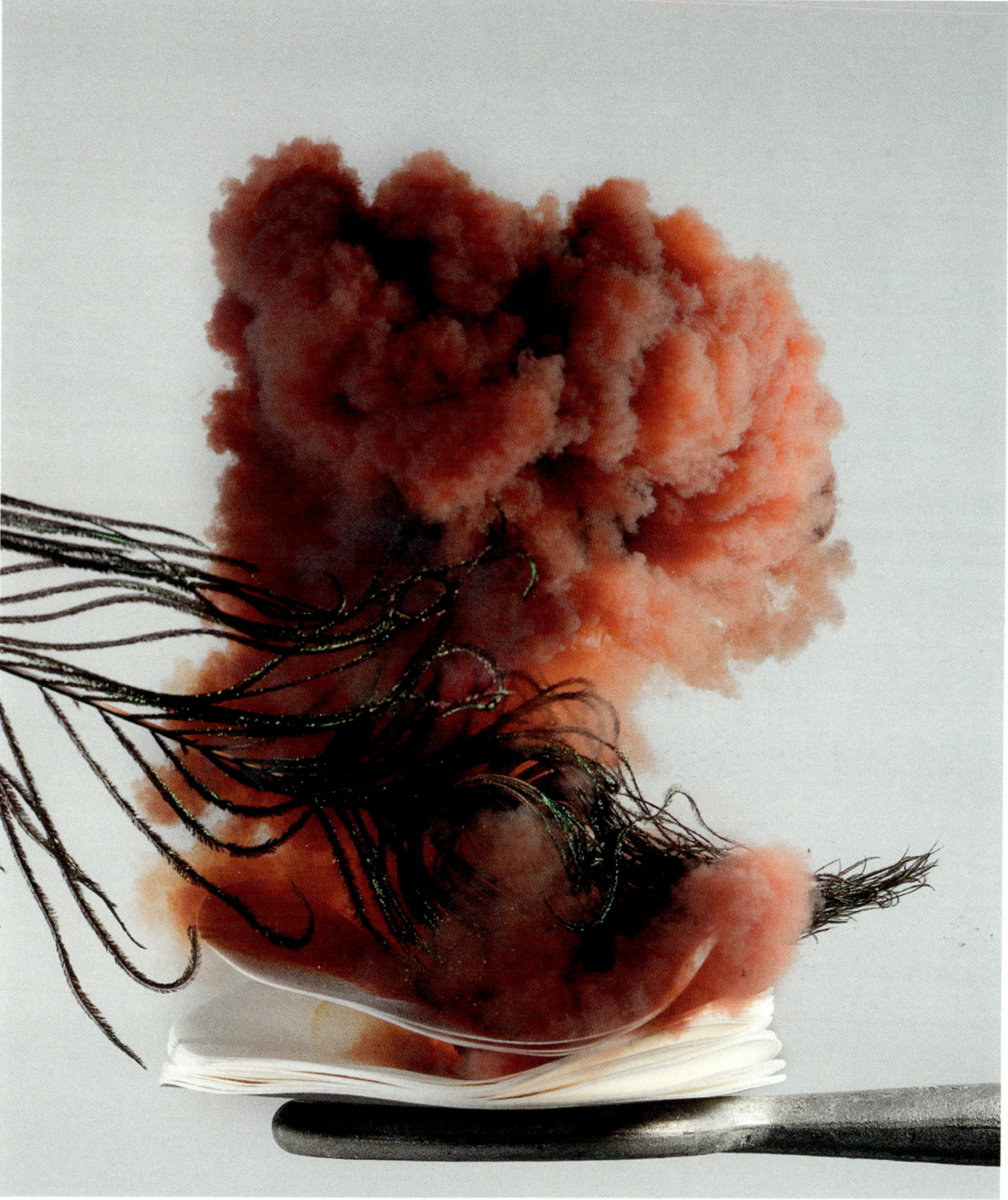

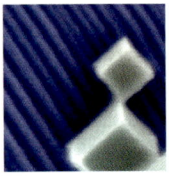

Daniel Mathys

MgO Crystal, 2018

Scanning electron photomicrograph; FEI Nova NanoSEM 230; image processing software to colorize image

Pharmaceutical Biology, University of Basel, Basel, Switzerland

---

The MgO (magnesium oxide) crystal is used as a high-resolution test for evaluating scanning electron microscopes.

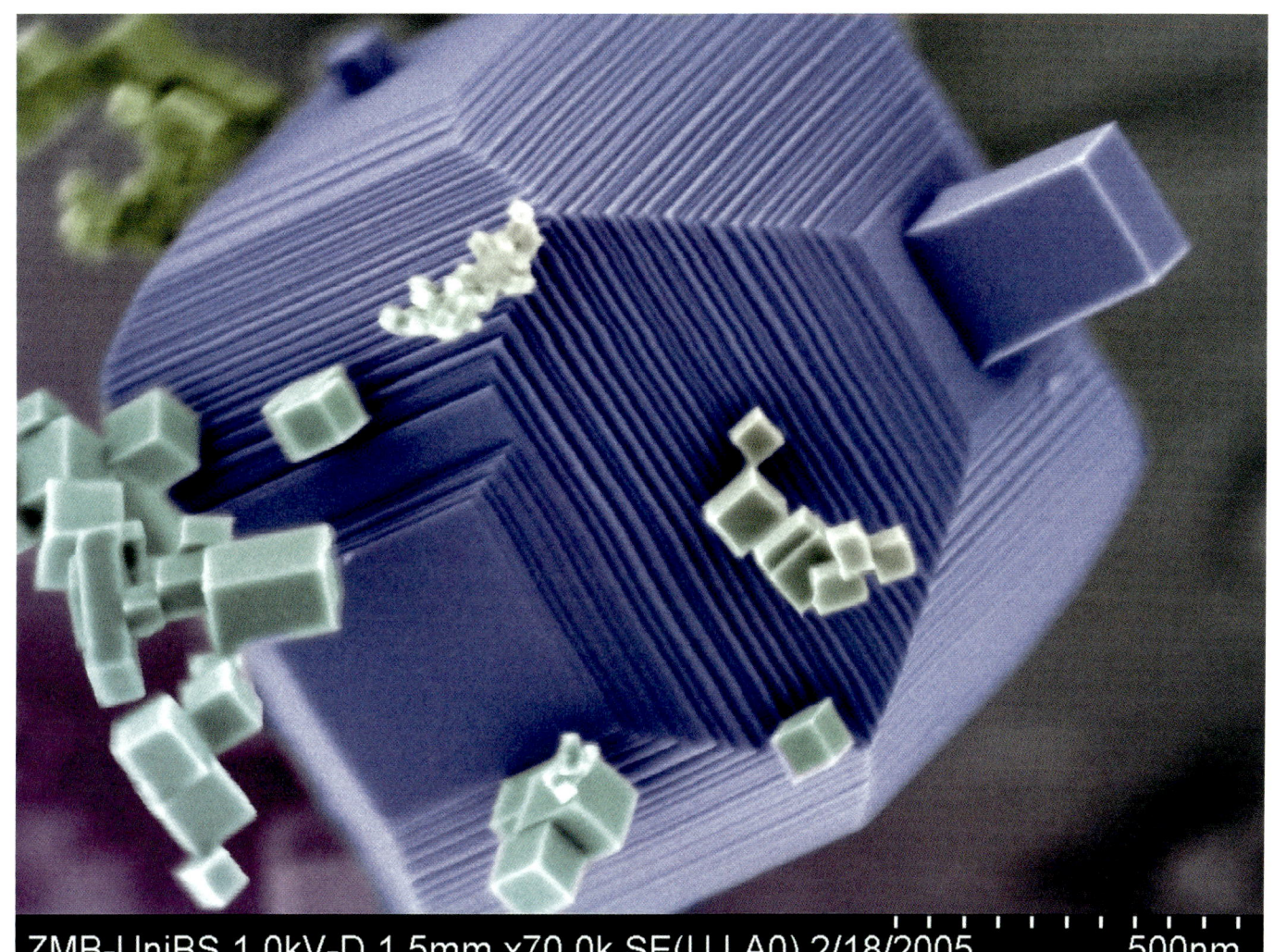

ZMB-UniBS 1.0kV-D 1.5mm x70.0k SE(U,LA0) 2/18/2005   500nm

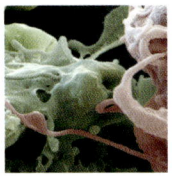

Oliver Meckes and Nicole Ottawa

Natural Killer Cells Attacking Cancer Cells, 2018

Colored scanning electron photomicrograph; FEI Quanta 250 scanning electron microscope; capture magnification ~x1000; digital colorization

Eye of Science, Reutlingen, Germany

This image shows the reaction of an immune system where natural killer cells attack cancer cells when encountered. In the photomicrograph, two natural killer cells (red) are located on a cancer cell (olive) and destroy it. The apoptosis (cell death) is already in process, which can be seen on the bubble-like vesicles. A second cancer cell in the background had been attacked, too. It also proceeds to apoptosis and will fall apart into droplets.

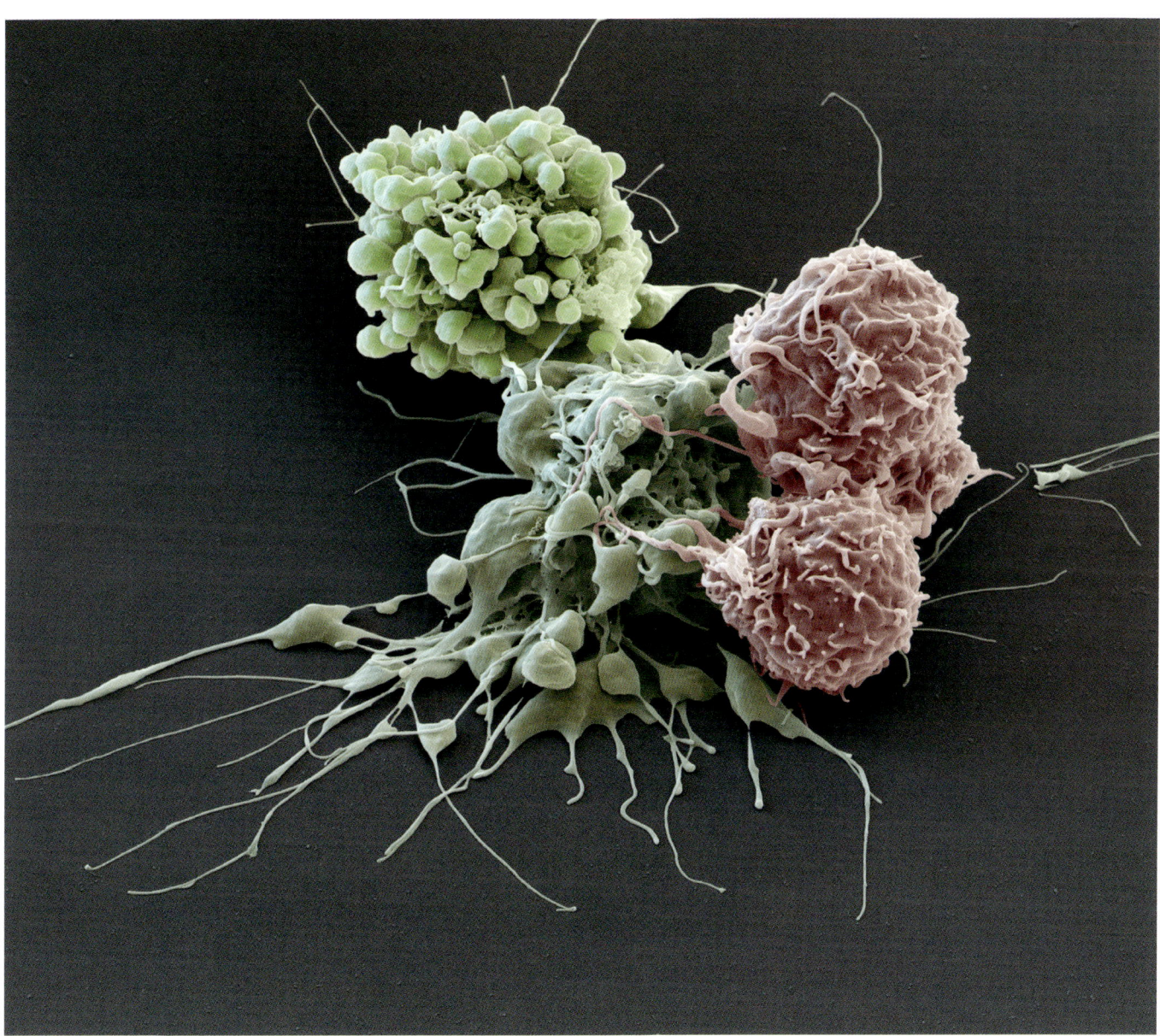

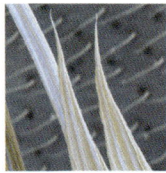

Oliver Meckes and Nicole Ottawa

Wing of a Mosquito, 2018

Colored scanning electron photomicrograph; FEI Quanta 250 scanning electron microscope; capture magnification ~x100; digital colorization

Eye of Science, Reutlingen, Germany

The picture shows a wing of a mosquito, revealing fine scales on its veins and edges. It is thought the scales reduce the noise of the wings in flight. In this image the signals of a secondary electron detector and two backscattered electron detectors were mixed, and the scales were separately colored.

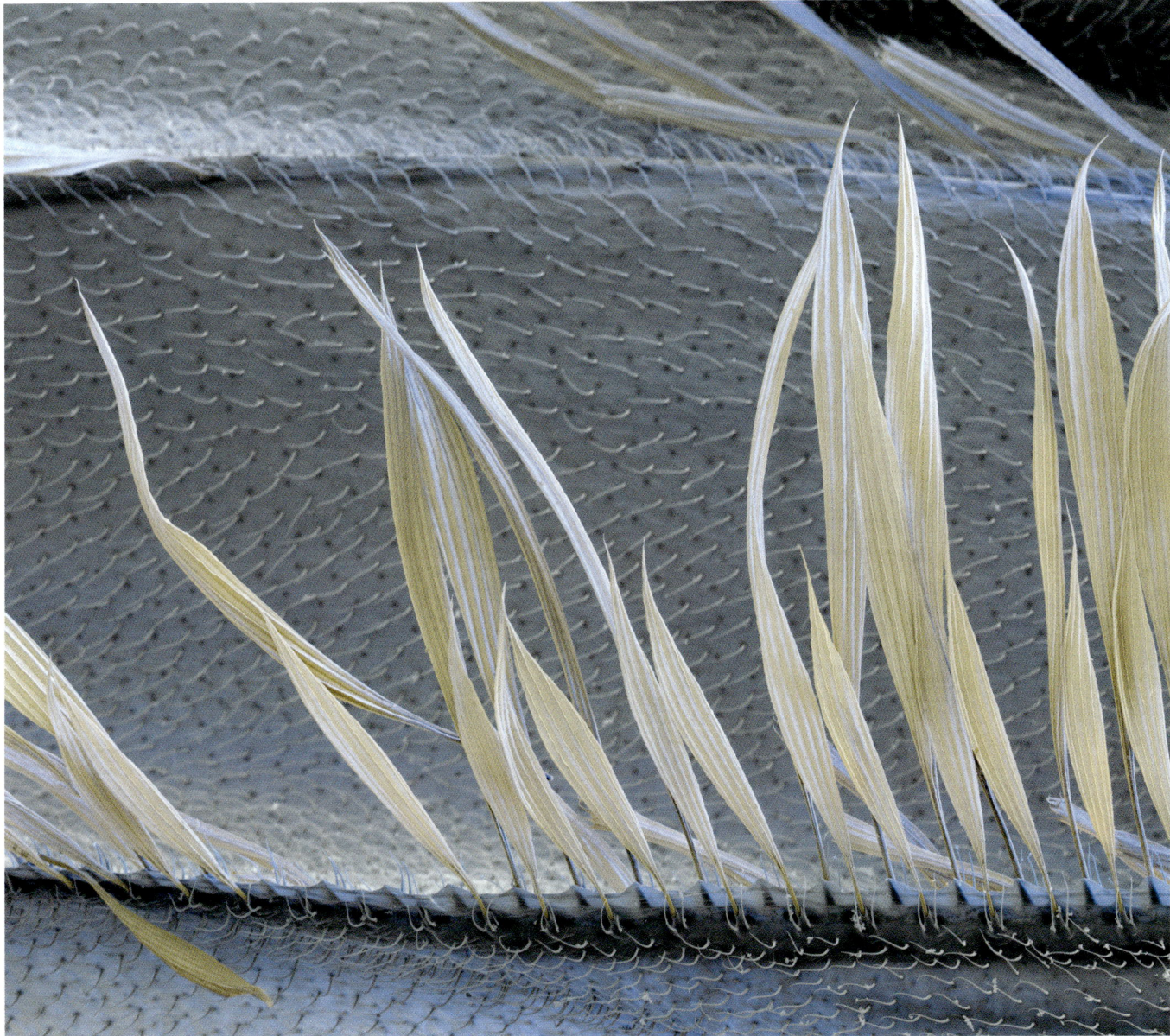

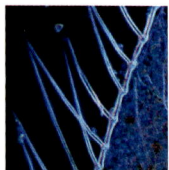

Marek Miś

Damselfly Caudal Gill, 2017

Photomicrograph; Olympus BH-2 photomicroscope; Mitutoyo Plan Apo 10X objective; Pentax K-1 DSLR camera

Marek Miś Photography, Suwalki, Poland

The photomicrograph represents the trachea and tracheoles located in a damselfly's caudal gill. The image was produced using darkfield illumination and polarized light.

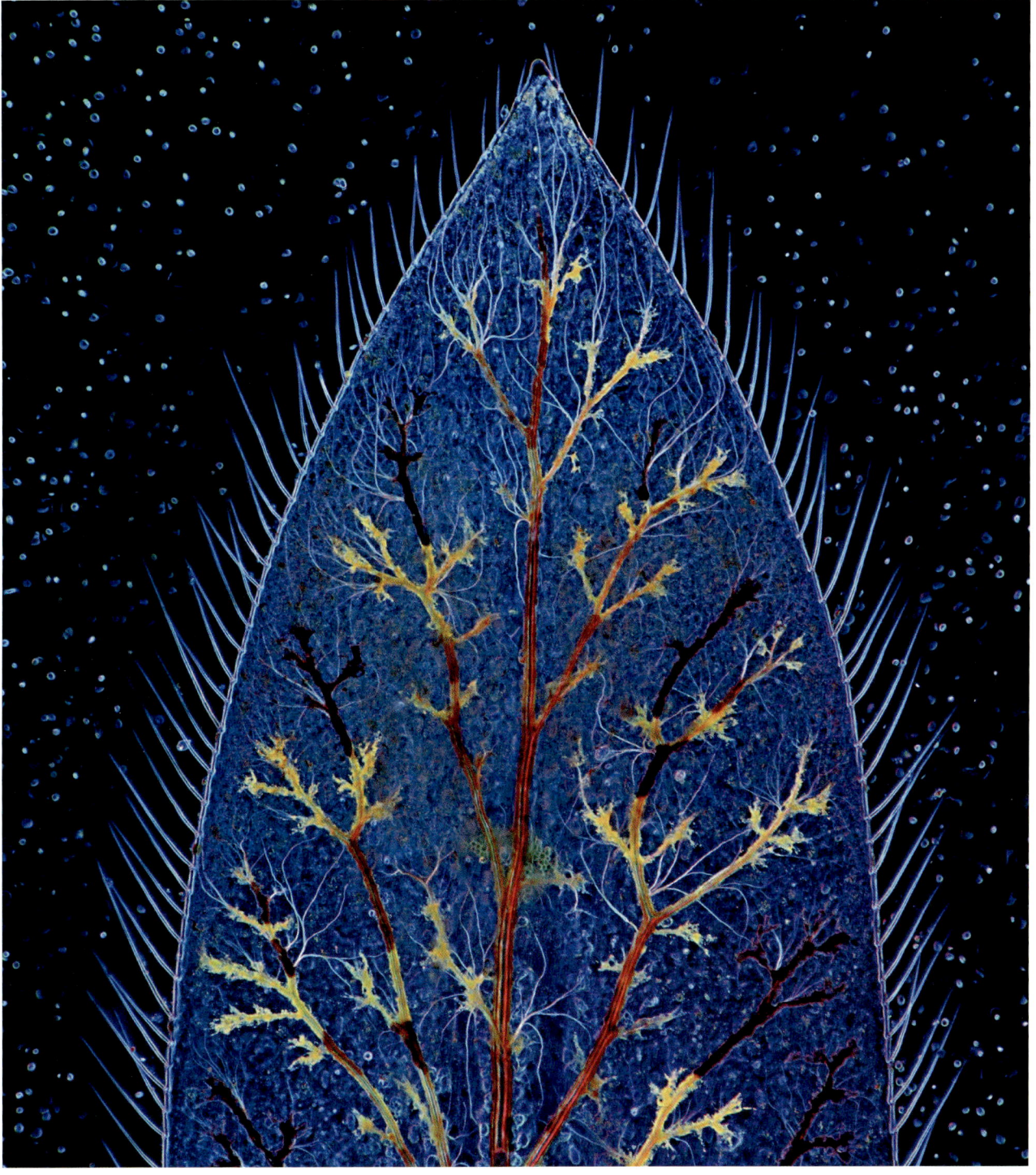

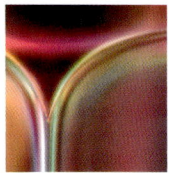

Marek Miś   **Juror Selection Award**

Strange Square Air Bubbles Formed on a Tea Bag, 2016

Photomicrograph; Olympus BH-2 photomicroscope; Mitutoyo Plan Apo 10X objective;
Pentax K-1 DSLR camera

Marek Miś Photography, Suwalki, Poland

The photomicrograph reveals air bubbles of a most unusual square shape.
They formed on top of a tea bag immersed in water. When the sample air
bubbles were covered with a cover slip, they connected with each other at
their corners. The image was produced using darkfield illumination and
polarized light.

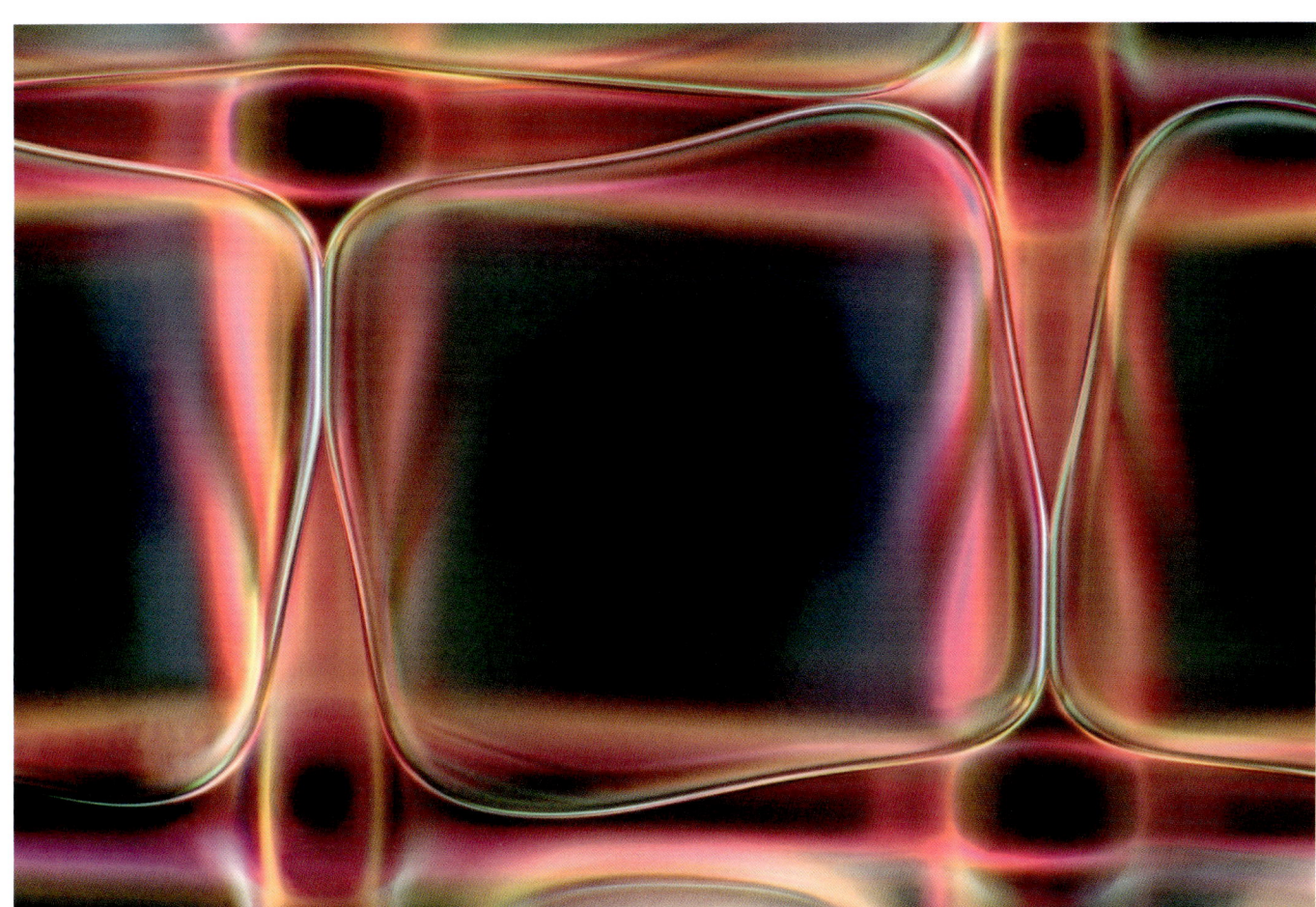

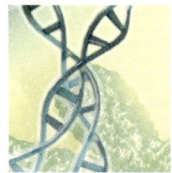

Mao Miyamoto

Drug Delivery of Cas9, 2018

Digital illustration; Maxon Cinema 4D; Redshift; Adobe Photoshop

Mao Miyamoto Scientific Visual Design, Boston, Massachusetts, United States

---

This illustration accompanies the article by Y. Li et al. "Intracellular Delivery and Biodistribution Study of CRISPR/Cas9 Ribonucleoprotein Loaded Bioreducible Lipidoid Nanoparticles" published in the journal *Biomaterials Science* (January 2019). The illustration depicts the finding that lipidoid nanoparticles promote the delivery of the Cas9 to mammalian cells. This delivery enhances the genome editing through the CRISPR/Cas9 system.

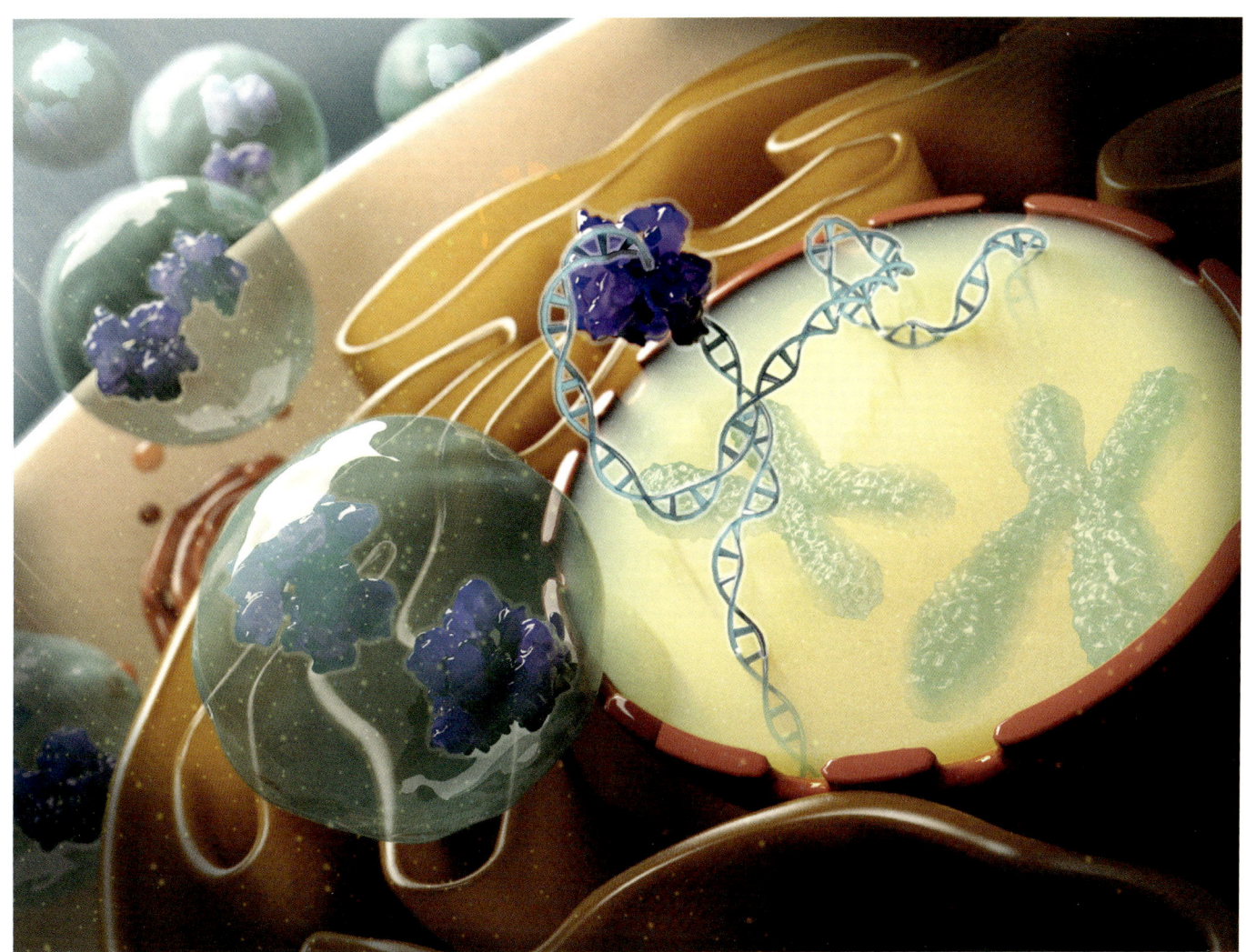

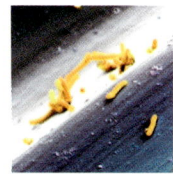

Martin Oeggerli, F. Schmidt, M. Cherepkova, and R. J. Platt

Escherichia coli on a Phonographic Record of Ludwig van Beethoven's "Moonlight Sonata" (Piano Sonata No. 14 in C-Sharp Minor), 2018

Colored scanning electron photomicrograph; colorized with image processing software

Pathology, University Hospital of Basel, and University of Basel, Biosystems Science and Engineering Dep., ETH Zürich in Basel, Basel Switzerland

---

This colorized scanning electron micrograph shows cells of the human gut bacterium *Escherichia coli* (*E. coli*) plated onto a phonographic record of Ludwig van Beethoven's "Moonlight Sonata" (Piano Sonata No. 14 in C-sharp minor). *E. coli* has been engineered to express the molecular components of another bacterium's CRISPR-Cas system, an adaptive bacterial immune system that enables the cell to write a permanent record of the RNAs within the cell into its own genome where it is safely stored. Much like the Beethoven composition, this record is preserved over many generations. Scientists can retrieve it at any time to reveal the mysteries of the bacterium's transcriptional history.

148

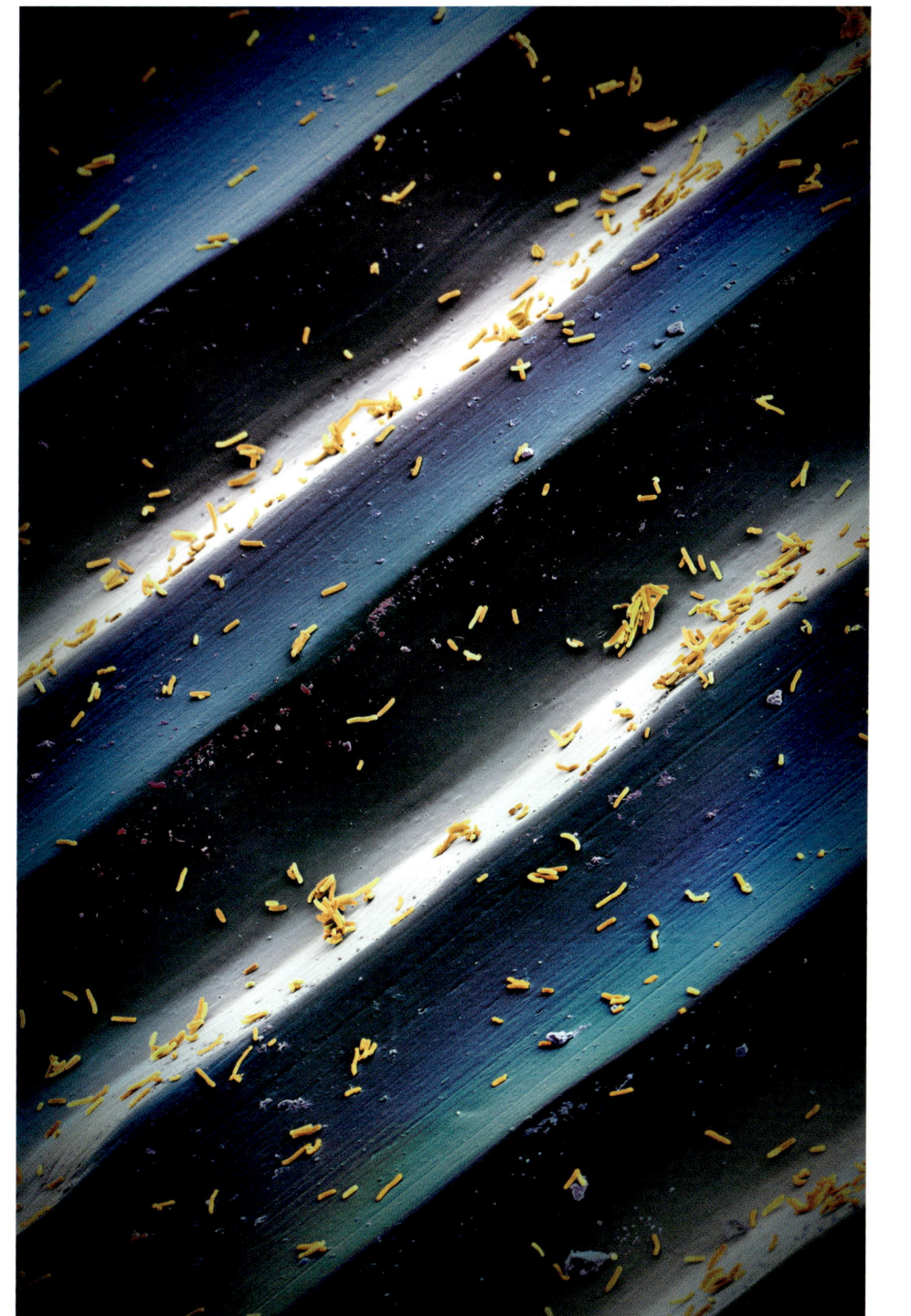

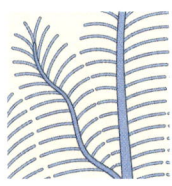

James Perkins

Astrocyte Biology, 2016

Digital illustration; Adobe Illustrator

Rochester Institute of Technology, Rochester, New York, United States

This illustration summarizes the structure and function of astrocytes in the central nervous system. It emphasizes their role in supporting neuron metabolism, regulating pH and ion balance, and contributing to the blood-brain barrier.

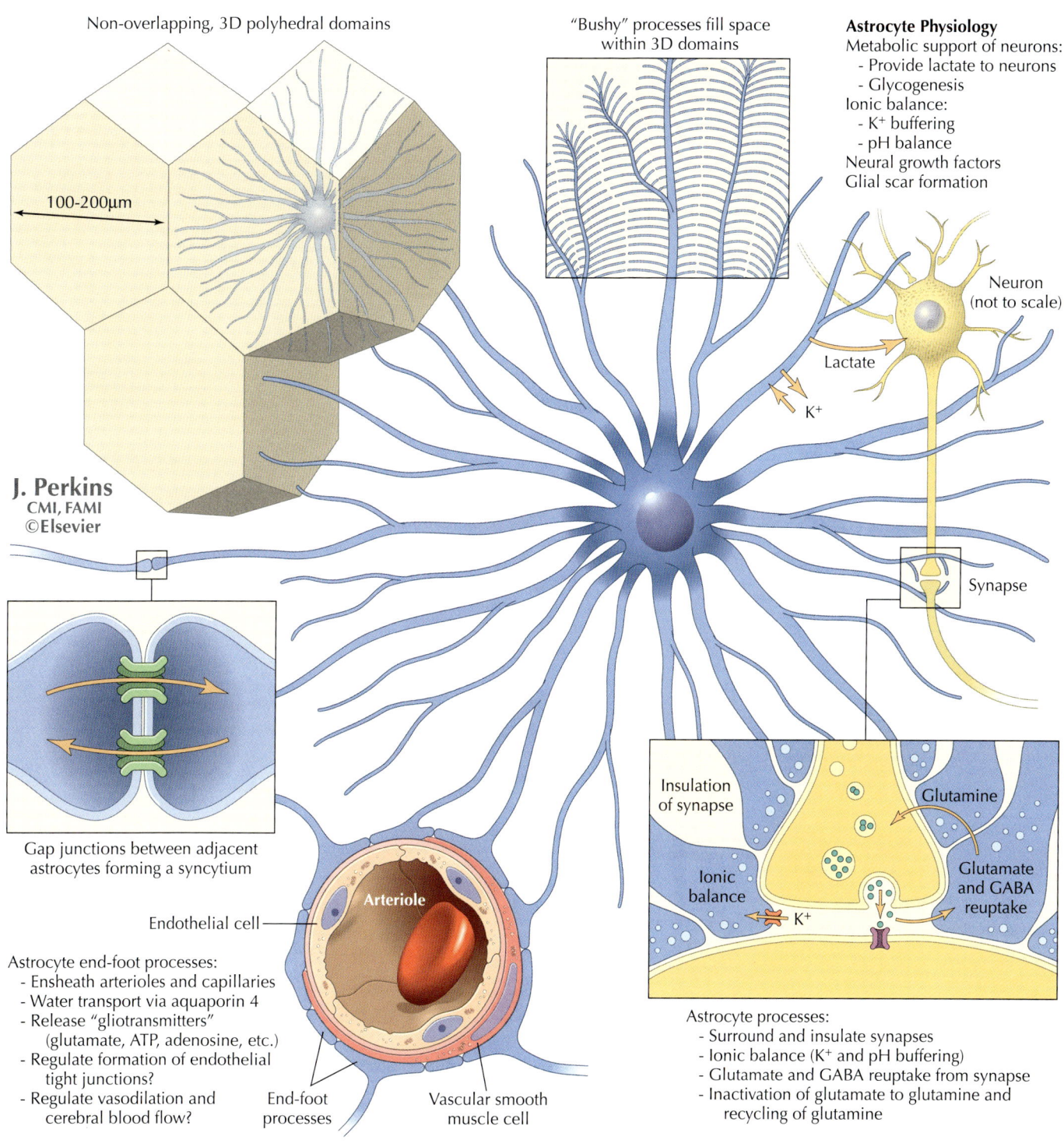

Non-overlapping, 3D polyhedral domains

100-200μm

"Bushy" processes fill space within 3D domains

Astrocyte Physiology
Metabolic support of neurons:
- Provide lactate to neurons
- Glycogenesis
Ionic balance:
- K$^+$ buffering
- pH balance
Neural growth factors
Glial scar formation

Neuron (not to scale)

Lactate

K$^+$

J. Perkins
CMI, FAMI
©Elsevier

Synapse

Gap junctions between adjacent astrocytes forming a syncytium

Insulation of synapse

Glutamine

Ionic balance

K$^+$

Glutamate and GABA reuptake

Arteriole

Endothelial cell

Astrocyte end-foot processes:
- Ensheath arterioles and capillaries
- Water transport via aquaporin 4
- Release "gliotransmitters" (glutamate, ATP, adenosine, etc.)
- Regulate formation of endothelial tight junctions?
- Regulate vasodilation and cerebral blood flow?

End-foot processes

Vascular smooth muscle cell

Astrocyte processes:
- Surround and insulate synapses
- Ionic balance (K$^+$ and pH buffering)
- Glutamate and GABA reuptake from synapse
- Inactivation of glutamate to glutamine and recycling of glutamine

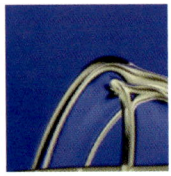

Phred Petersen

Glycerol Droplets Moving through a Salt Solution, 2018

High-speed video; Phantom VEO 640S camera; Micro-NIKKOR 200mm lens; 1600 fps; resolution of 2560x1440 pixels

RMIT University, Melbourne, Victoria, Australia

Two glycerol droplets were dropped, one after the other, into a solution of magnesium sulfate ($MgSO_4$) to visualize the flow and folding behavior of a viscous liquid moving through a less-viscous environment. This has relevance to the field of microfluidics. Rheinberg illumination was used to optically color the different liquids.

https://vimeo.com/313013192/e52ca95bcd

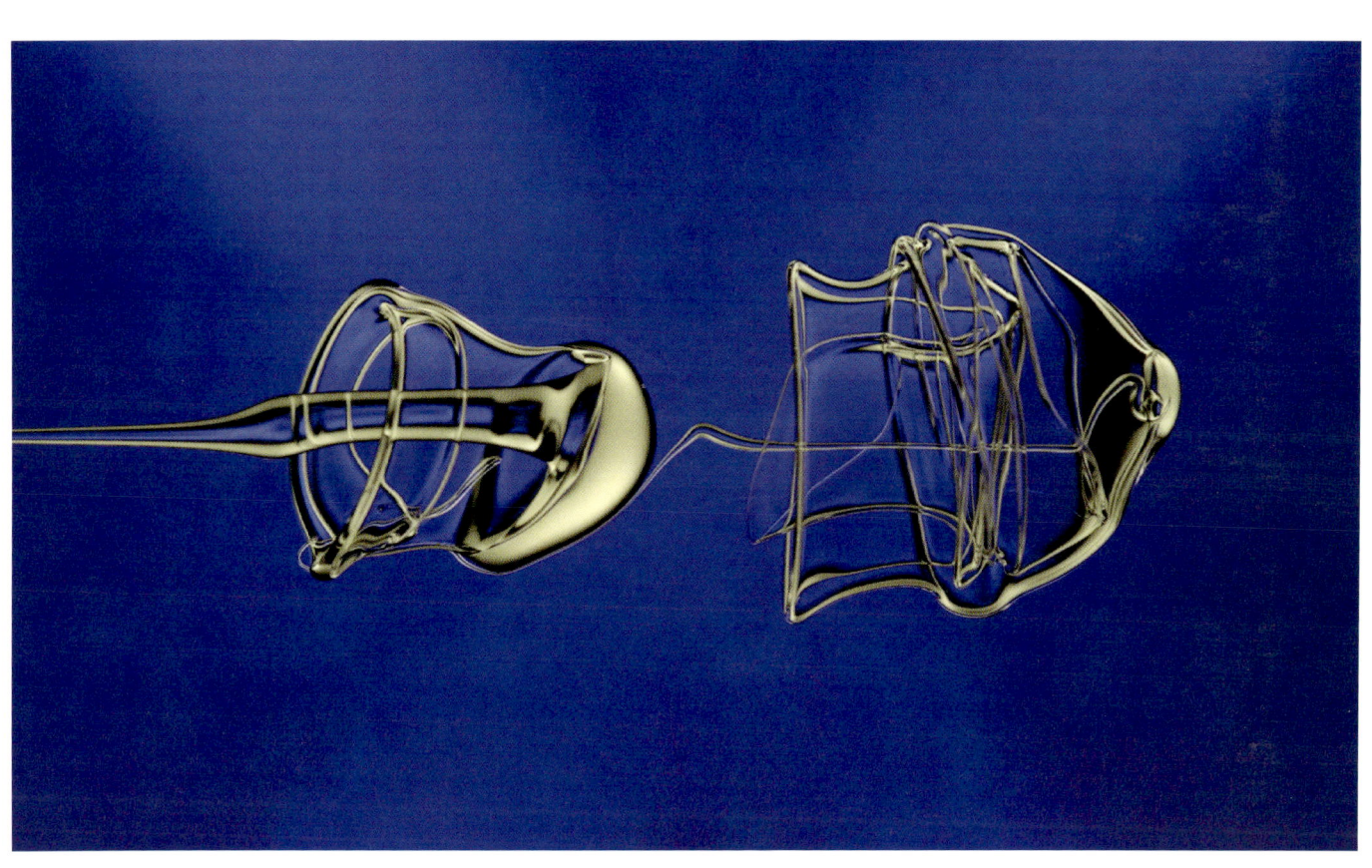

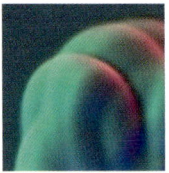

Phred Petersen

Schlieren Visualization of Airflow around a MAV, 2016

High-speed video; 300mm f/10 Z-mirror Schlieren system; Phantom v2511 camera; 10,000 fps at 1280x720 pixels

RMIT University, Melbourne, Victoria, Australia

A three-color, direction-indicating Schlieren setup was used to visualize the airflow around a Micro Air Vehicle (MAV). Alcohol vapor was used to see the downdraft at startup. At lift-off, hot air columns from two small butane torches tracked the surrounding airflow. This video contributes to understanding the aerodynamics of MAVs.

https://vimeo.com/313013634/bc188ac8f3

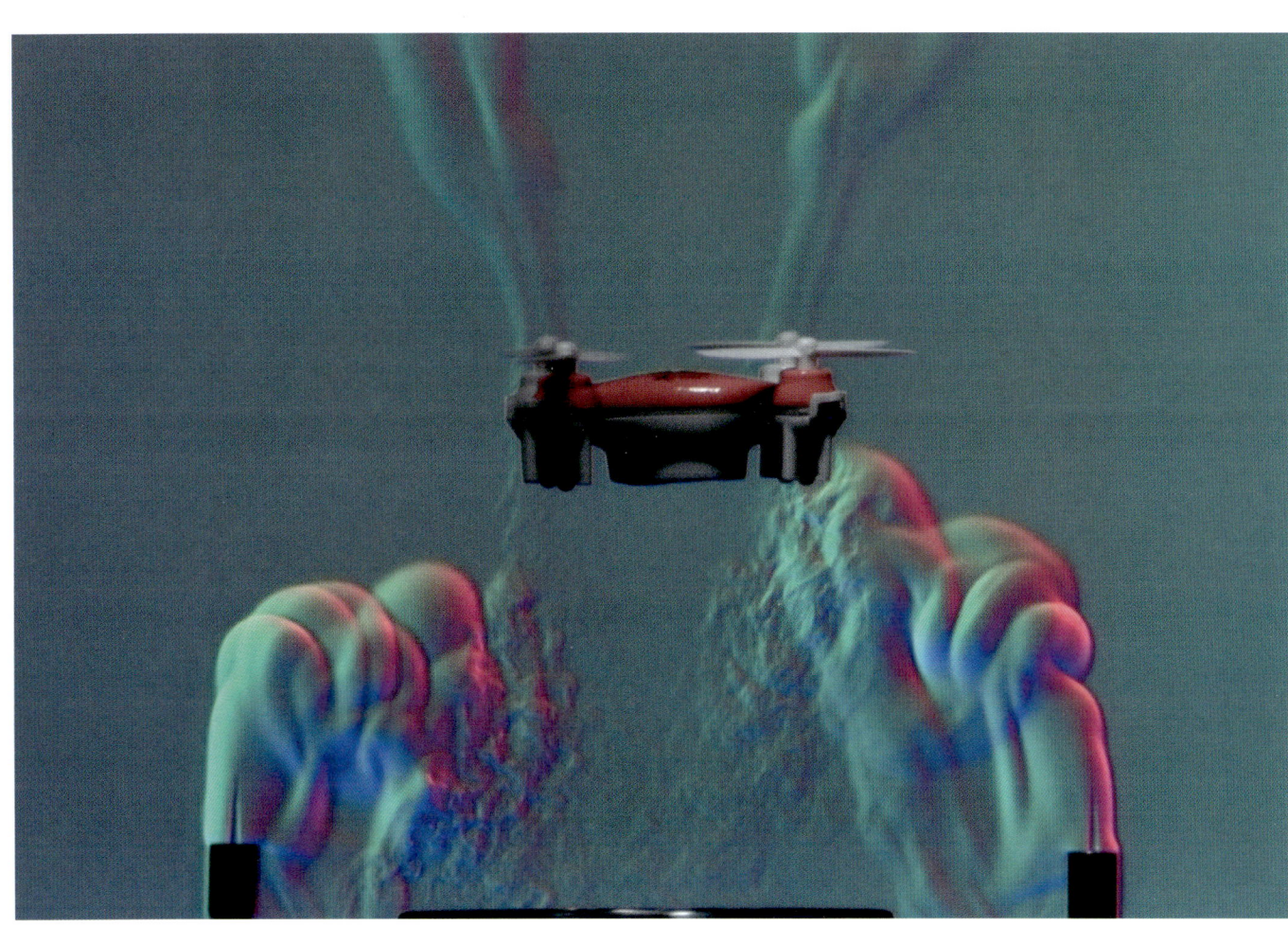

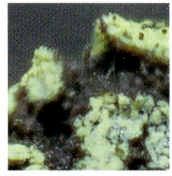

Alison K. Pollack

Physarum viride, 2018

Computational close-up photograph; Sony a7R II DSLR camera; Laowa 25mm Ultra Macro lens; a composite of 30 images that were focus stacked

San Anselmo, California, United States

Shown in this photograph are the fruiting bodies, or sporangia, of the Myxomycete *Physarum viride*. They are about 1 millimeter tall. Myxomycetes, or slime molds, are a group of amoeboid protists that help decompose wood and plants; there are about 1,000 species documented worldwide. When mature, the sporangia are bright yellow, encrusted with lime. The caps of these sporangia have opened up to reveal the spore mass within; when fully dry, the spores will be dispersed by the wind. The plant was photographed in San Anselmo, California.

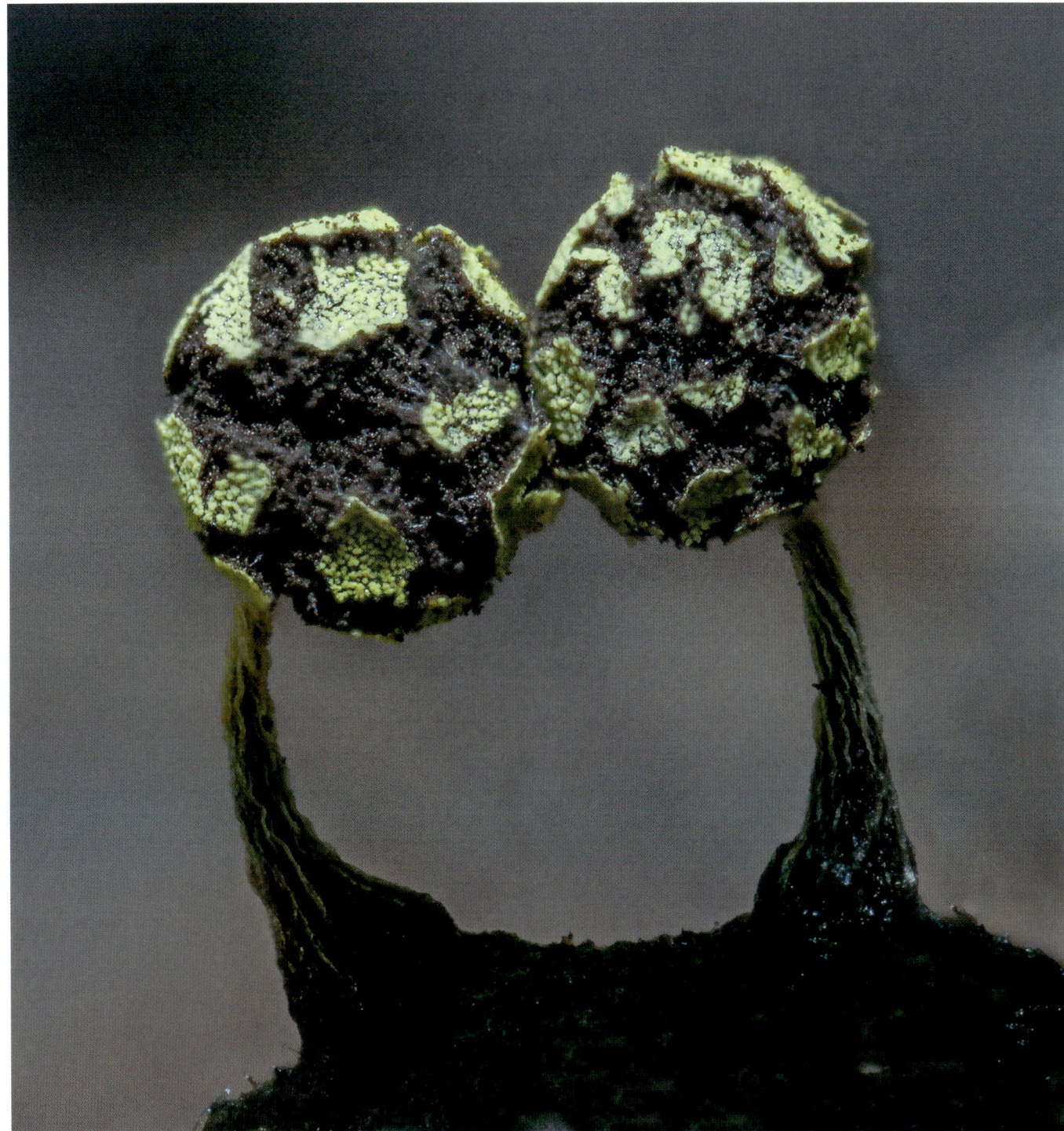

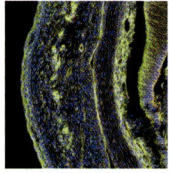

Alan Prescott

Mitochondrial Turnover in the Developing Mouse Eye, 2018

Laser scanning confocal photomicrograph

Dundee Imaging Facility, University of Dundee, Dundee, Scotland, United Kingdom

---

The tiled images in this photograph were taken from a frozen section of a developing eye harvested from the mitoQC mouse, a transgenic mouse with a pH-sensitive fluorescent mitochondrial signal. Under stable conditions, mitochondria fluoresce both green and red. However, when the process of turnover (self-destruction of damaged mitochondria) begins, the mitochondria are delivered to lysosomes, where the acidic environment of the lysosomes quenches the green fluorescence, guaranteeing specificity of the red autophagy (destruct) signal. Large red dots in the image are mitochondria in lysosomes demonstrating turnover of damaged or worn out mitochondria in active tissues in the developing eye. DNA-labelled nuclei are blue. This mouse model has revealed the distribution of the turnover process in diverse, metabolically active tissues, such as tissue of the kidney, heart, and retina. In addition, this mouse model unveils the tissue architecture as delineated by the distribution of mitochondria. At this developmental stage, the eyelids are closed and the posterior chamber still contains blood vessels to support the developing lens and retina.

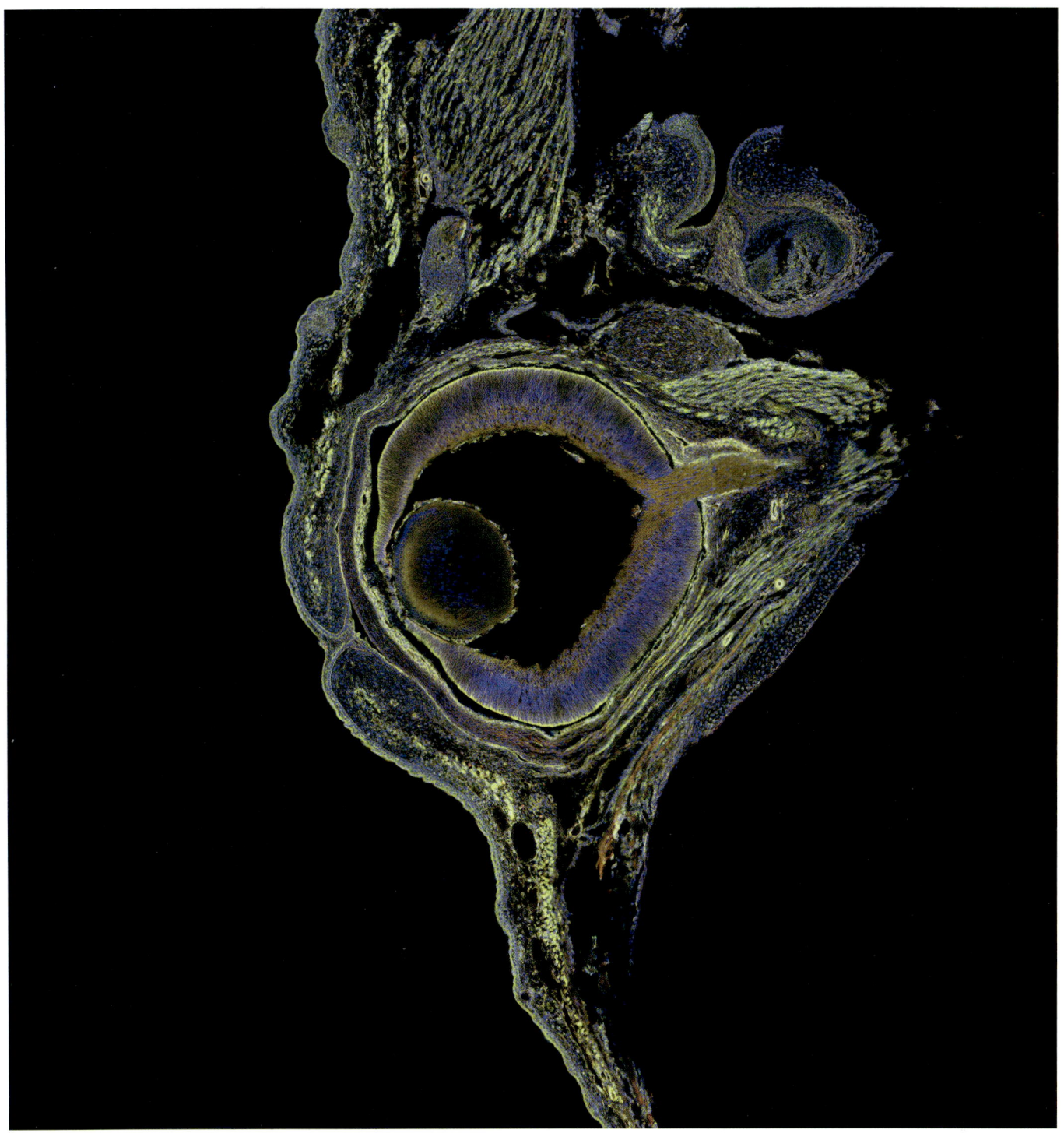

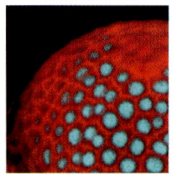

Nathanael Prunet

Arabidopsis Flower Buds, 2017

Confocal photomicrograph; Zeiss LSM 780 confocal microscope;
equipped with a 20x objective

University of California, Los Angeles; Los Angeles, California, United States

---

This photomicrograph features a confocal image of an Arabidopsis expressing a fluorescent reaction for the SHOOT MERISTEMLESS gene. This gene maintains cells in meristems, organs at the tip of the stems and flowers that produce leaves and floral organs in an undifferentiated state (shown in cyan). Cell walls were stained with propidium iodide (red). The recorded image was 2048x2048 pixels and corresponds to a physical sample size of 345x345 microns.

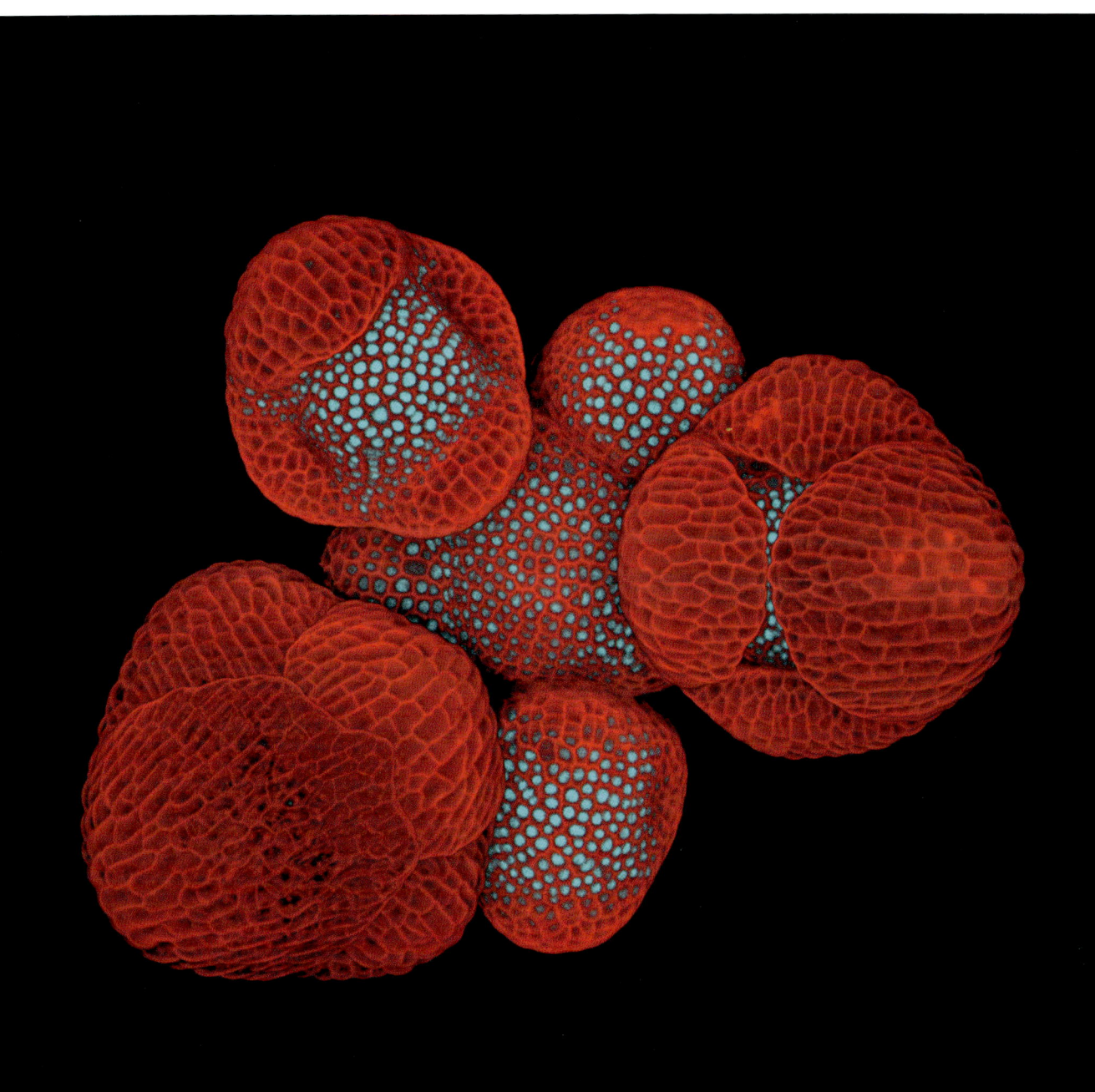

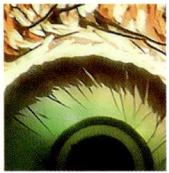

Danny Radius

Plexippus petersi Face, 2018

Composite macro photograph; Nikon D3200 DSLR camera; reverse mounted NIKKOR
18-55mm lens; manual focus rail; a composite of several images that were focus stacked;
capture magnification ~x4

Sukoharjo, Indonesia

This photograph was made from a dead specimen of *Plexippus petersi,*
commonly known as a jumping spider.

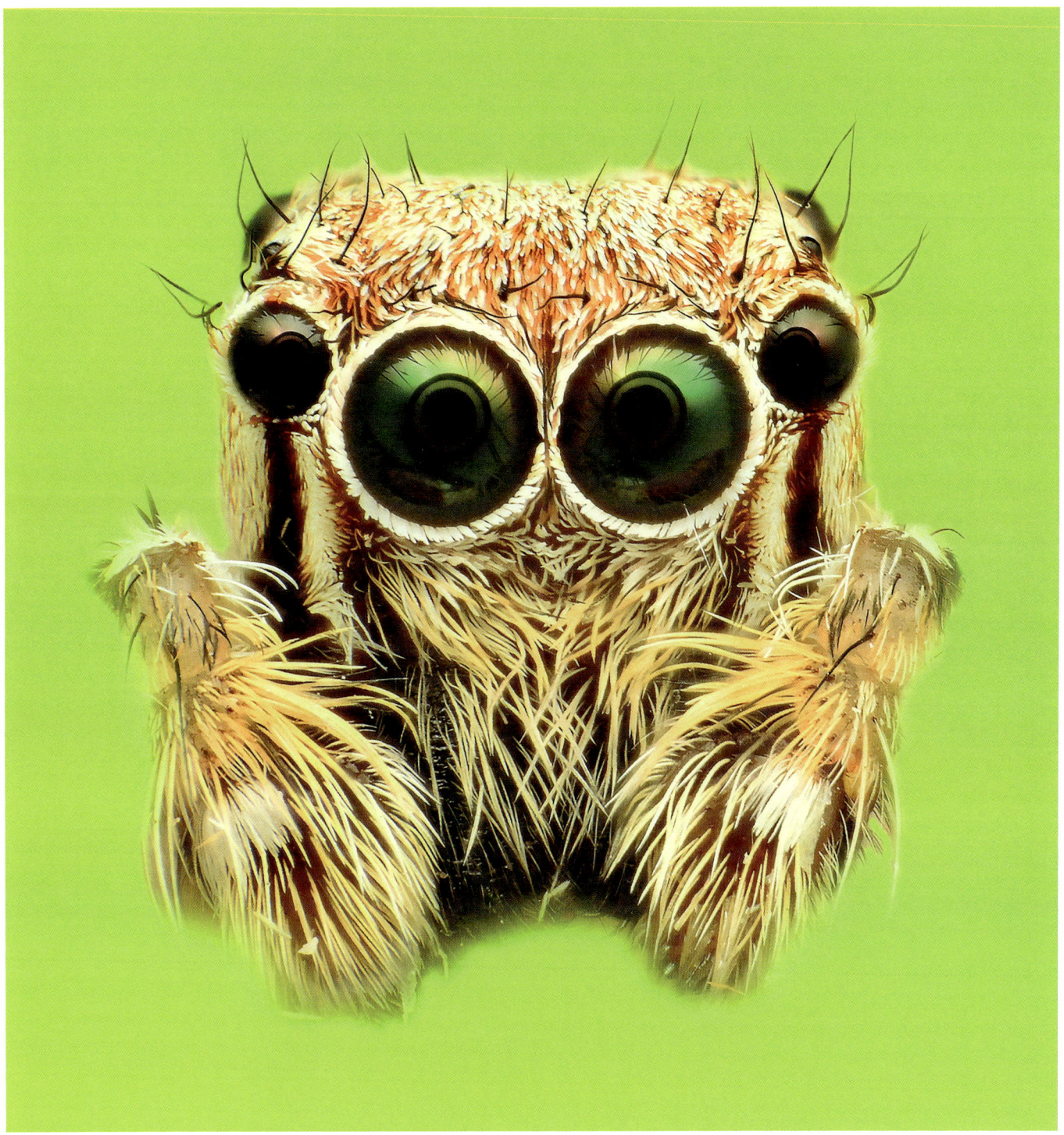

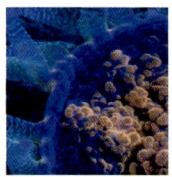

Nina Roepke

Lobed Brain Coral (*Lobophyllia*), 2016

Underwater photograph; Canon 6D DSLR camera; 100mm macro lens;
UV-rich radiation source

Rochester Institute of Technology, Rochester, New York, United States

---

Ultraviolet radiation reveals a coral's fluorescent pigments. *Lobophyllia* is a genus of corals with long sweeper tentacles that sting and damage other sessile animals (immobile animals that have no stalk). The photograph was taken in an aquarium.

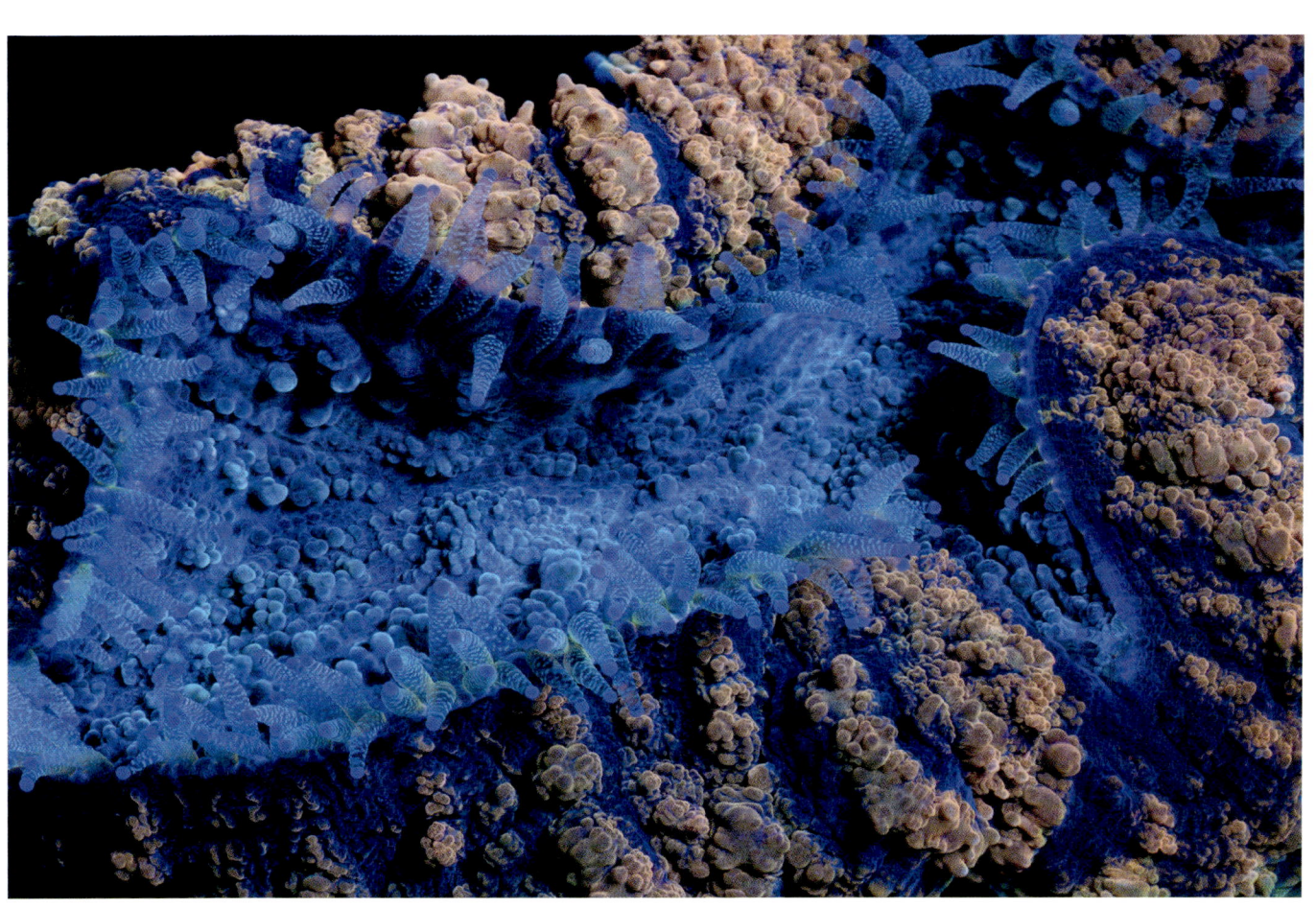

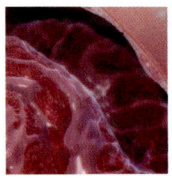

Joe Samson

Structure of the Renal Corpuscle, 2018

Digital illustration; ZBrush; Adobe Photoshop

University of Georgia, Athens, Georgia, United States

This illustration depicts the cellular structure of a renal corpuscle in the nephron of a kidney.

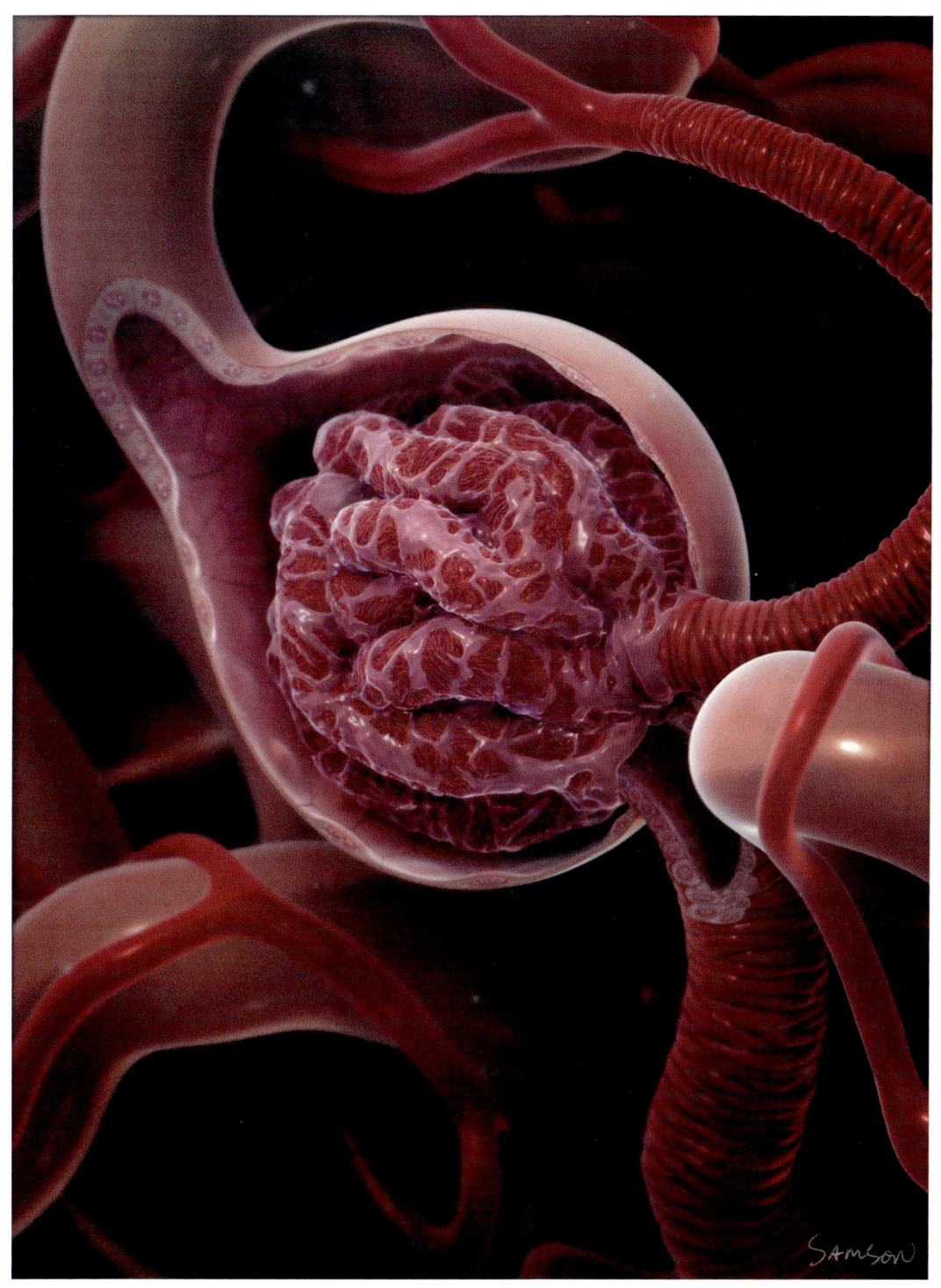

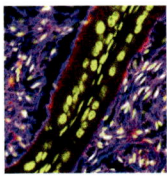

Derek Sung

Mouse Epididymis, 2017

Immunofluorescence confocal photomicrograph; Zeiss LSM 880 confocal microscope

Laboratory of Molecular Cardiology, National Heart, Lung, and Blood Institute of the National Institutes of Health, Bethesda, Maryland, United States

---

The epididymis is a long, tortuous tube that sperm must travel through after leaving the testes. In a mouse, the epididymis can be up to a meter in length, and in humans, it can be up to six meters. During this journey, the sperm mature and acquire motility necessary for fertilization. The epithelium of the epididymis contains special structures, called stereocilia, that absorb fluid to create a current that propels the sperm forward. Mutations or defects in the epididymis can result in infertility. This epididymis came from a dissected mouse, was preserved in paraformaldehyde, embedded in paraffin, thinly sliced, and then stained for PNA (red/magenta), WGA (blue), and nuclei (yellow).

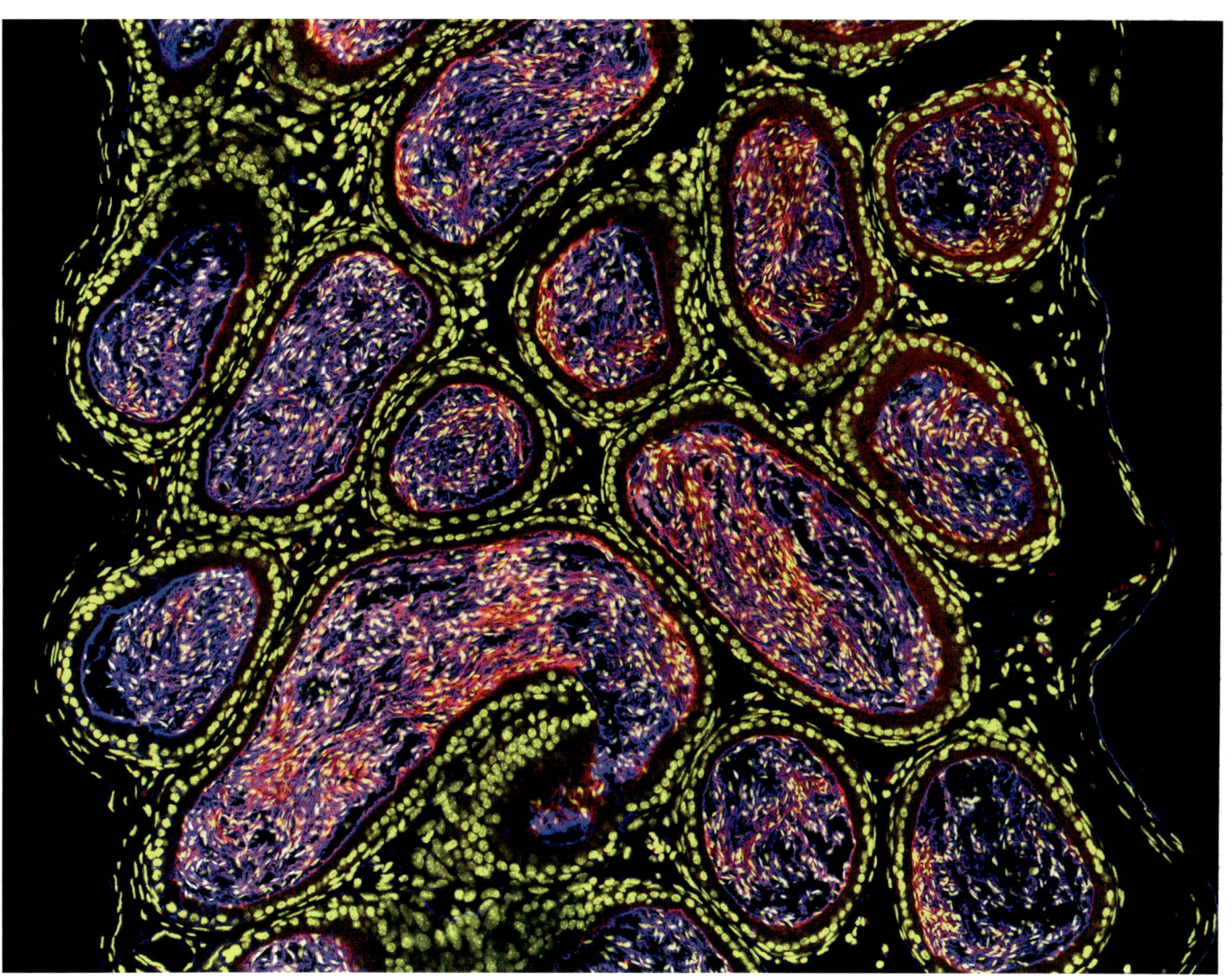

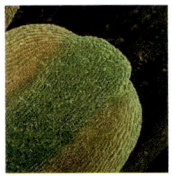

Viktor Sýkora

Nigella sativa Flower, 2018

Scanning electron photomicrograph; scanning electron microscope;
capture magnification ~x50

Charles University, Prague, Czech Republic

This pseudo-colored scanning electron micrograph features the *Nigella sativa* flower.

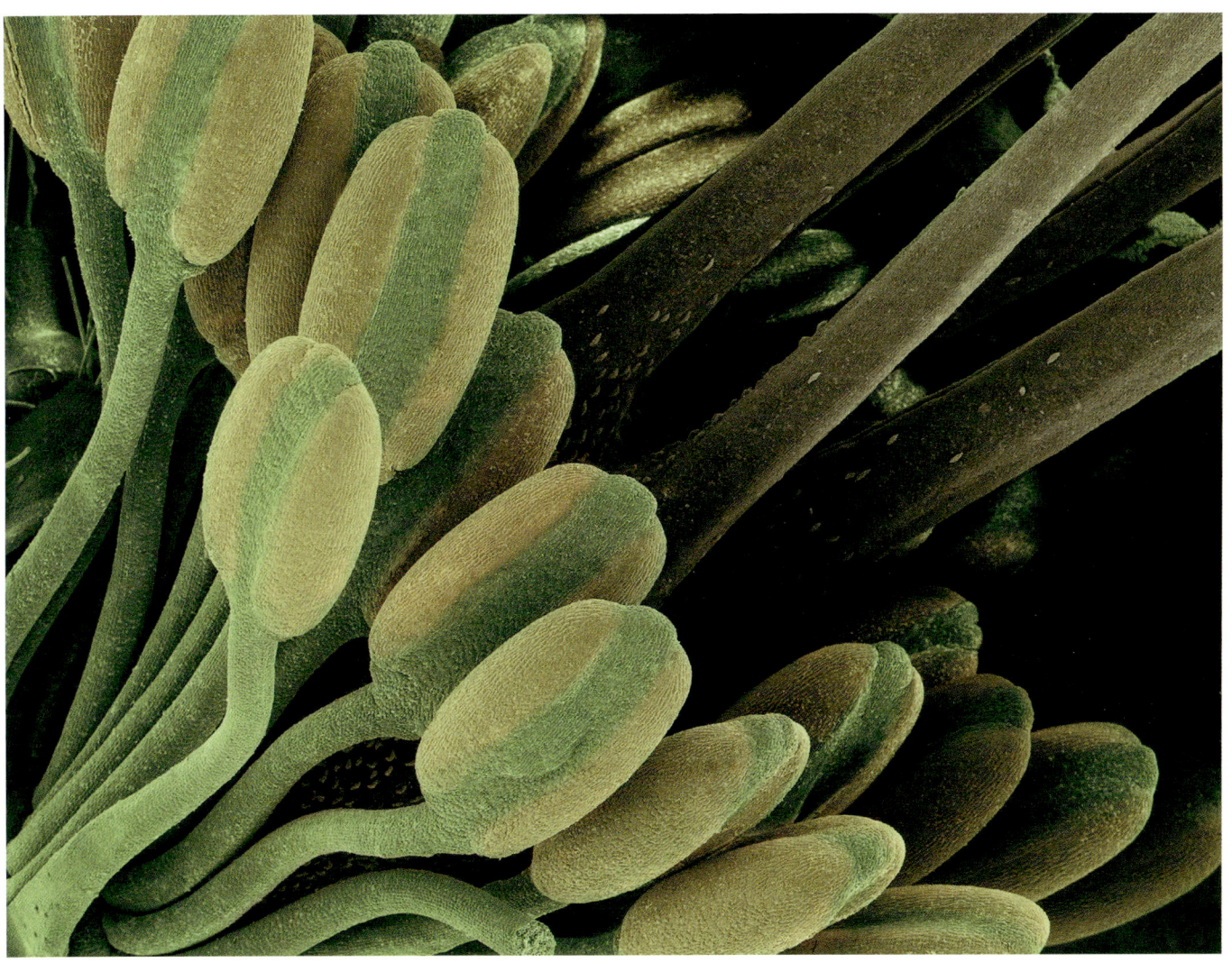

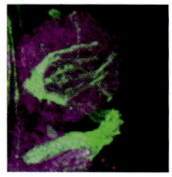

Darya Task   **Juror Selection Award**

Drosophila melanogaster **Maxillary Palp, 2018**

Confocal photomicrograph; Zeiss LSM 700 confocal microscope; 10X objective

Johns Hopkins University School of Medicine, Baltimore, Maryland, United States

The vinegar fly, *Drosophila melanogaster*, has many organs for sensing smell and taste. The noses (antennae and maxillary palps), the mouth (labellum and pharynx), the legs, and the wings all play a role in sense. The sensory neurons in these organs send this information along bundles of nerve fibers (axons) to the brain and ventral nerve cord. In this image, these nerve fibers have been genetically labelled with green fluorescent protein, and the brain and ventral nerve cord have been stained in magenta. The width of this brain is no more than a few grains of table salt.

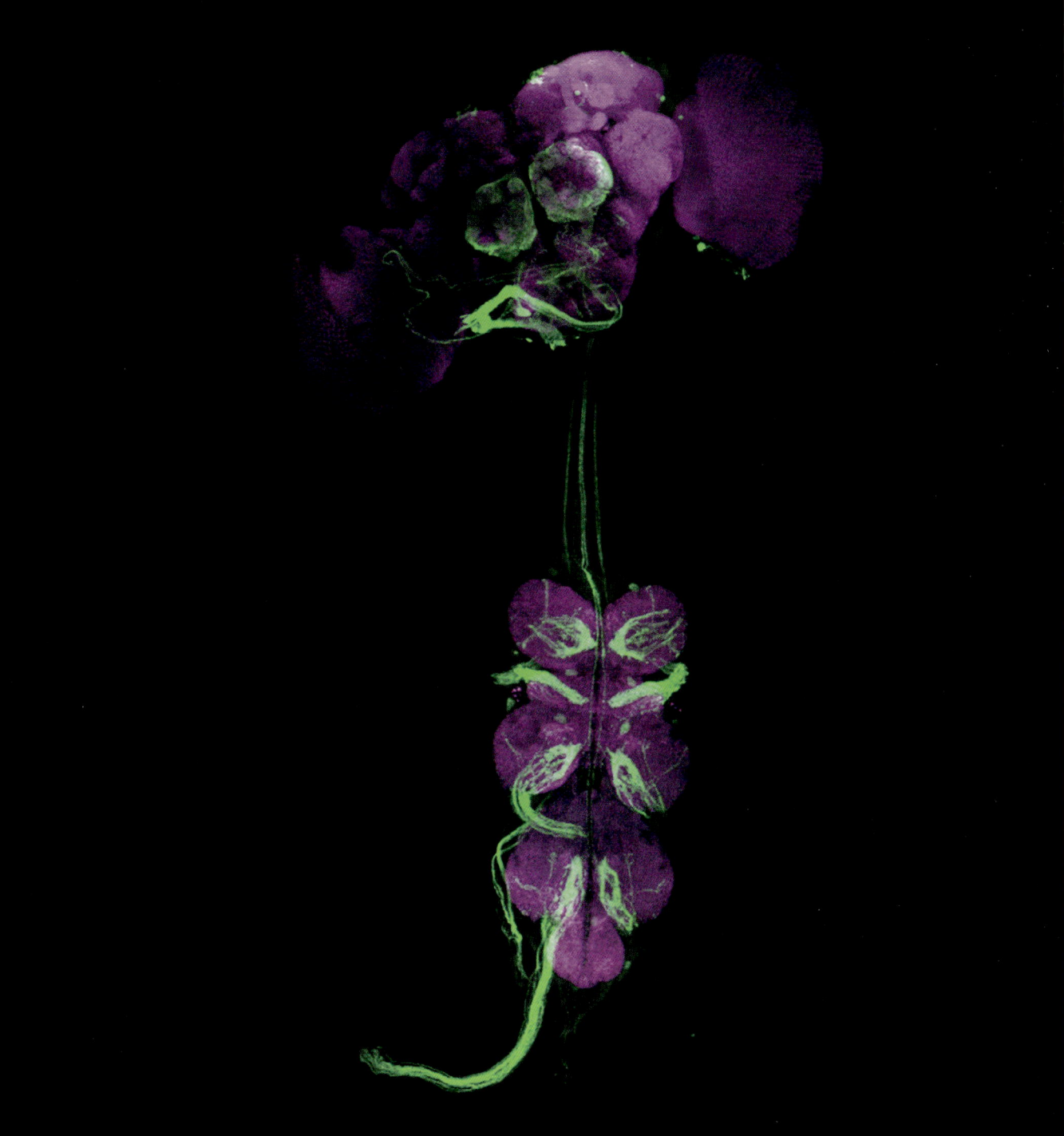

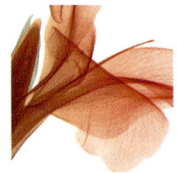

Jim Wehtje

Canna Lily, 2018

Radiography; X-ray machine with 0.5mm source size at approximately 23–35 kVp for 35–45 seconds; 60cm source-to-film distance; mammography film; a composite of multiple images, edited and colorized digitally

Lancaster, Massachusetts, United States

This colorized radiographic image of a Canna lily reveals the flower's interior structure; the image is for both scientific and artistic purposes.

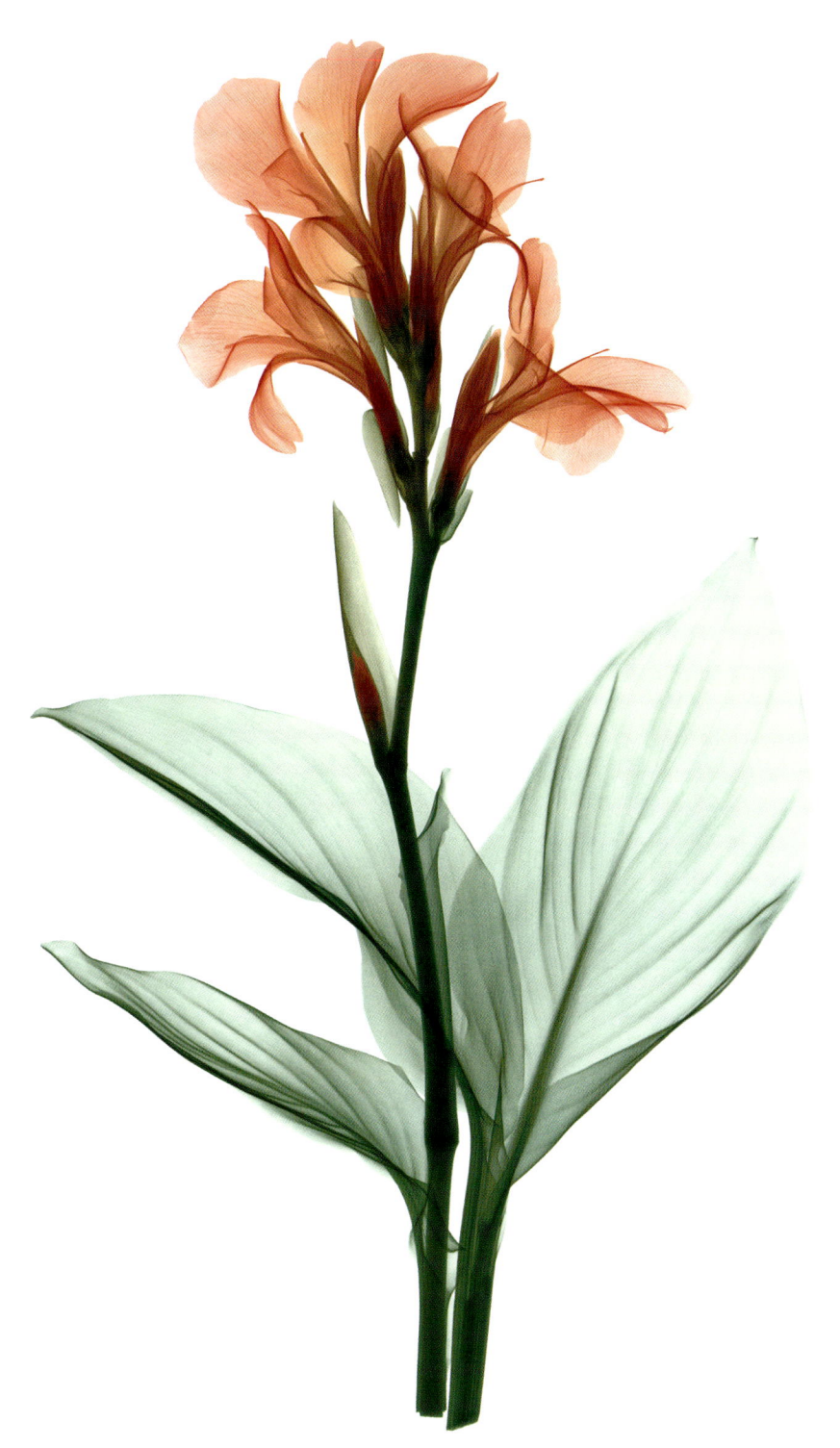

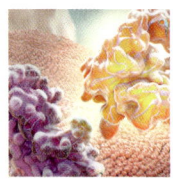

Gary Welch   **Juror Selection Award**

Targeted Antibody Therapy in Breast Cancer, 2017

Digital illustration; Maxon Cinema 4D; Adobe After Effects; Adobe Photoshop

Tipping Point Media, LLC; Malvern, Pennsylvania, United States

---

This illustration shows how the HER2 (blue molecule) and HER3 (purple molecule) receptors are found in abnormally large numbers on some cancer cells (red cells). They transmit signals that allow cancer to grow and spread. To do so, they must come together as pairs (or dimers). Pertuzumab (orange antibody) is a dimerization inhibitor that specifically targets HER2. By physically blocking HER2 and its partner HER3 from coming together, pertuzumab can stop the growth of certain cancer cells. This new therapy overcomes a key resistance mechanism that cancers employed against older HER2-targeting therapies, and is more selective than chemotherapies, which may be toxic to both cancer cells and healthy cells. Pertuzumab is typically used in combination with other therapies.

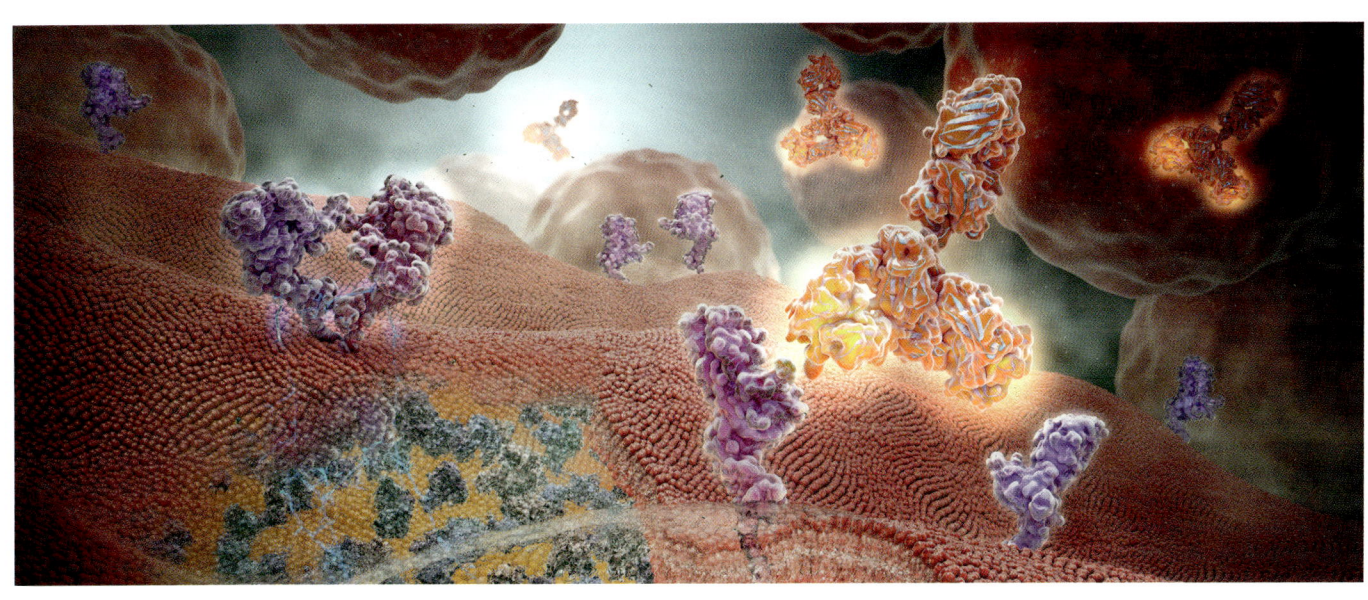

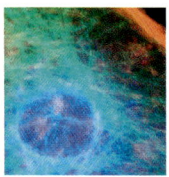

Ethan Whitecotton

BPAE Cells, 2018

Photomicrograph; capture magnification ~x63

Rochester Institute of Technology, Rochester, New York, United States

---

At a cellular level, an image can be surprisingly vibrant and mesmerizing. This photomicrograph features a colorized image of Bovine Pulmonary Artery Endothelial (BPAE) cells from a young cow. The image awakens a sense of wonder at the intricate beauty woven into the most minute aspects of life. Structures such as the mitochondria and proteins are visible in this picture. The colors in the photograph are the result of the way the sample interacted with different wavelengths of light.

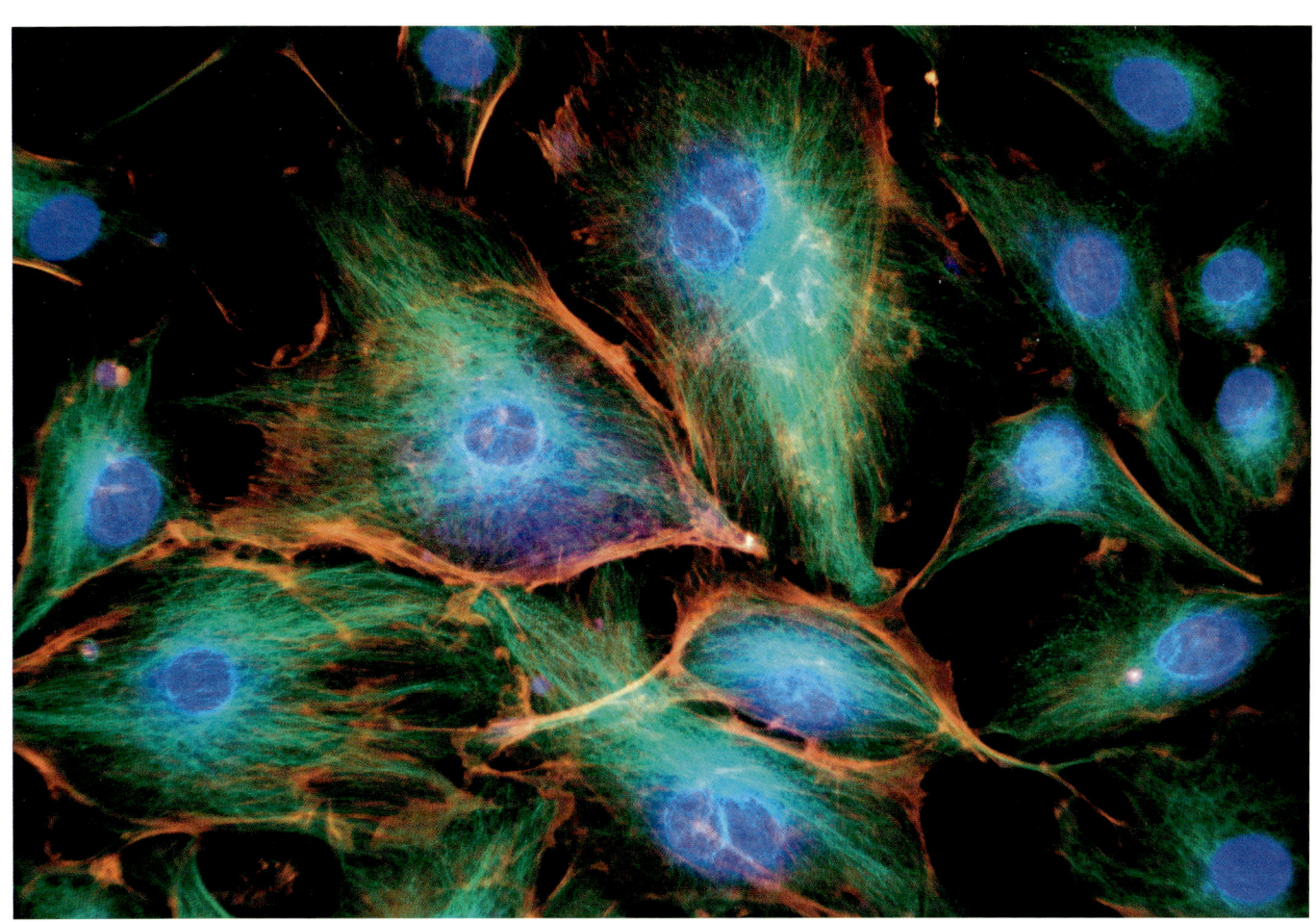

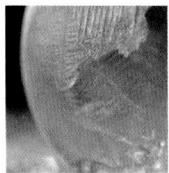

Paul Whitten

Frozen Soap Bubbles, 2018

Close-up photograph; Nikon D810 DSLR camera; Micro-NIKKOR 105mm lens; 1/200 sec; f/16; ISO 80

Paul Whitten Photography, West Nyack, New York, United States

---

This photograph features frozen soap bubbles on snow.

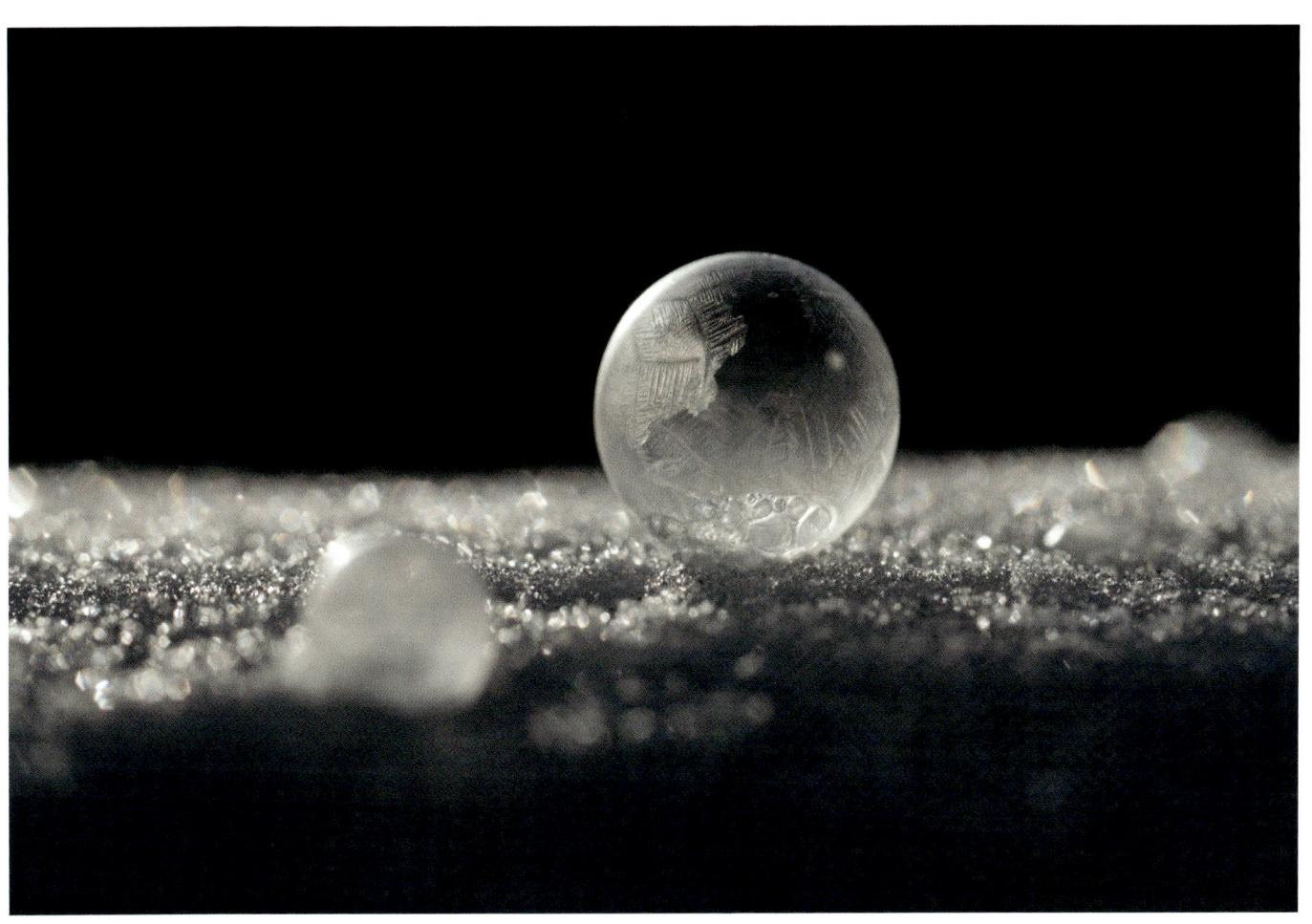

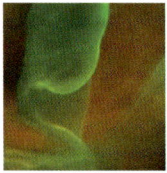

Paul Whitten

Giant Retinal Tear, 2018

Retinal fundus photograph; Optos 200Tx ultra-widefield retinal camera; a composite of multiple images

New York Eye and Ear Infirmary of Mount Sinai, New York, New York, United States

This photograph is a widefield mosaic showing a giant retinal tear and resulting detachment.

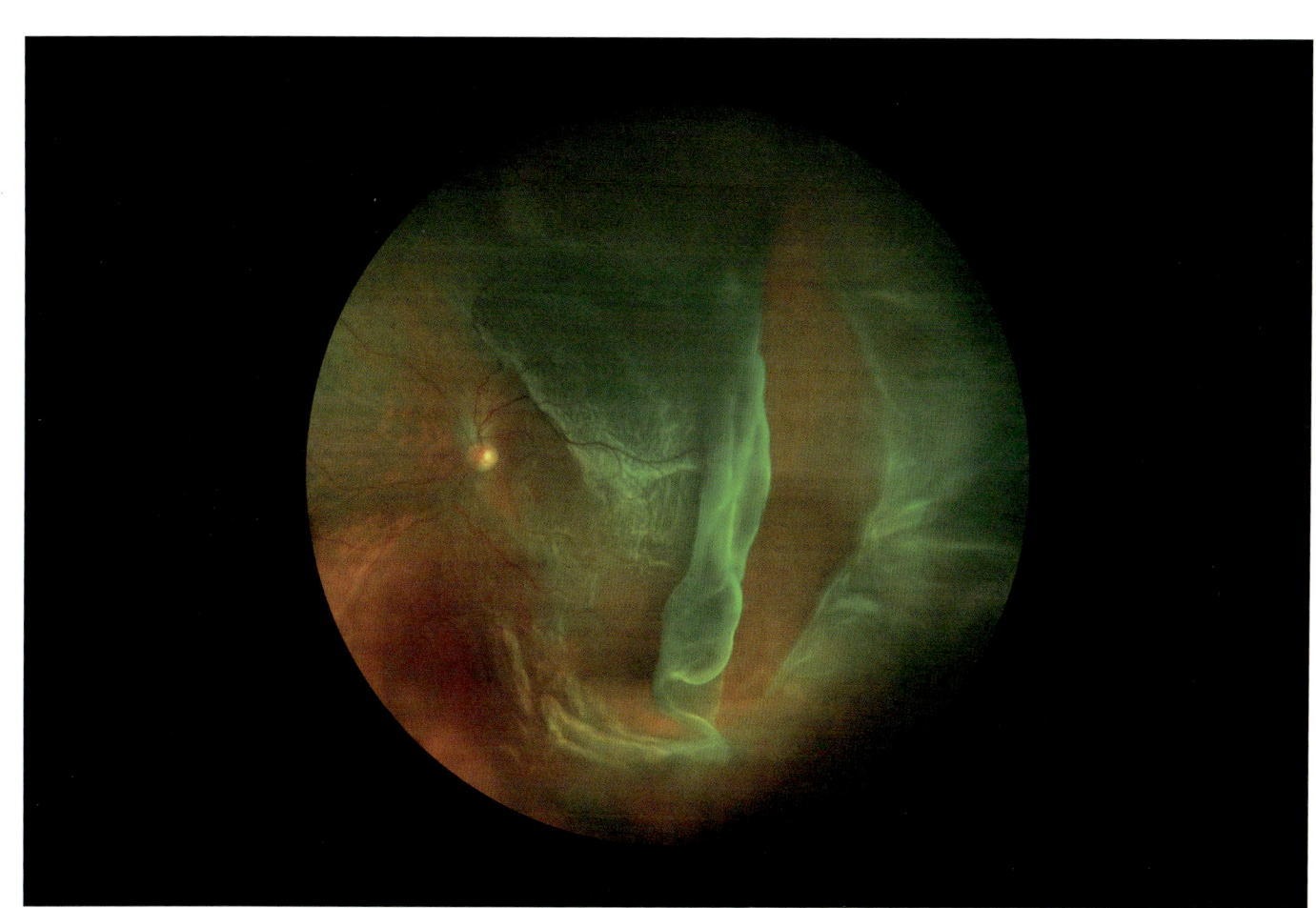

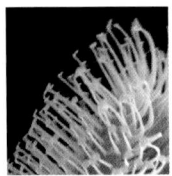

Jannicke Wiik-Nielsen

Hoverfly Foot, 2018

Scanning electron micrograph; scanning electron microscope; capture magnification ~x1050

Norwegian Veterinary Institute, Oslo, Norway

This photograph features a colorized scanning electron micrograph of a hoverfly foot. Hoverflies, also called flower flies or syrphid flies, are abundant on flowers and feed on nectar and pollens. The two claws and a single bristle (empodium) enable the fly to grip rough surfaces. The rounded pads (pulvilli) allow the fly to cling to smooth surfaces, as each pad is covered in tiny tubular structures that secrete an adhesive liquid.

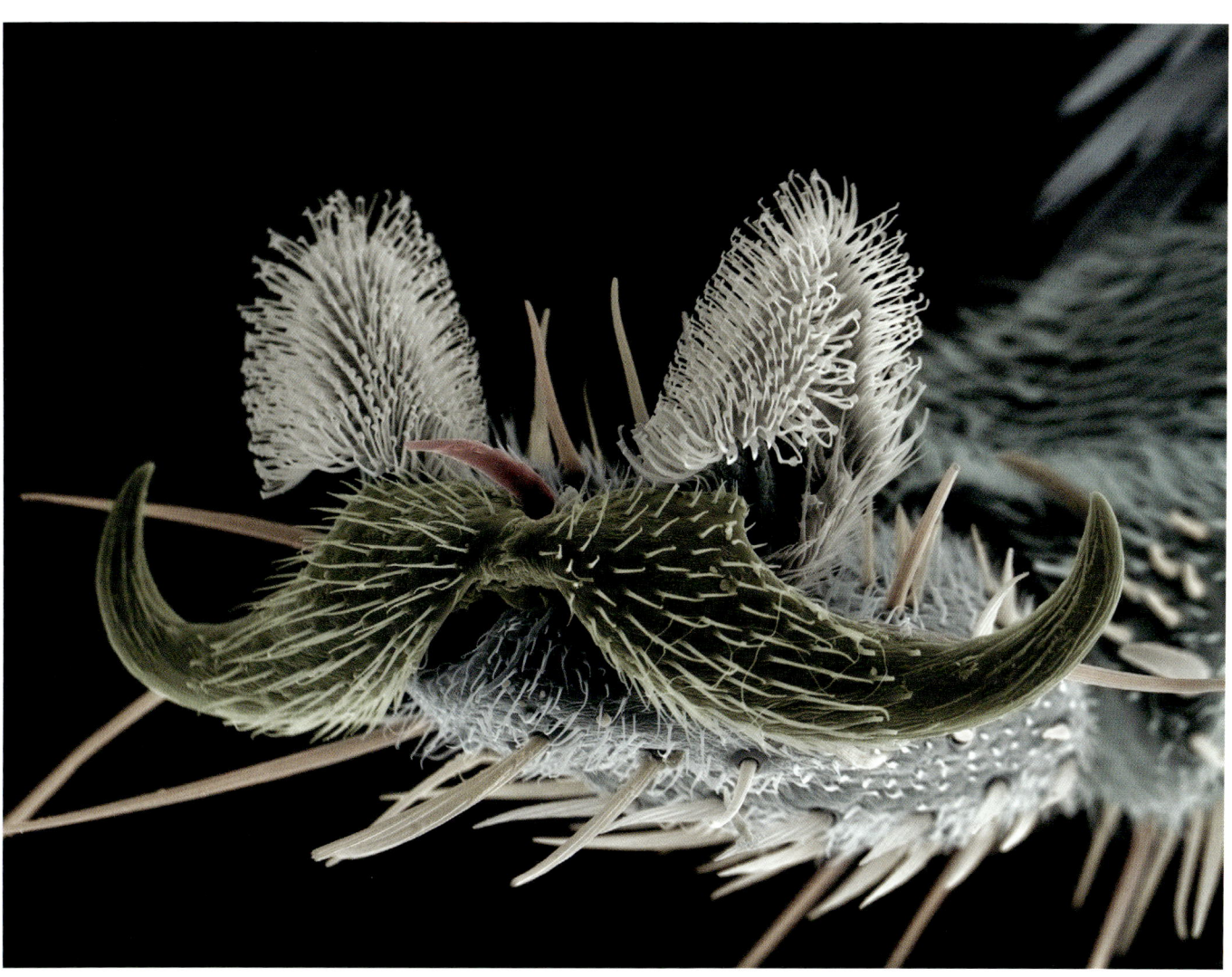

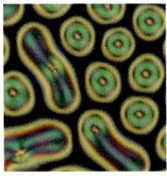

Vance Williams

Cholesteric Liquid Crystals, 2018

Photomicrograph; polarized optical microscope; Nikon D90 DSLR camera; field of view
1 x 0.7 millimeters

Simon Fraser University, Burnaby, British Columbia, Canada

This photomicrograph shares how the material found in mood rings and other
thermography applications appears when examined by optical microscopy.

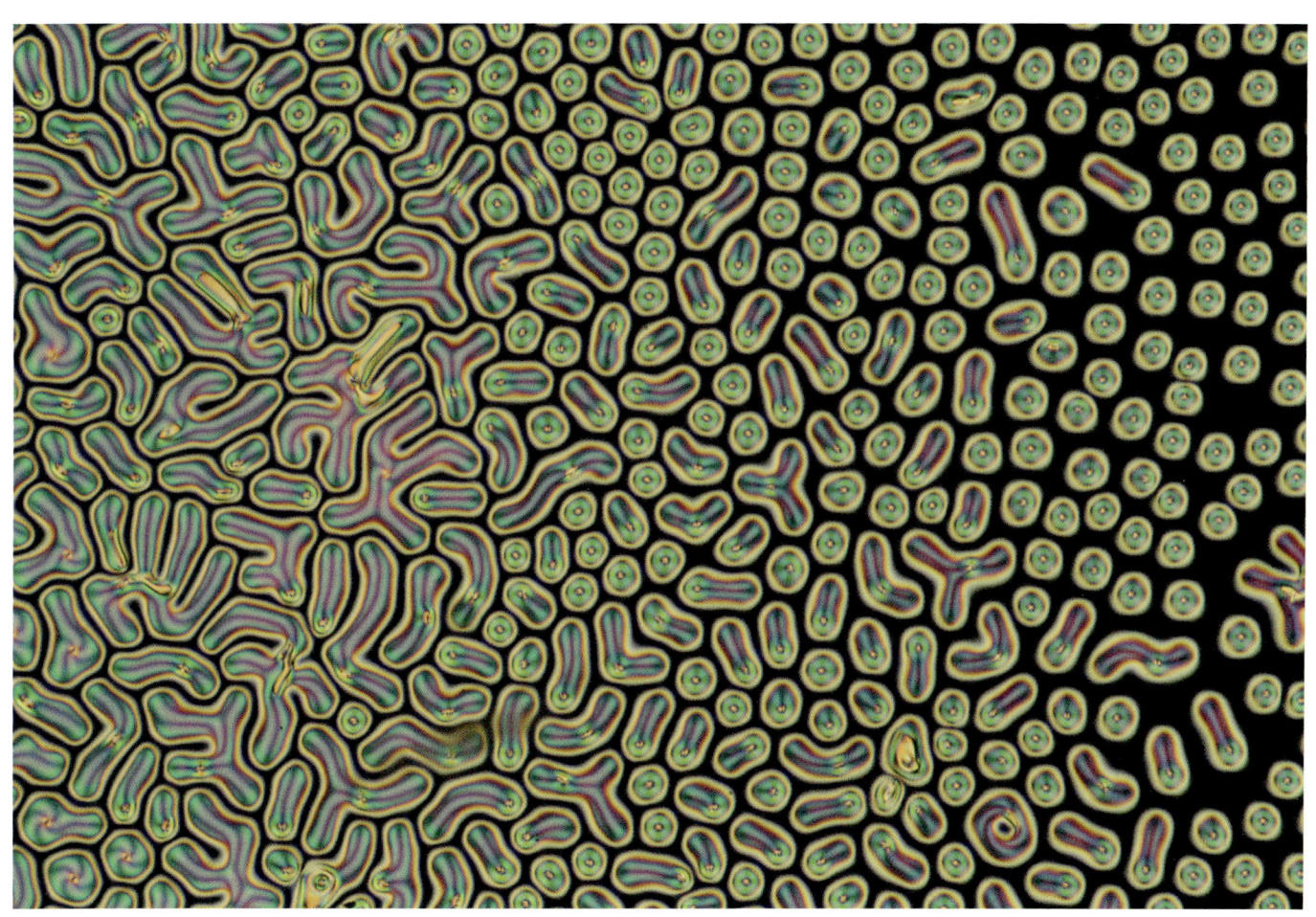

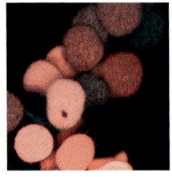

Teresa Zgoda

Cyclops Male and Female, 2016

Confocal photomicrograph; Leica SP5 confocal microscope

Philadelphia, Pennsylvania, United States

This photomicrograph shows the differences between the male and female Cyclops, or water flea, and shows the eggs attached to the female.

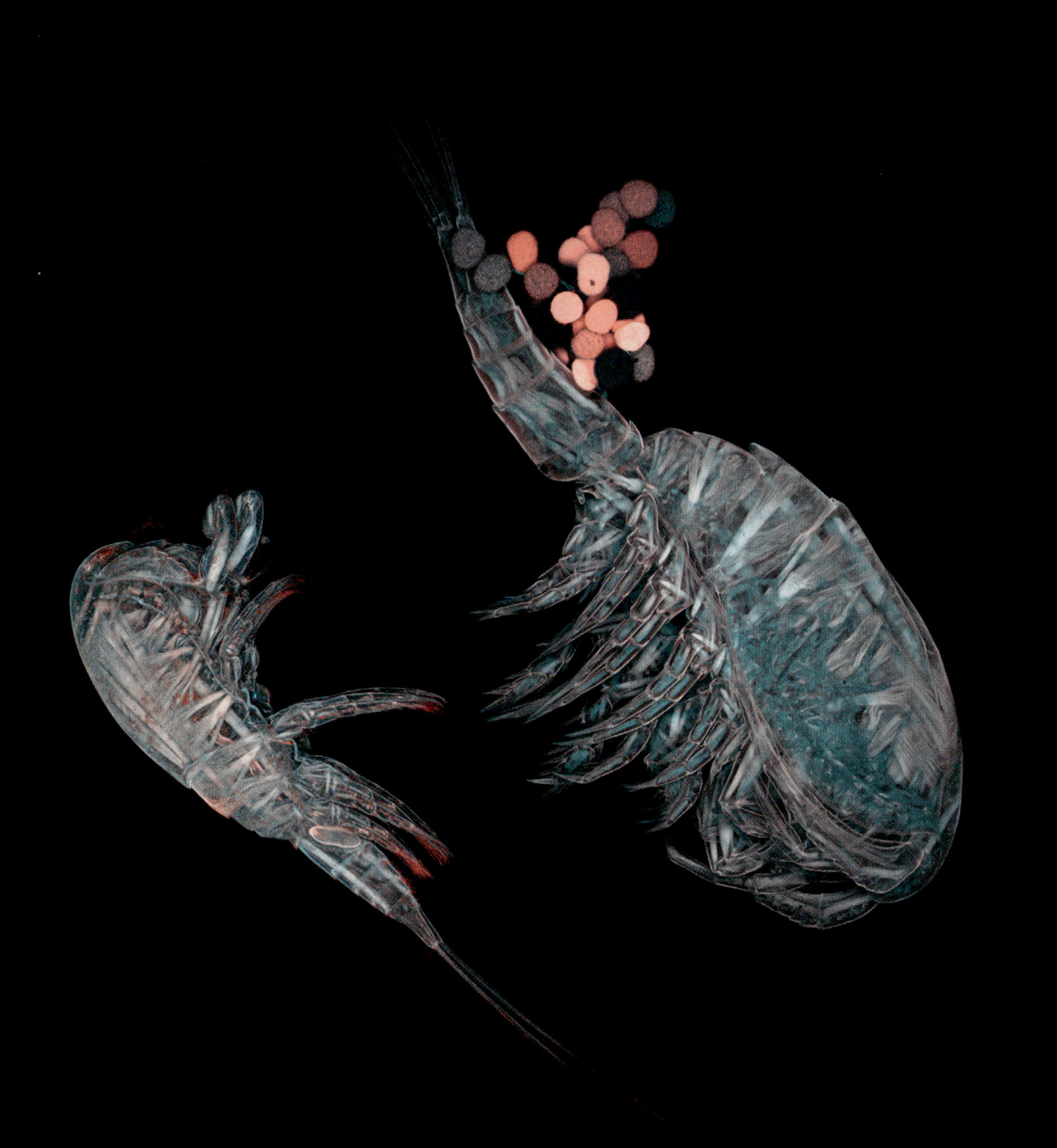

The Judges

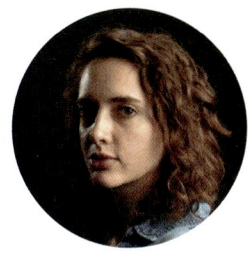

Chloe Coleman

Photo Editor
The Washington Post, Washington, DC, United States
www.washingtonpost.com/people/chloe-coleman

Chloe Coleman is an award-winning photo editor at *The Washington Post*, currently working on the international news desk. She is a contributing writer and editor for the paper's In Sight photo blog, where she has written about and featured contemporary photography, photo books, and exhibitions. Her career in photo editing began as an intern at National Public Radio, followed by her first staff position as a digital photo editor at *The Denver Post*. She attended the Columbus College of Art & Design and is a graduate of the photojournalism program at the Rochester Institute of Technology. Coleman also serves as a faculty member at The Kalish Visual Editing Workshop and has participated as a juror for several photography contests, including The Magenta Foundation's Flash Forward competition (2018) and New York Press Photographers Association's Year in Pictures.

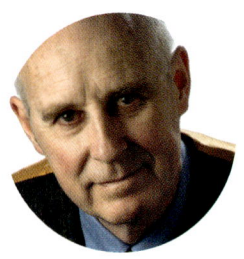

Paul Crompton

Medical Photographer, Author, and Researcher
University Hospital of Cardiff, Cardiff, Wales, United Kingdom
bca.org/resources/experts/crompton.html

Paul Crompton studied at Blackpool College of Art and then worked as a trainee medical photographer at the University Hospital of Wales. He quickly progressed to senior photographer, where he earned additional certificates. Crompton has explored different genres of photography and has exhibited his work in Wales' prestigious Ffotogallery. Crompton became a lecturer at the Cheshire School of Art and Design in 1985 and shortly thereafter became the leader of the vocational photography course. He earned an MA from Derby University in photographic studies, and he was a visiting lecturer in photography at Blackpool College.

Crompton returned to University Hospital of Wales in 1994 as Head of Photography, where he led the conversion from film to digital. He optimized the digital photography services, expanded into ophthalmic imaging, and created initiatives for developing the role of photography within the patient care pathways of dermatology and wound healing. He has written and lectured in the United Kingdom and the United States, and has won a number of awards. He served as a judge for the United Kingdom's Institute of Medical Illustrators' awards and for the BioCommunications Association's exhibitions. In 2014, Crompton was selected as a Louis Schmidt Laureate, a lifetime achievement award from the BioCommunications Association. In 2015 he was awarded an Honorary Fellowship of the Institute of Medical Illustrators. Crompton continues to produce new work and is part of a team documenting outreach projects in Africa. Currently he is working with the charity Mothers of Africa, and Cardiff University's Phoenix Project, an educational collaboration with the University of Namibia in southern Africa, where he produces multimedia digital stories.

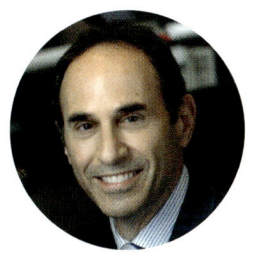

Jonathan Epstein

Professor of Pathology, Urology, and Oncology
Reinhard Chair of Urological Pathology
Director of Surgical Pathology
The Johns Hopkins Medical Institutions, Baltimore, Maryland, United States
urology.jhu.edu/jonathanepstein/

After receiving his MD, Jonathan Epstein received training in pathology at Johns Hopkins Hospital, with a fellowship at Memorial Sloan Kettering Cancer Center. He is the past president of the International Society of Urological Pathology. Epstein has published 898 papers, 68 book chapters, and 15 books. He has one of the largest surgical pathology consulting services in the world, with approximately 12,000 cases per year, covering the full range of urologic pathology. He trains four genitourinary pathology fellows each year, with 61 fellows trained to date. He has lectured 363 times outside of his institution, including in 41 different countries. His passion outside of his work is photography in the many countries he has been fortunate to visit.

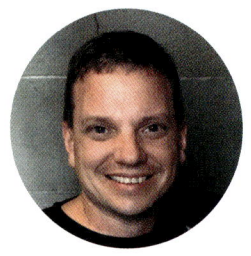

Steve Gerard

Director
Science Source Images
New York, New York, United States
www.linkedin.com/in/steve-gerard-78b7186/

For nearly three decades, Steve Gerard has been the director and editor of the science and medical collections at Science Source, a stock photo agency based in New York City that specializes in scientific, medical, and high-tech photography. In this role he is responsible for talent acquisition, photographer relations, and editing and maintaining the collection of over 500,000 images. Gerard also has extensive knowledge of publishing and of commercial, television, and film rights management. At Science Source Images, Inc., he has overseen the conversion of the original Science Division (which was started as Photo Researchers, Inc.) from slides and prints to a fully digital archive. Gerard also acquires and represents content for Science Source's new video division. He has a BS in biology from State University of New York at Binghamton.

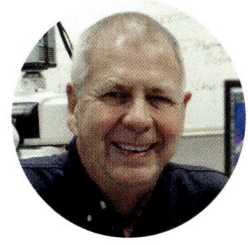

Staffan Larsson

Imaging Consultant
School of Engineering Sciences in Chemistry, Biotechnology and Health, and The Jonasson
Centre for Medical Imaging/3D Visualization Lab, KTH Royal Institute of Technology,
Stockholm Sweden
www.kth.se/profile/stla/

Staffan Larsson lives in Stockholm, Sweden, and earned an AS in photography in 1972 and a national certificate in digital image workflow delivery systems. In 2018, he earned a national Swedish master's diploma in photography.

Larsson has over 45 years of experience in medical and scientific photography. He has worked at Karolinska Institute, a medical university, and Stockholm County Council Healthcare. In 2009, he joined the faculty of the Royal Institute of Technology's School of Technology and Health and he joined Karolinska Institute's Clinical Science Intervention and Technology. Larsson has also worked in the arts, in photojournalism, and in nature. His photography has been included in countless science and medicine articles, featuring images created using new and interesting techniques. He has led workshops and courses for students across Sweden and the United States. Larsson was pivotal in the formation in 1997 of the Lennart Nilsson Award, and he developed initiatives supporting its mission for more than 15 years. He is a contributing author of *The Focal Encyclopedia of Photography* (4th ed., 2013) and *Laboratory Imaging and Photography* (2017). In 2017, he retired as a research engineer in medical and scientific photography at the School of Technology and Health, where he taught and assisted scientist working groups as a consultant for communications and public relations. He is currently a consultant to the Image Center located at The Jonasson Centre for Medical Imaging/3D Visualization Lab, KTH Royal Institute of Technology, Stockholm, Sweden.

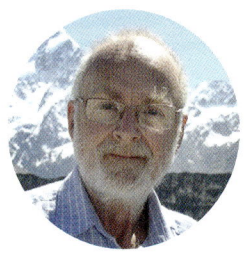

David Malin

Anglo-Australian Telescope, Sydney, New South Wales, Australia; and RMIT University, Melbourne, Victoria, Australia
www.davidmalin.com

Australia-based photographer and astronomer David Malin was born in England, studied chemistry, and explored photography early on. After working for a multinational company as a chemist using photomicrography, Malin went from exploring the infinitely small to the infinitely far away when he joined the Anglo-Australian Observatory as its photographic scientist in 1975. He remained there for 26 years.

In his photographic laboratory in Sydney, Malin invented new ways of extracting information from astronomical photographs, which lead to the discovery of two new types of galaxies. His novel image-enhancement techniques were incorporated into a method of making unique three-color photographs of previously unseen deep space objects. Malin's photographs have been widely published in books and magazines, including *LIFE* and *National Geographic*, and after being recognized for their scientific value, his chromogenic and platinum/palladium prints of the universe have been exhibited in major museums and galleries. His work is part of the collections of museums, institutions, and private collectors on an international level.

A well-known lecturer, Malin has published numerous scientific papers and popular articles on astronomy and photography, as well as nine books, including *The Invisible Universe* (Bulfinch Press/Little, Brown and Company, 1999), a large-format celebration of the beauty of the night sky, and *Ancient Light: A Portrait of the Universe* (Phaidon, 2009), in black and white.

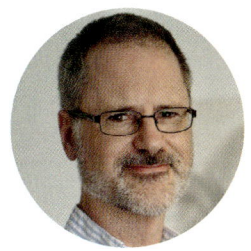

Nick Woolridge

Director and Associate Professor of Biomedical Communications
University of Toronto Mississauga, Mississauga, Ontario, Canada
www.linkedin.com/in/nick-woolridge-1a23b326/

Nick Woolridge received his MSc from the Institute of Medical Science at the University of Toronto in 1996. The topic of his thesis was the development and formative evaluation of a semi-immersive clinical simulation for medical students, which had been funded by SPAR Aerospace. He is the director and an associate professor of biomedical communications in the biology department of the University of Toronto Mississauga. He conducts research in the development of digital media as instruments of biomedical research, teaching, and patient assistance. He is the co-author of Anatomy 300/303 Interactive Lab Companion, a hybrid Web/CD-ROM program, as well as co-author (with Jason Sharpe and Charles Lumsden) of *In Silico: 3D Animation and Simulation of Cell Biology with Maya and MEL* (2008).

The Organizers

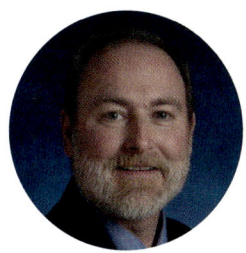

Norman Barker

Professor of Pathology & Art as Applied to Medicine
Director, Pathology Photography and Graphic Arts
The Johns Hopkins School of Medicine

Norman Barker is a professor of pathology and art as applied medicine at the Johns Hopkins University School of Medicine. He specializes in photomicrography, macro photography, and natural science photography. He is director of the Pathology Photography and Graphic Arts Laboratory.

Barker received his undergraduate degree from the Maryland Institute College of Art. He earned his MS in education from Johns Hopkins University and an MA in publications design from the University of Baltimore. He joined the Johns Hopkins faculty in 1983.

He is an Accredited Senior Imaging Scientist (ASIS) and a Registered Biological Photographer, as well as a fellow of the BioCommunications Association and a fellow of The Royal Photographic Society. Barker's work appears in textbooks, journals, and museums world-wide. His work is in the permanent collections of more than 40 museums, including the Smithsonian, the George Eastman Museum, the American Museum of Natural History, and the Science Museum in London.

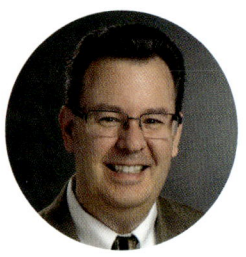

Chris Jackson

Professor and Project Designer
Associate Dean, College of Art and Design
Rochester Institute of Technology

Chris Jackson is the associate dean in the Rochester Institute of Technology College of Art and Design. He is also a professor in the School of Design and the former graduate director for the MFA Visual Communication Design program. With over 15 years of academic experience and 20 years of professional work in graphic design, instructional writing, multimedia design, and motion graphics, Jackson brings diverse expertise to his courses in interactive design and development for applied computer graphics, 2D and 3D animation, and motion graphics.

Jackson continues to create a body of work that contributes to the field of computer graphics design. He is the author of several books, including *After Effects for Designers, Digital Design in Action: Creative Solutions for Designers, After Effects and Cinema 4D Lite, Flash + After Effects, Flash Cinematic Techniques,* and *Flash 3D: Animation, Interactivity, and Games*, which have all been translated into foreign languages. His scholarly work has been featured in *Animation Magazine* and cited in Adobe's user manuals as a good resource for learning After Effects.

As an Adobe Higher Education Leader and Adobe Video Ambassador, Jackson's research and scholarly work have also been peer-reviewed, published, and presented at Adobe MAX, SIGGRAPH, TypeCon, the UCDA Design Education Summit, and the Society for Technical Communication's national and international conferences. He has been a featured speaker at Adobe MAX since 2008 and has been awarded the honor of MAX Master, which means he was a community favorite and was ranked as one of the top 20 speakers for his presentation. His professional work has received over 25 distinguished national and international awards for online communication. His interactive work is on permanent exhibit at the National Museum of Play at The Strong in Rochester, New York.

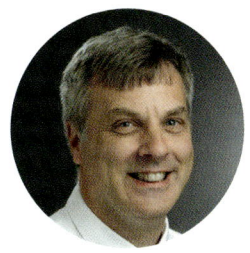

Ted Kinsman

Associate Professor
Photographic Sciences Program
Rochester Institute of Technology

Ted Kinsman has an AS in optics, a BS in physics, and an MS in science education.
He worked as an optical engineer, a physicist, and a physics instructor before coming to
Rochester Institute of Technology to teach the technical side of imaging.

Kinsman continues to explore imagery for books and magazines. His work has appeared on
The Discovery Channel, *Crime Scene Investigations (CSI), The X-Files, South Park, The Tyra
Banks Show*, ABC, NBC, PBS, CBS, and the British Broadcasting Corporation. Recently, he
has done work on *The Frozen Planet* series and on James Cameron's *Avatar* movie.

In 2015, Kinsman won the National Science Foundation's Imaging Science Contest with an
X-ray image of a turtle with eggs. Kinsman's work predominantly focuses on using images to
teach science. Kinsman's latest book is *Cannabis: Marijuana under the Microscope* (Schiffer
Publishing, 2018). His fresh and visually stunning survey celebrates the extraordinary beauty
and diversity of the world's most controversial plant, *Cannabis sativa.*

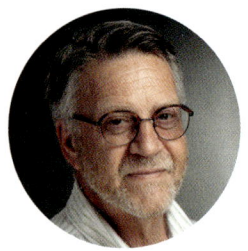

Michael Peres

Professor and Associate Chair
School of Photographic Arts and Sciences
Rochester Institute of Technology

Michael Peres is an award-winning photo-educator, author, and science photographer.
Peres is a professor of biomedical photographic communications at Rochester Institute of
Technology and teaches photomicrography, biomedical photography, and other related appli-
cations of photography investigating science.

Peres has enjoyed a varied photographic career which began in 1973. He has actively published throughout most of his career and recently wrote *Laboratory Imaging and Photography*
(Focal Press, 2016), as well the *Focal Encyclopedia of Photography* (4th ed., 2013). He also
co-authored *Michael Photographs a Snowflake*, a children's book (Fossil Press, 2016).

Peres was a 2003 RIT outstanding faculty award winner, and he has been twice awarded
the Gitner Family Prize by the RIT College of Art and Design for outstanding achievement in the graphic arts. In 2007, Peres was selected as a Louis Schmidt Laureate by the
BioCommunications Association for lifetime achievement in the field of biocommunications.
Peres earned an MS in instructional technology and a BS in biology and biomedical photographic communications. He is also a Registered Biological Photographer.

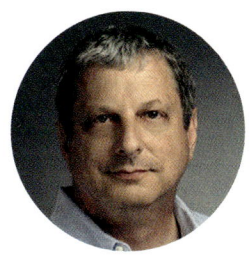

Bob Rose

Assistant Professor
Photographic Sciences Program
Rochester Institute of Technology

Bob Rose graduated from Rochester Institute of Technology in 1978 and was hired in 2015 by his alma mater, bringing more than 35 years of experience in the industry as a photographer, educator, and consultant. In 1999, he opened his own company, VMI, to provide innovative solutions and act as a technology resource for corporations and others. His worldwide contributions have allowed companies to make better products and to promote their products more effectively by increasing brand awareness, and have made it easier for people to use photographic equipment. During his career, he developed new photographic devices and techniques, directed the use of new technologies, and helped make good things happen for photography.

He serves as editor-at-large for *Photo District News* and *Rangefinder* magazines, overviewing new products and technologies, and assisting companies in making important business decisions, such as when a new product or technology should be shared. Rose has photographed on six continents and underwater in four oceans. He has published countless articles and has two patents. He earned an MS in education from the American Intercontinental University School of Education specializing in online training in 2004. He earned his BS in professional photography from the RIT School of Photographic Arts and Sciences in 1978.

Sponsors

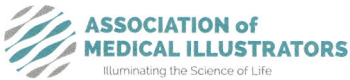

Association of Medical Illustrators

www.ami.org

In 1945, 30 medical illustrator delegates gathered in Chicago for the purpose of organizing a society, which they named the Association of Medical Illustrators. The objective of the AMI is to promote the study of and to encourage the advancement of medical illustration and allied fields of visual education. Through cooperation with the medical and dental professions, including public health and nursing practitioners, AMI helps members present concepts in medicine, healthcare, and the life sciences by being cognizant of the impact visual communications have on people and institutions, through a worldwide network of specialized interdisciplinary professionals.

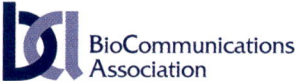

BioCommunications Association

www.bca.org

The BioCommunications Association (BCA) is an international professional association of people working in the biological communications field. The BCA was founded at Yale University in 1931 as the Biological Photographic Association by 38 photographers who recognized the need to exchange technical information and to acknowledge professional excellence. BCA's vision is to maximize the success of all creators and users of visual communication media in the life sciences and medicine. The BCA's mission is to enhance the professional competency of its members and advance the profession by educating and developing creators and users of visual communication media in the life sciences and medicine.

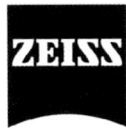

Carl Zeiss Microscopy, LLC

www.zeiss.com/microscopy

Zeiss Optics, founded as a business in 1846, is a world leader in lenses and other optical products; it is a large, research-oriented enterprise that distributes products around the world. Carl Zeiss Microscopy is a leading provider of microscope solutions in the life sciences and materials research markets and QA/QC and also manufactures optical sensor systems for integrated process analysis. As the pioneer of scientific optics, Carl Zeiss continues to challenge the limits of human imagination. With a passion for excellence, Zeiss creates value for its customers and inspires the world in new ways.

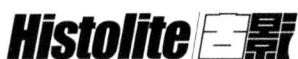

Histolite

www.histolite.com

Histolite, founded in 2017, has been the only independent institution in China dedicated solely for the preservation and conservation of photographic objects. With a strong belief in research and education, it has established an inclusive sample set illustrative of the historical stages of photography and its technological evolution. Histolite is not only actively involved in programs that help the general public become aware of the aesthetic, historical and, more importantly, scientific value of photographic objects, but also works with museums, archives and other institutions to enhance their cultural heritage professionals' understanding of diverse photographs and assist their practice in conservation and preservation.

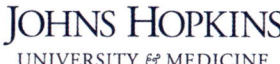

Johns Hopkins University and School of Medicine

www.jhu.edu

Johns Hopkins University, located in Baltimore, Maryland, opened in 1876. Its first president, Daniel Coit Gilman, believed that teaching and research go hand-in-hand—that success in one depends on success in the other—and that a modern university must do both well. He also believed that sharing knowledge and discoveries would help make the world a better place. Johns Hopkins University, America's first research university, includes the university press, the hospital, and the schools of nursing and medicine. The mission is to educate its students and cultivate their capacity for lifelong learning, to foster independent and original research, and to bring the benefits of discovery to the world.

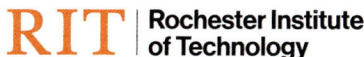

Rochester Institute of Technology (RIT)

www.rit.edu

Rochester Institute of Technology (RIT), a private university in upstate New York, enrolls more than 19,000 undergraduate and graduate students. As a future-focused university, it is internationally recognized as a leader in professional and career-oriented education. RIT is well-known for breaking the mold and recreating it in new ways. With academic programs in engineering, technology, business, the arts, and design, its creative environment adapts the newest technologies and launches brand new ways to experience them. RIT is a student-centered research university with rich ties to partners in the worlds of art, design, graphic communication, and technology.

RIT | College of Science
Chester F. Carlson Center for Imaging Science

RIT Chester F. Carlson Center for Imaging Science

www.cis.rit.edu

The Chester F. Carlson Center for Imaging Science at RIT is a highly interdisciplinary university research and education center, dedicated to pushing the frontiers of imaging in all its forms and uses. Offering BS, MS, and PhD degrees in imaging science, CIS produces the next generation of educators and researchers who develop and deploy imaging systems to answer fundamental scientific questions, monitor and protect the environment, help keep the nation secure, and aid medical researchers in their quest to conquer disease. Imaging science addresses questions about every aspect of systems that are used to create, perceive, analyze, and optimize images.

RIT | RIT Press

RIT Press

www.rit.edu/press

RIT Press is the not-for-profit scholarly book publishing enterprise at Rochester Institute of Technology. RIT Press is dedicated to the innovative use of new publishing technology while upholding high standards in content quality, publication design, and print/digital production. Established in 2001, the Press produces content supporting all academic disciplines offered at RIT. The Press also provides specialized titles for niche academic audiences, trade editions for mass-market audiences, texts for deaf studies, regional interest titles, limited editions with unique, aesthetic standards, and gift items.

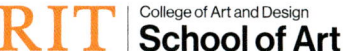

RIT School of Art

http://artdesign.rit.edu/schools/art

The School of Art's professionally oriented BFA and MFA options in art education, ceramics, expanded forms, furniture design, glass, illustration, medical illustration, metals and jewelry design, painting, printmaking, and sculpture are accredited by the National Association of Schools of Art and Design. The School of Art provides well-equipped, up-to-date classrooms and studios, and students have many opportunities to exhibit work, both on campus (in a variety of galleries and student shows) as well as at RIT's City Art Space, a new, student-run exhibition and event venue in downtown Rochester, New York. By offering a specialized curriculum and professional working environment, the School of Art prepares its students for successful careers as artists, illustrators, and educators.

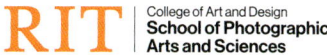

RIT School of Photographic Arts and Sciences

http://artdesign.rit.edu/schools/photographic-arts-sciences

The School of Photographic Arts and Sciences molds imaginative visual artists, practitioners, and technologists through its unsurpassed compilation of degree programs, including Bachelor of Fine Arts, Bachelor of Science, Master of Fine Art and Master of Science. It is recognized as among the finest colleges in the world with unique professional courses of study, as well as a one-of-a-kind educational community that consists of critically regarded faculty, state-of-the-art facilities, an unmatched repository of equipment, and co-operative education and internship opportunities. This strong community-based environment allows students to engage in image creation in a professional atmosphere known for its excellence.

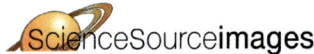

Science Source Images, Inc.

www.sciencesource.com

Science Source and its parent company, Photo Researchers, Inc., have been specializing in imagery from all fields of the natural, physical, and life sciences for over 50 years. Providing access to medical and scientific stock and custom images and video, Science Source serves a broad range of clients in book, magazine, and electronic publishing, as well as in advertising, corporate communications, and multimedia. Top clients include Commonhealth; Cline Davis Mann; Sudler Hennessey; Pearson Education; Scholastic, Inc.; Houghton Mifflin Harcourt; The McGraw-Hill Companies; National Geographic; and Time Warner, Inc.

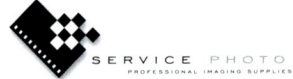

Service Photo, Inc.

www.servicephoto.com

Service Photo was founded in 1948 to serve the photography needs of the local neighborhood and Baltimore-area consumers. With a focus on high-quality products and a dedication to excellent customer service, Service Photo has grown into a local, regional, and national source for a broad range of photographic, darkroom, and digital products. Recognizing that professionals rely on their equipment every day for their careers, their hobbies, and their art, Service Photo is an authorized dealer for major photographic and digital equipment manufacturers and only sells equipment that is protected under a manufacturer's US warranty.